Psychosocial Studies

There is expanding global interest in the relationship between the psychological and the social. The bringing together of affect, emotion, and feeling with social, political, and cultural forces offers a creative, innovative, and rich set of ways of understanding the links between personal troubles and public troubles developed by Charles Wright Mills in his 1959 book *The Sociological Imagination*.

This book is an introduction to psychosocial studies. Drawing on different approaches to the field, the book introduces the main theoretical influences on psychosocial studies and their development and impact, through – for example – concepts such as the unconscious, self and identity, affect, emotion, and the cultural and social unconscious. It explores the theoretical frameworks of psychosocial studies and psychosocial research methods. The book offers examples of case studies that illustrate the diversity of psychosocial studies and what makes them distinctive. It asks: what is social about the inner worlds of the psychological? What is psychological and psychic about social worlds and social life?

This clear, accessible introduction will be of interest to students and researchers across the social sciences and humanities, in particular in sociology, psychology, cultural geography, social policy and politics, and cultural studies.

Kath Woodward is Professor of Sociology at the Open University. She has published extensively in interdisciplinary fields, including the developing psycho-social approaches, theoretically and methodologically. She is a founding member of the Association for Psychosocial Studies. Her publications include: *Understanding Identity* (2002), *Questions of Identity* (2004), *Boxing Masculinity and Identity* (2006), *Embodied Sporting Practices* (2009), *Social Sciences: the Big Issues* (2014 3rd edition), *Why Feminism Matters* with Sophie Woodward (2009), and the reflexive, innovative *Sporting Times* (2012) written in the 'real time' of the 2012 Olympics, which inspired the "Chasing Time" exhibition at the Olympic Museum, which Kath curated.

This book is essential reading for anyone seeking an introduction to the relatively new field of psychosocial studies. It is both scholarly and yet remarkably accessible, providing state of the art coverage of current thinking. There are few people who could produce a book of such scope and with this degree of balanced coverage. Without doubt, it is set to become a key text within the field.

Dr David Langdridge, Existential Psychotherapist,
the Open University, UK

In this timely and well-crafted book, Kath Woodward maps the chief current concerns of the expanding field of psychosocial studies, deftly illustrating what a psychosocial approach can contribute to a number of contemporary issues. The book will be invaluable to students and teachers looking for a lucid overview of the conceptual and methodological resources, drawn upon by psychoanalytically informed psychosocial scholars. Kath Woodward devotes a chapter to a psychosocial take on politics which is grounded in the personal and which carries forward the feminist inspirations which have been so central to psychosocial work. In providing a synoptic overview of the field, this book provides a valuable platform for scholars to build upon as they continue to challenge disciplinary orthodoxy.

Paul Stenner, Professor of Social Psychology and Co-Director
of the Psychosocial Programme of the Centre for Citizenship,
Identity and Governance, the Open University

Psychosocial Studies

An introduction

Kath Woodward

Routledge
Taylor & Francis Group

LONDON AND NEW YORK

First published 2015
by Routledge
2 Park Square, Milton Park, Abingdon, Oxon OX14 4RN

and by Routledge
711 Third Avenue, New York, NY 10017

Routledge is an imprint of the Taylor & Francis Group, an informa business

British Library Cataloguing-in-Publication Data

A catalogue record for this book is available from the British Library

Library of Congress Cataloging-in-Publication Data
Woodward, Kath.
   Psychosocial studies : an introduction / by Kath Woodward.
      pages cm
   1. Social psychology—Study and teaching.   2. Social sciences—
Study and teaching.   I. Title.
   HM1019.W66 2015
   302.071—dc23
   2014031124

ISBN: 978-0-415-71883-7 (hbk)
ISBN: 978-0-415-71885-1 (pbk)
ISBN: 978-1-315-86782-3 (ebk)

Typeset in Perpetua
by Apex Covantage, LLC

To Steve

Contents

Acknowledgements

I would like to thank Gerhard Boomgaarden, Emily Briggs and Alyson Claffey at Routledge for all their support on this project; Sheri Sipka and the team at Apex CoVantage for their patience and professionalism in getting the book into print.

Much of what I have written here draws upon the inspiration I received from the psychosocial group at the Open University where Peter Redman, Wendy Hollway, Gail Lewis, Margie Wetherell, Joanne Whitehouse Hart and I spent happy times grappling with Big Brother and the unconscious. What I have written is my responsibility, but this group of people was incredibly productive in the development of ideas.

Thanks to Steve Woodward for his diligence and dedication in creating the index for the book.

chapter 1

Introduction

Introduction

When I was working on the Introduction to *Psychosocial Studies* early in 2014, I was invited to talk on a BBC UK radio station about a report on the gendered nature of 'caring'. The report showed that women were much more likely than men to be carers. Carers are those who care for other people who cannot look after themselves for a large number of different reasons, such as babies, children, the very elderly who might need help with a range of household and personal care, and those with illnesses and disabilities. Sometimes this is paid work, and sometimes it is not, which may account for the blurring of the boundaries between caring *for* and caring *about* someone. Caring *for* is the daily work of caring, not so much caring about other people and feeling love and affection towards them but performing the routine tasks of daily care with respect and professionalism. The researcher asked me to offer some explanations of why caring should be undertaken primarily by women. Most caring work such as looking after babies and children, whether one's own or other people's, relatives with disabilities or the elderly in care homes, or more locally caring for neighbours is empirically – and emotionally – seen as women's work, which can be voluntary or (usually low) paid. The interviewer was keen to focus upon the nature-nurture dichotomy with little regard for the diversity among women and among men, as well as between women and men, and the different situations and social contexts in which caring takes place. Is it because it is natural that women want to care *for* as well as *about* people? Are women naturally and biologically suited to caring work? Are women taught to perform caring work whilst men are not? These are not really quite the right questions, though. They are not the only questions. The fact that women make up the larger proportion of carers is not simply because women learn these roles and feel that they want to undertake them and feel guilty if they don't; caring is not *only* about culture and tradition and the structure of the labour market, nor is it only restricted to a biologically, 'natural' emotional state or to innate inner drives. Caring also occupies the space between social practices and social systems and personal inner worlds. In the complex mix of factors that includes the particularities of culture, ethnicity, racialization, and social class, through which social relations and intimate **feelings** and practices are forged and experienced, the intensity of feelings of guilt and love make those relations and are made by them.

In the phone-in that followed my radio interview there was a wide range of callers, one of whom reiterated the binary logic of the nature versus nurture dichotomy, but most wanted to talk about the particularities of the their own situation and the lived experience of caring with its pleasures and pains and routine banalities, and they wanted to challenge the simplification of abstract explanation. This focus upon experience and of personal testimony, which is never entirely removed from the social context that feelings and **emotions** constitute and in which those feelings are made and remade is a key aspect of psychosocial approaches (Lewis, 2010). This is what this book is about. A choice does not have to be made between the personal and the social or between nature and nurture. It is an exploration of the processes and the relationship that provides a means of understanding and of making sense of what is happening and of why and how people do what they do and feel what they feel.

As a psychosocial approach shows, this discussion, which challenges the simplicity of nature versus nurture, is not just about complexity. What is the nature of the connections, and what is happening in the spaces between the social and the psychic? These are feelings and emotions that are expressed and experienced in caring work, like other work. How are emotions and feelings like love, guilt, compassion, disgust, anxiety, and shame implicated in the context of work? For example, it is through iterative everyday practices of caring that women might subjectively experience the possibilities of containing and managing the range of emotions and feelings such as frustration and anger that those who are being cared for may experience. Caring involves intersubjective processes.

In the example above of my own experience, the journalist's dichotomies of nature and culture, of innate drives and processes of socialization, are clearly not the only possibilities, as carers who rang in to the programme demonstrated. Feelings of guilt (or lack of such feelings) are inextricable from the social situations in which they are lived, but there are contradictions in the spaces that psychosocial approaches endeavour to address. Caring is psychosocial, as is a whole range of interventions and experiences: for example, in areas of health care, medicine, welfare, and education.

It has increasingly become evident that even medically defined conditions such as HIV, AIDS, and cancer, as well as mental health issues across a wide range, are not wholly the **subject** of medico-scientific intervention but have social elements that combine to produce the whole experience and to which carers and practitioners need to pay attention. Many of the practical issues that are involved in psychosocial studies have their origins in the provision of medical and social care and education as part of a move towards recognizing that dealing with the whole person, in the promotion of healing and well-being, includes not just the individual's social circumstances but a whole range of interactions within a person's biography and the situated self as well as the more obvious socioeconomic factors associated with ill health or dependency and underperformance in education.

What sort of connections are there between inner and social worlds if the link is not simply causal? For example, if people's actions and feelings and even their physical and mental health are not simply caused by a social factor like economic circumstances, such as poverty or a biochemical condition, what else might be going on? How are social forces and ideas lived and experienced and translated into people's lives in the world? The processes in which the different elements are connected are psychosocial. A psychosocial approach is able to attend to **unconscious** forces and **psychodynamics** and social elements of contemporary life (Roseneil, 2007) and go beyond binary oppositions and ask questions about what is going on under the surface of behaviour and social organization. How do people see themselves, and are they recruited through a process of **interpellation** into subjectivities, as the French social theorist Louis Alhusser, who used psychoanalytic theories in his work argued (Althusser, 1971)?

Many of the observations and issues that trigger debate cite their relevance in the 'contemporary' world, which on the whole suggests particular forms of social relations and organization that are associated with liberal democracies and what have often been often called 'western' societies. I have used the idea of 'the west' to provide a loose classification in preference for some of the other terminology, such as the global north, whilst acknowledging the orientalism that might be inherent in the use of the west. The term is avowedly used loosely and as part of an imprecise rather than explicitly political classification, which often refers to geographical locations in which western values and norms are robustly challenged. The term is deployed with full awareness of the challenges of a world after orientalism in which western cultural supremacy can no longer be asserted (Isin, 2014; Isin and Nyers, 2014), The 'west' also has to accommodate multi-ethnicity and the diversities of mobility.

An area of experience like caring has wide policy implications, and a psychosocial approach offers a route into making sense of much wider political and social issues. Care and compassion are expressed and experienced on the global stage too. One example could be the increasingly ambivalent attitude of the public to the frequency and scale of humanitarian disaster as communicated in their high visibility in the world's media. Whilst still responding generously to humanitarian emergencies, as demonstrated by public donations following typhoons, earthquakes, and other natural disasters, the public seems to be increasingly critical of and reluctant to commit to ongoing support of humanitarian and international development agencies. These tensions between compassion and care and reluctance to contribute 'yet again', which is sometimes construed as 'compassion fatigue', raises several questions that have interdisciplinary psychosocial implications. For example, the media coverage evokes different reactions, some of which might attribute responsibility to those who are most in need of support. What are the ideological, emotional, and biographical underpinning of audiences' responses and actions on a global scale as well as in the case of individuals?

What is the relationship between the public and providers of support such as national governments and nongovernmental organizations or charities' expectations and understandings?

There are assemblages of different elements that are in play in the case of care and caring at all levels, which offer examples of the puzzles with which this book engages, and this combination of different interrelated factors is a feature of psychosocial studies.

What is the psychosocial?

The field of psychosocial studies is one that is emerging and developing and includes a wide range of debates and ideas that put affect, emotion, and feeling into public as well as personal spaces. This field of inquiry has also generated some innovative methodologies and interdisciplinary methods. What is largely known as the psychosocial in the UK has different labels in different parts of the world as an exciting, innovative, and very productive interdisciplinary mode of inquiry into social life and relationships in the contemporary world. Psychosocial studies are constituted by past legacies and new questions and debates. More and more areas of everyday life and increasingly, public, political life are subject to inquiry that can be categorized as psychosocial because they bring together the personal and the political and the individual and the social in new ways. As Jem Thomas pointed out in his editorial comment in the *Journal of Psycho-social Studies* in 2013, '[T]he heart of psychosocial studies is invariably the idea of *relation*. . . . And if we are always in relation, we are also always *dependent*' (Thomas, 2013:5). Caring is a particular example of dependency, although dependency is a feature of virtually all human relationships. This book explores what is involved in psychosocial studies and addresses some of the questions raised in this fast-developing field.

What do we mean by psychosocial, and what makes this field of research distinctive? It is the purpose of this book, firstly, to demonstrate what marks out the psychosocial from other fields of research and inquiry and to demonstrate some of the productive connections of psychosocial studies' interdisciplinary projects. There are clearly interdisciplinary and multidisciplinary concerns in this field of study that draws upon many different subject areas and schools of thought, although this field is nonetheless particular and recognizable in its approaches.

Secondly, this book aims to demonstrate what is distinctive about psychosocial studies through examples of the kind of areas of life that are included in the psychosocial and subject to psychosocial research methods. The book uses examples in order to show the range of issues and ideas that are part of what can be called psychosocial studies and, in particular, to engage with the processes through which the field of the psychosocial is reproduced, enacted, experienced, and understood. A major focus is everyday experience.

The particular features of psychosocial studies identified in this book are organized around two important aspects of this field of inquiry. Firstly, there are the relationships between the social and the psychic, which in psychosocial studies are inextricably interrelated but through particular processes that can be explored and analyzed. In the example of caring above, there are social, demographic factors that shape experience, as well as disrupting expectations of what is routine and taken for granted (Frosh and Emerson, 2005). There are demographic factors such as population growth, increased longevity, and improved health care and consequently a greater proportion of the population needing care because of the longer life span, and a rising birth rate generates greater demand for child care and education. A variety of factors including the pace of contemporary life has also led to increased numbers of people experiencing mental health difficulties. The care traditionally undertaken by families and in communities is no longer possible. Caring, especially in some contexts, such as for those suffering from drug or alcohol dependency, is stressful as well as demanding. Conflicting and often strong emotions are involved in all acts of caring, whether for professional carers or for those who have made choices, such as to bring children into the world, as anyone who has had children will know, however much you want them and love them.

Psychosocial studies bring together the micro and the macro, the personal and the social, inner worlds and outer worlds, which combine in different ways. It is not a matter of adding on the social to a psychological approach or one that explores the social with an added psychological perspective. Psychosocial studies are innovative because both elements are always in play, although not always in the same ways. Secondly, the psychosocial involves the exploration of processes and of different points of connection and disconnection. The psychosocial deals with what is in the middle, in the spaces that can be described as liminal (Stenner and Moreno, 2013), as points of connection, which have been theorized in a range of ways to capture some of the complex and sometimes mysterious nature of the interstices between inner and outer worlds, such as Wilfred Bion's ideas about the 'third' space in group dynamics (Bion, [1961]2004). Psychosocial studies seek to go beyond the limitations of binaries such as those between nature and nurture and the personal and the social as illustrated in the example of caring cited above, in a variety of different ways, in order to accommodate the possibilities of change and offer a dynamic understanding of the relationship between the personal and the social in a wide variety of contexts.

The aim of the book is to map out some of the concerns of psychosocial studies as an expanding field of inquiry and scholarship. Given the speed of change, this book cannot be definitive or comprehensive, but it can demonstrate what sort of questions, puzzles, and issues matter in psychosocial studies and give some indication of the empirical areas that are being covered. My aim is also to show what psychosocial approaches can contribute to key issues in the contemporary world. Empirical work in psychosocial studies covers all the major areas of contemporary personal, social, and political concern, including sexualities (Roseneil, 2007, 2010, 2013), intimacies, health, mental health education, welfare (Lewis, 2010), conflict, risk, and trauma (Byford, 2008; Rashkin, 2009) as well as conceptual engagement with areas such as power, equality, inequality, love, hate, guilt (Frosh, 2003), and **bodies** and enfleshed experience (Woodward, 2012b).

What is crucial is the relationality of psychosocial studies, which includes intersubjective relations that make up the experience of inner and outer worlds as well as the affectivity of all human relations. This relationality extends beyond human relations, although psychosocial studies tend to focus upon human relations and human activity and the agency of the human subject (Frosh and Baraitser, 2008; Hollway and Jefferson, 2005a), although there is increasing recognition of connections between the human and the nonhuman in a variety of forms; **objects** and things play a part in the generation of affects and in making sense of dependency and relationality (Pollock, 2013; Bennett, 2010).

Writing the psychosocial

In this book I use the first person to refer to my aims and intentions and to locate myself as a researcher and a teacher. I also use the first person plural, which seems to be quite customary in psychosocial studies and within the psychoanalytic literature, although in the rest of my life in the university the use of the first person plural is seen as problematic. 'We' is used as a device to bring the reader in and to demonstrate that this is collective project, which is a quite acceptable strategy. 'We', however, also suggests a universal humanity, which is more problematic since the use of the plural pronoun can be seen to override differences and suggest a universal norm, which has traditionally meant a white, able-bodied heterosexual man. Similarly within women's and gender studies there has been considerable discussion, not to mention controversy, about the assumptions being made when the category 'woman' and the first person of 'we women' have been seen as guilty of the same universalizing tendencies. The homogenous category of all women suggests a largely white norm. These arguments are well rehearsed, and the contributions of queer theory and especially Judith Butler's work have been most influential and effective. Some of these issues are addressed in the discussion of methodologies in relation to some of the strategies that have been adopted, rather than the debate about categories. Thus it is more a matter of how difference, and collectivities and sameness, might be expressed.

In this book 'we' is used to encompass some commonalities in relation to the psychoanalytic concepts that are used to explain what people do and who they are. This strategy does not for a moment underplay or fail to acknowledge social, cultural, political, and economic differences. The idea of the unconscious as creative, chaotic, and disruptive itself defies uniformity. There remains, however, the criticism of psychoanalysis as presenting a fixed and universal structure to the psyche and the failure of psychoanalysis to accept its own role in producing that knowledge, rather than uncovering it. Psychosocial approaches seek to avoid this problem, whilst using the conceptual frameworks of psychoanalytic thought, by focusing upon the processes through which inner and social worlds are always interconnected and combined.

What's in a name?

The term 'psychosocial' has been used for some time, especially in the context of practical application, for example, in health care, in dealing with the 'whole person' rather than the presenting symptom and its associated anatomical part. Psychosocial has been used to describe the development of strategies to deal with the implementation of health and social care through achieving some understanding of the complexity of the psychodynamic processes that are part of making sense of experience. In this literature the term itself has been largely unproblematic, but there has been more recent discussion within psychosocial studies about how this psychodynamic relationship should be described and classified, with considerable attention paid to the presence or absence of a hyphen.

The use of the term 'psychosocial' as a single word in this book is not ideological but is intended to provide as broad a remit as possible for psychosocial studies. There are several variants in the labels that are used, and there are debates about which element in the relationship should come first – the psychic or the social and societal (Wengraf, 2004). Psychosocial is recognizable, and, even if most psychosocial departments and research centres are not in psychology, this term acknowledges the intellectual legacy and the role of the psychoanalytic. Psychosocial studies has a particular relationship with psychology (Stenner et al., 2011). It is also my concern not to be too closely linked to one strand within the psychosocial whilst retaining its broad, distinguishing features. There are different approaches to the psychosocial, but this book attempts to be as wide ranging and all-embracing as possible. There are also different labels, such as the psycho-social or the psycho-societal (Wengraf, 2004).

Wendy Hollway argues for the use of the hyphen, as in 'psycho-social' in order to capture the dynamic of the psychosocial relationship because the social is always multiply mediated by the psychodynamic and vice versa. Hollway suggests that the hyphen is necessary for this version of the psychosocial, which is heavily dependent upon **object relations** and the assertion of some reality or truth that can be uncovered, which represents a strong strand in psychosocial studies but is not the only one.

> We are psycho-social because we are products of a unique biography of anxiety- and desire-provoking life events and the manner in which their meanings have been unconsciously transformed in internal reality. We are psycho-social (Wengraf, 2001) because defensive activities affect and are affected by discourses and also because the unconscious defences that we describe are inter subjective processes (that is, they affect and are affected by others). We are psycho-social because the real events in the external, social world are desirously and defensively, as well as discursively appropriated.
>
> (Hollway, 2004:3)

What Hollway's discussion most usefully demonstrates is the focus on the processes, which are internal and external, and the ways in which psychic forces and investments like **defence** mechanisms and **desires** operate at the wider level of society and even global politics. Her approach includes the researcher and issues about how the researcher is implicated in the process of producing and especially interpreting knowledge. What matters is the inextricable combination of elements, of the unconscious and the discursive at the level of the society and the individual in the making of subjectivities, which is embraced by the psycho-social. There are advantages in presenting the two main strands of the psychic and the social as one, in this distinctive new field of inquiry.

Stephen Frosh and Lisa Baraitser (2008) argue for the unhyphenated psychosocial to capture its critical approach and the dynamic interplay of the psychic and the social. They agree that although the field of study remains ill defined, the priority of psychosocial studies is reflexivity, understood as interactively critical 'practice that is constantly reflecting back on itself and is suspicious of the productions of its own knowledge' (Frosh and Baraitser, 2008:350).

These differences in nomenclature are less significant than the distinctiveness of the psychosocial or the psycho-social, whichever term is used. I have used the unhyphenated psychosocial for pragmatic reasons, as an increasingly familiar description that embraces a range of different approaches. Although this is a sometimes eclectic mix, the psychosocial is nonetheless distinctive and recognizable and includes approaches that share particular intellectual and methodological concerns, and it has the potential for developing new and productive research strategies.

This book is informed by the following broad questions:

- What is distinctive about the psychosocial?
- Where do psychosocial ideas and approaches come from – what is their history?
- What sort of questions and puzzles do approaches that identify – or that can be identified – as psychosocial address?

- How do psychosocial approaches engage with these intellectual and methodological issues, and how effective are they?
- In what is largely an emerging field, where is the psychosocial going, and what are the future possibilities for psychosocial studies, for example, in relation to current concerns with affect, emotion, risk, trauma, collective action, politics, and policy?

These more specific questions are also central to the book's discussion of psychosocial studies:

- Why do people do what they do?
- How can the researcher access and understand psychosocial relationality; how do you get into those relational spaces as a researcher?
- Why are people attracted towards some things and people and repelled by others, often in irrational ways that may not be in their own best interests?
- How useful are psychoanalytic concepts across a range of encounters and different relations, outside as well as inside the clinical context?
- How do the emotions associated with intimate and personal life operate in the wider context of international politics? For example, how might hurt, affection, and hatred operate among and between nations as well as individuals?

Questions form an important part of this book, especially in terms of the questions that are raised by taking a psychosocial approach. Each chapter concludes with a set of questions related to the material that has been covered in the chapter.

The book starts with an exploration of some of the repertoires upon which the psychosocial draws. From the start this has been an interdisciplinary field, but there are particular disciplines that have played a significant role, notably psychology, psychoanalysis, sociology, feminism, queer studies, postcolonialism, and cultural studies. Some strands have also drawn upon social policy and politics with their focus upon the policy implications of psychosocial phenomena and the ways in which power operates in psychosocial encounters.

The next three chapters of the book, chapters 2, 3, and 4, trace some of the connections that contemporary psychosocial studies have with earlier attempts at exploring the entanglements of the psychic and the social and the impact of the social in the psychic and the psychic in the social. These three chapters explore different aspects of the psychosocial: intellectually, by thinking about different theoretical approaches, and methodologically, in chapter 3, which includes some of the innovative approaches to finding out that are being developed. Approaches to the self, subjectivity, and identity in chapter 4 are part of the genealogy of psychosocial studies and remain central to its engagements. The following five chapters each highlight a different (but nonetheless interrelated) concern of the psychosocial. This book is not definitive or comprehensive, and more and more aspects of contemporary life are being included in psychosocial research, but each of the sets of ideas covered here shows what is distinctive about taking a psychosocial approach and opens up possibilities.

Chapter 2, *Ideas*, traces earlier attempts at engaging with the intersection of the psychological and the social and with personal worlds and social worlds, many of which come from within the tradition of sociology and cultural studies. The strongest links have been with psychology and psychoanalysis (Parker, 2011), but within the social sciences, especially, sociologists have demonstrated the limitations of what Dennis Wrong first called 'the oversocialized conception of man', to quote from the title of Wrong's famous 1961 article in *American Sociological Review* (Wrong, 1961). Wrong argued for more complex, dialectical approaches to sociological theory than those implied by socialization theories because the process is always incomplete. Wrong was critical of other sociological solutions to the problem of the relationship between individuals and their inner worlds and social forces, such as some of the ideas of functionalism. Functionalists like Talcott Parsons developed the work of US sociologist Robert Merton within the Durkheimian tradition to explore a theory of **internalization**, as the mechanism whereby people take in social norms and values and internalize them (Parsons, [1951]2001).

Most of the major theorists whose work has been of particular importance come from some form of psychoanalysis, based on the work of Sigmund Freud, Jacques Lacan, and the object relations approach of Melanie Klein, albeit moving beyond much traditional psychoanalysis (see Mitchell and Black, 1995). Specific engagements with the connecting or liminal spaces of the psychosocial, however, come from sociology going back to Karl Marx and Marxist critiques such as the Frankfurt School, which has recently offered productive links, for example, in the work of Judith Butler (1990, 1993, 1997, 2005). Louis Althusser is also included as a Marxist theorist who uses psychoanalytic concepts to address some troubling aspects of political subjectivity. Marxist analyses such as those of Althusser (1971) and in different ways Stuart Hall (Hall 1992, 1997) and Slavoj Žižek's explorations of Lacanian psychoanalysis have offered different approaches to the understanding of inner worlds and social systems that provide a focus on power and its imbalances. Franz Fanon's famous critiques of colonialism and racism (1952, 1961) draw upon different strands of psychoanalysis and have been influential in postcolonial psychosocial studies. This chapter maps out some earlier engagements with the psychosocial and shows how they lead into more contemporary approaches, including those of feminism and postcolonialism, becoming a distinctive field of its own.

Chapter 3, *Methodologies*, is central to psychosocial studies. This chapter explores some of the methodological concerns of the psychosocial and highlights some of the particular approaches that have been developed within the field, including a range of qualitative approaches such as narrative (Clarke and Hoggett, 2009), ethnography, discourse analysis auto-ethnography, and biography (Chamberlayne et al., 2012). Narrative and variants of this form of getting under the surface are central to psychosocial approaches (Buckner, 2005; Wengraf, 2000, 2004; Hollway and Jefferson, [2000]2013). In more clinical encounters, analyses have been developed by object relations and Kleinian approaches and by Wilfred Bion ([1962]1991) and Christopher Bollas (1995, [1961]2004), through clinical encounters or analyses of different forms of cultural expression. Psychoanalytic concepts that address some of the ambivalences and contradictions of human experiences such as the **life drive**, the **pleasure principle**, and the **reality principle** have some purchase in exploring some psychosocial processes and relationships, even if the original application of these ideas lay in the therapeutic encounter. The chapter looks at methodologies that identify explicitly with a psychosocial approach. For example, Wendy Hollway and Tony Jefferson have developed a particular version of open-ended interviewing in qualitative research, free association narrative interviews, which provide a route into extending the depth of **analysis** in empirical work to explore some of the psychoanalytical dynamics in play (Hollway and Jefferson, [2000]2013). Narrative in various forms has been used extensively in psychosocial studies, including research using a single respondent to explore the rich, thick data that can be gathered from in-depth analyses. Ideas developed from object relations in particular have been developed to make distinctively psychosocial methodologies, and object relations can be seen as particularly influential in the development of contemporary psychosocial approaches.

Chapter 4, *Selves*, traces some of the relationships between concepts of the self, the subject, and identity and explores the centrality of some understanding of the self within psychosocial studies. The use of particular concepts, such as self, subject, and identity (see Lawler, 2014), has a complicated history (Hall, 1990, 1996; Hall and Gay, 1996), but psychosocial approaches all include recognition of a self who can be reflexive and autonomous, for example, in reinventing that self (Elliott, 1992, 2001, 2004, 2013). The debate has focused upon the emergence of a rational or bounded autonomous self and theories that explain the self as subjected to social and institutional forces, thus lacking any agency. The other aspect of this debate is the matter of boundaries, which psychosocial approaches have addressed by acknowledging the notion of a human, relational self with the capacity for reflection and taking responsibility, whatever the extent of social, economic, political, and cultural constraints. This chapter maps out some of the debates that inform contemporary psychosocial studies including social psychological and sociological work such as the work of US pragmatists such as Charles Horton Cooley ([1902]1964) and William James ([1892]1961), George Herbert Mead (1934), and more recently empirical work such as Charles Taylor's (1989) and David Reisman's (1950), which engages directly with transformations of the self in contemporary western society. More explicitly psychoanalytic accounts draw upon Freud and, in the case of cultural studies, on the work of Jacques Lacan and feminist developments of these approaches such as Luce Irigaray (1985) and Juliet Mitchell (1974, 2003) and explorations of synergies between more discursive,

Foucauldian work and psychoanalytic theory such as Judith Butler's (Butler, 1990, 1993) and more critically, Stuart Hall's work on cultural identity (Hall, 1992). Contributions of social theorists such as George Herbert Mead have also been influential especially in shaping more sociological accounts such as those of Erving Goffman (Goffman, 1959, 1967), which in turn feed into other accounts of the self, the subject, and identity.

Chapter 5, *Affect*, explores the contribution of psychosocial studies to the 'affective turn' (Clough and Halley, 2008; Gregg and Seigworth, 2010; Hoggett, 2010a, 2010b, 2012; Wetherell, 2012) through discussion of the role of emotion and feeling (Frosh, 2011) in both everyday personal lives and in the wider terrain of more collective experiences and demonstrations of feeling (Wetherell, 2012). The purpose of the chapter is to pose some of the questions that psychosocial approaches might deploy in the context of affect and to open up the discussion. There are very different approaches to affect, ranging from those deriving from Barach Spinoza and Gilles Deleuze (Carry and Kwinter, 1992), which appear antithetical to the humanism of psychosocial studies, to views that see affect as emotion and feeling. Some theorists of affect draw upon Deleuzian posthuman ideas (Massumi, 1996), which incorporate the intensity of emotions into their accounts, for example, of trauma (Clough in Harvey et al., 2014). Affect can be located specifically within the field of psychosocial studies, but the field is changing, so my aim is not to be prescriptive but rather to think about possibilities, for example, through conversations between psychoanalytic and sociological theories and those within the broad remit of cultural studies. This chapter also uses the idea of 'being in the zone' (Woodward, 2014) to suggest ways of reconciling different versions of affect and to emphasize the centrality of relationality through the dynamic interaction of affect and sensation and conceptualizations of liminal spaces (Brown and Stenner, 2009; Greco and Stenner, 2013). These approaches go beyond more traditional psychological approaches to the zone that is based on the idea of flow (Csikzentmihalyi, 1997, 2003).

Chapter 6, *Intimacies*, looks at how psychosocial approaches address intimate relations and explores psychosocial responses to changes in this area of experience, which is not confined to the personal. Intimacies embrace a whole range of relationships of family and friendship as well as sexual relationships. This is a field in which psychosocial approaches have had considerable impact, both in challenging the perceived certainties of intimate relations as well as contributing to new ways of thinking about intimacy (Brown, 2006; Roseneil, 2013). Intimate life has been seen as created through individualization and reflexive modernization (for example, Giddens 1992; Beck and Beck-Gernsheim, 1995, 2002; Bauman, 2001). More recently, work on gendered practices of interdependency and care have been included within the study of intimate relations (Brown, 2010, 2012, Finch and Mason, 1993; Jamieson, 1998; Smart, 2000; Ribbens-McCarthy and Edwards, 2003; Tee et al., 2012), which have been influenced by the work of Teresa Brennan (2004), Jane Flax (1993), Jessica Benjamin (1995), Judith Butler (1997), and

Nancy Chodorow (1999). Such approaches build on Butler's view of the psyche as a source of **resistance** to constraining social identities in the making of the self in these areas of life that matter so much but that can be so conflictual that individuals have to do emotional work in reconciling different conflicts (Craib, 1995). Sometimes this emotional work takes place in the more public sphere of policy-directed social care.

Chapter 7, *Risk*, concerns the extent to which risk and anxiety are central to contemporary societies (Bauman, 1989; Beck, 1992). Risk generates anxieties about security and about the self (Hoggett, 2013). Exploring the processes involved in risk raises questions about how anxiety and fear operate within social as well as individual, inner worlds (Hoggett, 2000). Risk is strongly linked to anxiety, and the management of anxiety in which social systems increasingly play an important part as has been recognized for some time (Menzies Lyth, 1960).

Physical and existential dangers threaten the confidence with which nations assert their identity and the security of their boundaries as well as the boundaries of the self and well-being. Risk is particularly interesting because the fear generated by risk is real and motivates collective and individual action, often of an extreme nature, but the perception of risk is also discursive and could constitute a regime of truth or a moral panic in its manifestations in the contemporary world. Risk ranges from concerns about food additives and obesity and routine engagement with risk assessment techniques in most corporations and public organizations to fear of terrorist attack (Seidler, 2013). Risk is a major concern in the contemporary world, even though life expectancy has been extended in most parts of the world and morbidity rates have fallen. Risk and anxiety cannot be explained adequately without being attentive to the psychodynamics of anxiety and the perception of risk as well as its socially quantifiable dimensions. Chapter 7 explores the connections between risk and the making and remaking of the self, especially among the personal, the psychic, and the social, which leads into the next chapter's focus upon a particular manifestation and outcome of the risk society, trauma.

Chapter 8, *Trauma*, deals with what may appear to be a personal and psychic experience that nonetheless has implications for collective and social experience (Rashkin, 1992, 2005, 2009) and includes the representational systems, such as film, in which trauma is so central (Cooper, 2012). Personal trauma is recognized within psychoanalysis in the clinical setting (Mann and Cunningham, 2009; Parens, 2008). Contemporary psychosocial studies bring together the psychic trauma of experiences such as the Holocaust (Rashkin, 1992, 2009; Byford, 2008), which are translated into cultural memory and where trauma is manifest as a personal experience and as one that is collective. This chapter brings together the psychosocial insights of the clinical encounter and historical, social, and cultural manifestations of trauma, which can have global implications, as in the case of 9/11 (Seidler, 2013).

Chapter 9, *Politics*, develops the feminist claim that the personal is political within the scope of psychosocial studies. Psychosocial approaches go much further to explore the connecting space between the psycho and the social in the political arena (Frosh, 1987). The chapter uses a number of different examples, which include exploring social exclusion using a psychoanalytically informed approach (Auestad, 2012a, 2012b, 2014). The unconscious, especially the **collective unconscious**, and feelings, affects, and emotions play a big part in political debates at all levels. The collective unconscious derived from Jung's work (Jung, 1991) has been reinterpreted in different ways. The chapter engages with the politics of 'othering', for example, in psychoanalytic understandings of racism and racialization and of social exclusion and social inequalities. Psychosocial approaches to everyday experiences of the political and the affective dimensions social exclusion include social class and the affective as well as the economic aspects of class-based inequalities (Froggett, 2002). Politics is about exclusion and inequality: politics also involve the promise of change and the challenges of resistance. Psychosocial approaches are not restricted to the individual and self-transformation but also offer the possibilities of political change and the making of new subjectivities. Big contemporary debates such as climate change can also be most productively explored using psychosocial approaches.

Chapter 10, *Conclusion*, offers some reflection upon the scope of psychosocial studies as well as suggesting some possibilities for future developments, intellectually and empirically, in relation to the fields that could be explored and the new questions that could be asked. The Conclusion lists some of the distinguishing features of psychosocial studies, whilst accepting that the field is dynamic and changing and that concluding is really just a start. Reflection includes revisiting some of the puzzles and contradictions of psychosocial studies as well as identifying possibilities for future growth of psychosocial approaches.

There are different ways of looking at psychosocial studies. You could consider what sort of empirical fields are included, or how researchers approach their work, or what sort of theoretical frameworks inform the field. This is where we are going to go next. Where do psychosocial studies come from? What sorts of ideas and theories lead into contemporary psychosocial studies?

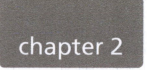

chapter 2

Ideas

This chapter:

1 Explores some of the conceptual routes that the psychosocial has taken in its development.
2 Selects particularly influential ideas, theories, and approaches from the psychoanalytic theories, for example, of Freud and Lacan.
3 Looks at the contribution of object relations following the work of Melanie Klein.
4 Establishes some of the key concepts and developments of psychoanalysis that have been taken up by psychosocial studies.
5 Considers recent developments including the work of Judith Butler in addressing psychosocial questions about the relationship between the social and the psychic.

This chapter explores some of routes that the psychosocial has travelled and considers some of the layers of thought and the kinds of questions that have been addressed, which have led to the main focus of this book, psychosocial studies. As was suggested in the Introduction, there are different disciplinary areas that have attempted to engage with the interrelationship between inner and outer worlds and between the personal and the social, notably psychology, especially social psychology, psychoanalysis in various forms, sociology, and more recently cultural studies.

Psychoanalysis has a long relationship with sociology, for example, in the US in the twentieth century, even if it has not always been a happy marriage and has even resulted in an 'unhappy divorce' (Chancer and Andrews, 2014). Functionalists like Talcott Parsons developed the work of US sociologist Robert Merton within the Durkheimian tradition to explore a theory of internalization, as the mechanism whereby people take in social norms and values and internalize them (Parsons and Shils, [1951]2001).

Connections have been severed more recently, leading to reluctance to deploy psychoanalytic concepts such as the unconscious, anxiety, and defence mechanisms by US sociologists, although things are beginning to change. This chapter begins by setting out the intellectual context of the debate before looking at earlier attempts at engaging with the intersection of the psychological and the social and with personal worlds and social worlds, which may not have been labelled psychosocial and which might not come strictly within the boundaries of contemporary psychosocial studies, but they are discussed in this chapter for three reasons:

1   To demonstrate the conceptual and theoretical legacy of psychosocial studies today; to show which concepts are particularly useful and where psychosocial studies come from.
2   To show examples of how the puzzles and issues with which contemporary researchers grapple have been approached before. Some of the problems remain but these productive attempts at exploring relationality and connections remain influential.
3   To pick out some of the limitations of some past attempts at exploring and reconciling inner worlds and social worlds in order to demonstrate the need for a distinctive approach to the psychosocial and an identifiable field of inquiry and research.

Psychology and psychoanalysis have focused upon the personal and the individual and inner world connections, but nonetheless the big questions about the relationship between inner and outer worlds have always been important. For psychology the question may largely have been posed as: how do outer social worlds operate within the inner world of the psyche? For social theorists and sociologists the question has been more: how does the psyche operate within social worlds, and do unconscious forces play any part in social worlds? Within social sciences, sociologists have demonstrated the limitations of what Dennis Wrong first called 'the oversocialized conception of man' (Wrong, 1961). At a time when socialization theories were particularly dominant, Wrong argued for a more complex, dialectical approach to sociological theory because the process is always incomplete. Charles Wright Mills addressed a similar issue when he asked the question about the point at which a personal trouble becomes a public issue and posited the sociological imagination as a route into understanding how these spaces are related. To understand the interconnections and the spaces in between we need to think creatively and recruit the imagination.

Sociologists have engaged with the dilemma of the space between inside and outside and the puzzle of the inner world, which has led them to explore different possibilities such as the concept of internalization. Wrong was critical of other sociological solutions to the problem of the relationship between individuals and their inner worlds and social forces, especially as expressed in the work of functionalist sociologists who had attempted to explore the connections between individuals and society within a Durkheimian paradigm, which, ultimately, whatever the nuances and complexities, could be seen as resulting in social order. Theories of internalization, as the mechanism whereby people take in social norms and values and internalize them so that it appears that these are the thoughts of the individuals concerned (Parsons, [1951]2001) might seem to be a route into understanding the relationship. In Parsons' work this is a somewhat one way process however, with individuals always internalizing social norms and accepting social values. The association between individuals and society and between the psychic and the social could be more troubling and disruptive. How adequate is an approach that suggests that social factors are internalized? Is this about a relationship, or are these two distinct spaces?

One weakness is the one-sidedness of this relationship, if it is a relationship. The social occupies the inner space. There is little about any influence of the unconscious of inner worlds on the social space. Secondly and most importantly, it works. It is a functional arrangement whereby social norms become internalized so that people believe that these are their thoughts and act accordingly. Inner worlds appear not to be spaces of resistance within this framework.

Most of the major theorists whose work has been of particular importance in the genealogy of psychosocial studies have come from psychoanalysis, based on the work of Sigmund Freud, Jacques Lacan, and Melanie Klein. I am going to start with psychoanalysis, partly because sociological and social theories have specifically engaged with psychoanalysis. The earlier twentieth-century attempts to explore personal, inner worlds, by sociologists in the US drew upon Freud's work most directly (Chancer and Andrews, 2014). It is also useful to select some of the features of psychoanalytic approaches that have been particularly influential in shaping the psychosocial. The discussion that follows is highly selective but seeks to highlight some of the concepts that have been seen to be useful to explorations of the relational space between psychic and social.

Psychoanalysis

Psychoanalysis has played an enormously influential part in western societies, not least in the shift towards self-reflection of late modernity (Giddens, 1991) – so much so that Freud's insights have entered into the common sense of everyday speech. People without any particular familiarity with psychoanalysis refer to 'Freudian slips' or 'slips of the tongue', the name given to parapraxis, the **Oedipal complex**, the **interpretation** of dreams, and make pronouncements about hysterical women and sexual dysfunction, albeit often based upon oversimplifications of Freud's work. Although in the twenty-first century there is some hostility towards psychoanalysis, for example, with the rise of alternative therapies such as CBT (cognitive behavioural therapy) and more substantively a distrust of the therapist who has access to the meaning of our thoughts and actions that we cannot grasp ourselves and reveal our innermost drives, many of Freud's ideas have become routine in everyday life. Other challenges to psychoanalytic thought have been offered within the social sciences and the arts and humanities from a number of very different perspectives, from the growing popularity of 'big data' and grounded empirical work to critiques of interpretation that might seem to present an imbalance that privileges the expert voice of the researcher (or the analyst). These criticisms have been taken on board by psychosocial approaches, which see interpretation as a more collaborative project, but these aspects of the debate need to be highlighted here because they inform later developments and are issues to which the psychosocial has to be attentive.

Psychoanalysis has been very influential in clinical therapeutic practice, in social and cultural intellectual life, and in social theories and in connections among them; the insights of therapeutic encounters have generated productive ways of exploring social relations and have contributed greatly to psychosocial studies. Freud's own work was certainly not confined to the consulting room, and he attempted to explore and explain major social and political phenomena such as the trauma of the First World War and anti-Semitism in his own lifetime, which nonetheless impacted upon everyday life.

The everyday could be the key to understanding the enduring relevance of psychoanalysis and its contemporary translations and reinterpretations. Psychoanalysis has changed and reinvented itself in response to social, political, economic, and cultural transformations and continues to speak to people's everyday concerns and the things that matter to most of us as human beings. Psychoanalysis, like literature, speaks to relationships, feelings, and emotions, which are always in conversation with and implicated in sociocultural change.

Questions and quandaries about psychoanalysis

Psychoanalysis, however, remains intensely controversial, not least because of the claims it makes to reveal inner, underlying truths, which critics, following Michel Foucault (1981), argue could be produced rather than uncovered. Rather than revealing the truth about 'who we are' and our 'true' feelings, psychoanalysis might produce those feelings and anxieties and complexes and give them a label that thus makes them **real** and makes it possible to think that this is what is real. Psychoanalysis itself contributes to particular social relations including sexual difference and heterosexual normativities, rather than revealing the truth about what is naturally and empirically the case, for example. People experience a range of emotions and feelings and a set of knowledge like psychoanalysis organizes these disparate and chaotic feelings and sensations into normalized and accepted categories and those who might be classified as deviant. There is also some disquiet in the clinical context about the privileged position of the therapist who, following Freud, has the status of the all-knowing patriarch who can interpret our thoughts for us. This, however, may be more about particular clinical practices that are framed by the society in which they take place. What matters, however, are psychoanalysis's fundamental assertions about the unconscious and the inter-relationships between the unconscious and social and cultural contexts (Bainbridge, Radstone, Rustin, and Yates, 2007).

Some feminists, especially in the US and from radical and material feminist perspectives, have been very critical of psychoanalytic thought, although it is also the case that feminism has generated some of the most exciting applications and developments of psychoanalytic theories and practices in a very wide range of ways (Brennan, 2004; Butler, 2000; Chodorow, 1989, 1999; Mitchell, 1974; Mitchell and Rose, 1982; Kristeva, [1974]1998; Irigaray, [1977]1985, 2004). The centrality of sex and sexuality psychoanalytic theories has both enhanced their appeal in western cultures, which appear saturated by sexuality in its representational systems as concerns, and generated criticisms for the normative assumptions made, for example, in Freud and Lacan about heterosexuality and family.

The reference to patriarchy as bearer of patriarchal values expresses a major problem with psychoanalysis, especially as developed by both Freud, particularly in his earlier work, and Lacan, for its privileging of male power and male sexuality. These aspects of psychoanalysis have been both challenged and reinterpreted, through the development of alternative approaches to the development of the self and the operations of the unconscious, for example, in prioritizing the role of the mother rather than the 'law of the father' or of new understandings of the unconscious reinvented for changing times – sometimes both. Freud's ideas remain appealing, especially in times of perceived risk, insecurity, and trauma in societies characterized by conflict, externally and internally. Modern societies, such as neoliberal democracies, are marked by individualism, competition, and the dominance of free markets, yet those individuals can be deeply troubled and dependent. The individualism that also makes possible personal projects, which are promoted and facilitated by self-knowledge is a significant feature of **neoliberalism**. The psychoanalytic notion of a contradictory and fragmented self, which is subject to and the subject of unconscious forces, desires, and drives, has considerable purchase in contemporary societies. So what does psychoanalysis bring to psychosocial studies?

Psychoanalysis has a great deal to contribute to both personal life and reflection upon the self and, importantly, social relations, politics, and the operation of power especially as expressed in the contradictory and often conflictual forces of late modernity. Psychoanalysis provides ways of understanding what is irrational and conflictual: feelings of anger, hostility, and hatred as well as affection and love. Hatred can be expressed as racism and misogyny, and love can be irrational and misdirected, whether on the part of individuals or much larger groups. Psychoanalysis offers ways into understanding where contradictory feelings and actions come from and how they are expressed, as well as the possibility of change and remaking of relationships.

Psychoanalytic theories can suggest explanations and are not necessarily normative. For example, by offering an explanation of the mechanisms through which patriarchal power operates and oppresses those who are subordinated to its dominant systems, it can be challenged as feminist critiques such as those of Juliet Mitchell have shown (1974).

Psychoanalysis provides some of the conceptual tools for understanding psychosocial processes. Psychosocial approaches are eclectic and selective, but some of the mechanisms and conceptualizations of psychoanalysis have been particularly productive, especially the unconscious.

The unconscious

> The unconscious changes everything; 'when Freud introduced the notion of the unconscious, he brought a demon into the world which will not let anything alone, but which continually disrupts the things we take for granted and subverts the things we take to be true'.
>
> (Frosh, 1997:242)

What distinguishes psychoanalysis from other psychological theories is the place accorded to the unconscious. The unconscious is made up of the powerful desires, often unmet, which arise in Freudian psychoanalysis from the intrusion of the father into the relationship between the child and the mother. It is rooted in unacknowledged desires that have been repressed, so that the content of the unconscious is forbidden to and by the conscious mind. These are the feelings you don't really want to acknowledge, and social normative pressures in the form of your superego try to stop you from thinking about or acting upon them. They do of course find expression, in the form of dreams, mistakes, or slips of the tongue, which are popularly known as 'Freudian slips' when you reveal what is happening in your unconscious. Jokes and humour are based upon the innuendos that can take us by surprise. The unconscious is also the source of deep, and often dark, contradictory feelings, which can erupt and trigger conscious actions. The unconscious is dangerous territory, but Freud argues that it is not unknowable, and, through therapy, for example, it is accessible.

Different forms of psychoanalysis and psychoanalytic theory have taken a variety of paths following Freud, but all agree that there is some dynamic energy that is the unconscious, which is characterized by its own structures that make it distinct from the conscious mind. There is, however, disagreement about those structures including the extent to which the unconscious is driven by instincts or their representations. The unconscious might be developed in response to loss and the psychic location of unmet desires rather than a primordial force. What is repressed depends upon the cultural context in which such repression takes place, which presents an interesting relationship between inner and outer worlds rather than a more straightforward set of instincts and drives. Also the dominance that Freud accorded to sexual instincts has been challenged. Not all repression is of sexual feelings. Object relations theorists have stressed the relationality of the unconscious, which is based on early childhood experience, especially of the infant's relationship with the mother and with external objects. This is not to say that innate drives are not important: they are in object relations theories. The unconscious remains of central importance in psychoanalytic approaches as an internal area, which is both inside and outside, organized and yet out of control and enormously important in our lives through its often erratic and disruptive emergence at different moments, often with considerable impact upon each of our life stories.

However chaotic and anarchic the unconscious may seem with its unpredict-able eruptions and disruptions, the unconscious has a structure, which can be accessed and understood in different ways, including, and primarily, in Freud's work, with the assistance of psychoanalysis, which provides guidance on the organizing mechanisms of the unconscious and is able to trace repression and **sublimation**. The analyst has some understanding of these processes within the unconscious and the relationships among **id**, **ego**, and **superego** and the apparatuses of the unconscious and the nature of repression and its links to the wider social world.

Freud's Oedipus complex presents a particularly powerful expression of the unconscious. The Oedipus complex is about the incest taboo, which he saw as one of the most powerful forces governing human behaviour and rooted in the psyche. The transgression of this taboo invokes strong feelings of shame and disgust because other passions and desires are implicated in incest. People do not just abide by the incest taboo the same way as they obey other social rules. There is something else going on. The inspiration for Freud's conceptualization of the Oedipus complex was the work of the Classical Greek playwright Sophocles, writing in fifth-century BCE Athens. Sophocles's play *Oedipus Rex* tells the tragedy of Oedipus, who unknowingly kills his own father and marries his mother: the ultimate taboo is broken because Oedipus destroys his father and has sex with his mother. Oedipus is devastated when he realizes what he has done and that he has fulfilled the prophecy of killing his father and mar-rying his mother, and towards the end of the play he blinds himself in his remorse. The inevitability of the outcome is expressed in the prophecy of the oracle, which cannot be resisted, but Oedipus's fate is sealed even more effec-tively by unconscious desires, which carry equivalent force to divine interven-tions and predictions in the ancient world for Freud. Freud is less interested in the power of the taboo and more in the inner world in which infants experience incestuous desire.

The Oedipus complex is seen as central to Freudian psychoanalysis as it accounts for the infant's negotiation of sensuous desires, which are initially directed towards the parents, largely towards the parent of the opposite sex of the child. Different commentators have attributed different values to the idea of the Oedipus complex in Freud and Lacan, including the claim that its focus on male desire can be challenged and that even if little boys desire their mothers and feel threatened by their fathers (with whom they ultimately identify), for little girls there is a more circuitous route to adult sexual maturity.

These ideas, which draw upon a somewhat particular set of cultural traditions, have been heavily criticized on a number of counts, not least cultural specificity and the patriarchal assumptions that underpin Freud's argument. Feminist critics have been strongly critical and have suggested that Freud's (and even more so Lacan's) notions of sexual desire as masculine are deeply flawed. Nonetheless the unconscious and those desires that are repressed play a powerful role in shaping desire and sexual feelings along with other powerful motivating forces.

Feminism and psychoanalysis

Given the emphasis that both Freud and Lacan place on sexual difference and the primacy of patriarchal or **phallocentric** power, it may seem surprising that feminists have been so interested in their work. Nonetheless, feminist work, especially using object relations as well as, particularly within particular branches of cultural studies and film studies, Lacanian psychoanalysis, has been enormously productive, especially in exploring the processes through which representational systems, like film, connect the psyche and social and cultural forms. Feminist psychoanalysis has also subverted the assumed norm of the male subject and demonstrated the fragility and fragmentation of all subjectivities as well as their interconnectedness. Psychoanalysis provides the concept of the unconscious as an explanatory framework for making sense of what is not necessarily rational, does not immediately seem comprehensible at all, and appears illogical to the rational mind, but which nonetheless is an immensely strong energy, shaping actions, connections, and relationships in the social world as well as understanding the self. Sexuality is one such area of human experience. The specificities of particular social arrangements and systems do not constrain the unconscious for all time. What is more important than any claims to the universality of particular forms of social organization is the nature of the unconscious and its mechanisms.

Freud was clearly hostile to feminist sexual politics, but this does not devalue the possibilities of psychoanalysis, and Freud was himself enmeshed in a particular culture. As Lynne Segal has argued, 'Freud did not invent the dread and repudiation of "feminists" in his patients (and in himself) though he did begin to take account of its dangerous and damaging consequences' (Segal, 1997).

As Juliet Mitchell so strongly argued (1974), psychoanalysis can destabilize the cultural fictions of sexual difference and male power. Freud was not only imposing and assuming social and cultural values about sexuality and sexual difference, he was describing lived inequalities and a particular social world that has not only persisted in many social institutions and practices into the twenty-first century but also survives within the unconscious, collectively and individually. It is not a justification of heterosexuality and phallocentrism; it can be used to explore the mechanisms through which these power geometries play out in the lives and feelings of individuals, most forcefully through the unconscious.

Feminist challenges have often taken on board the overemphasis upon patriarchy and the 'law of the father', especially in Lacanian psychoanalysis, and have sought to redress the imbalance by focusing upon the pre-Oedipal stage of development and upon the role of the mother in a variety of ways. One set of approaches is object relations, which is discussed later in this chapter, but what have very loosely been termed 'French feminisms' including the work of Luce Irigaray provide another approach, which challenges Lacanian phallocentrism but retains the psychoanalytic stages of development and the centrality of the unconscious.

Irigaray provides a critique of Freudian and Lacanian phallocentric, male-dominated desire and argues for a different approach, which includes women as desiring subjects and puts motherhood into culture. She also claims that psychoanalysis is itself governed by unconscious phantasies, which it cannot analyze. Lastly her work points to the specifically patriarchal qualities of psychoanalysis, which focus upon the transmission of culture from father to son, with a premium on identification with the father and his law.

Irigaray turns her attention to the pre-Oedipal stage and the infant's relationship with the mother and puts this relationship back into culture as a dark continent, which has been so significantly silenced and underrepresented in western culture. Irigaray presents a particularly turbulent relationship between mother and infant and makes the case that Freud's use of the Oedipus myth demonstrates how myths reflect particular cultures and not universal qualities and capacities. She challenges Freud's claim in *Totem and Taboo* that the murder of the father is what founds the primal horde, arguing that, rather, the archaic murder of the mother is what establishes the patriarchal polis.

Irigaray particularly critiques Lacan for his claims that even if the power of the phallus is illusory, the category and subject 'woman' is constituted in terms of lack, of not being a man. Irigaray seeks a female **imaginary** and the expression of desire for women in **jouissance**, which belongs to the pre-Oedipal phase before the infant enters the patriarchal culture, as outside the patriarchal symbolic order.

> [T]he relationship with the mother is a mad desire, because it is the 'dark continent' par excellence. It remains in the shadows of our culture; it is its night and its hell. But men can no more, or rather less, do without it than can women. And if there is now such a polarization over the question of abortion and contraception, isn't that one way of avoiding the question: what of the imaginary and symbolic relationship with the mother, with the

woman-mother? What of that woman outside her social and material role as reproducer of children, as nurse, as reproducer of labour power?

(Irigaray, [1977]1985:35)

In this short quotation there are a number of elements that resonate with other feminist challenges to and reworkings of psychoanalysis. Irigaray focuses upon mothers and the mother–child relationship rather than giving primacy to the father. This focus involves an engagement with social practices and processes including familial relationships and those of caring as well as the social control of women's bodies. This also suggests the need to recognize the entanglement of psychic and social worlds and the contingency and specificity of the social world.

The critique is still within a psychoanalytic framework in that inner worlds are shaped by and shape social worlds. The unconscious is subject to different forces of which Irigaray demands fuller analysis and recognition. She argues that the silence enjoined on the mother perpetuates dreadful fears and phantasies, including the mythical figure of the mother as devouring monster, which arise out of 'the unanalysed hatred from which women as a group suffer culturally' (quoted in Whitford, 1991:25).

What is relevant to psychosocial studies about this discussion is the acknowledgement of the particularities of the social world and the problem of reconciling shifting patterns of social relations including those between infants and carers. Irigaray also emphasizes the role of the maternal body in the processes of relating to the child and consequently in her conceptualization of sexual difference. Although Irigaray has been criticized for 'essentializing the capacities of the body in shaping women's experience, there are strong arguments that what she is doing is integrating corporeality and the flesh into an account that combines the social and the psychic. Following the 'corporeal turn' (Howson, 2005), there has been more engagement with the role of bodies (Butler, 1993) and in the making of enfleshed selves and as part of a psychosocial understanding of difference (Woodward, 2009, 2012b; Woodward and Woodward, 2009). Human beings are sentient and the affective nature of the psychosocial includes the senses and the body as part of the relational processes combining the psychic and the social. Some of this discussion has been taken up in the exploration of feelings and of affect, which is the subject of chapter 5.

Others have taken different paths in exploring the possibilities and in developing approaches that are more explicitly psychosocial, but some of the discussion in this chapter includes influential approaches, which might not be classified as psychosocial although they deal with what are big psychosocial issues and the everyday puzzles of relationality.

Judith Butler also draws upon psychoanalytic theories and explores the interconnectedness of inner and outer worlds in a variety of different ways including a particular engagement with psychoanalysis and Foucauldian social constructionism. What matters here is that this work raises the questions and poses new ones that are the focus of the psychosocial.

Judith Butler: The psyche and the social

From *Gender Trouble* (1990) onwards, psychoanalytic theory has played an increasingly important role in Butler's work. Psychoanalytical theory, especially Lacanian theory with its emphasis upon symbolic and representational systems rather than naturalistic bodies, has been a resource for Butler's deconstruction of gender binaries. Other feminist critiques have emphasized the role of systems by drawing upon different theoretical frameworks (Coleman, 2013), but Butler's work is particularly important for my purposes in this book because she addresses psychoanalysis directly. By reiterating the normative discursive practices that constitute heterosexual masculinity and femininity, the subject is materialized as a socially intelligible and acceptable subject. In this way both sex, as anatomical and a naturalistic set of corporeal properties, and gender are all about performance. Performance involves the repeated citation and embodiment of compelling norms. The repetition of sex and gender produce a semblance of something that seems to be self-evidently biological and natural, but that is nonetheless part of the social embodiment of sexual difference (Braidotti, 1994). Thus it appears that binary gender and heterosexuality are facts of nature. Reiteration is also a process of continuous change, although the dominance of the heterosexual matrix and the relegation of oppositional forms of sex and sexuality, for example, in practices like drag, to the margins might reinforce the idea that the system of making and remaking sexual difference and heterosexuality largely works through social and cultural systems. The repetition of norms, depending on context, may emphasize or reduce or confirm or undermine the power and meaning of the cited norms.

Although Butler's work on gender performativity has been enormously influential, her direct engagement with exploring the psychic and the social attempts at reconciling a social constructionist, discursive Foucauldian approach with that of psychoanalysis have been less obviously successful. Psychoanalytic theories are, however, rather than an aberration, central to Butler's work (Lloyd, 2007), especially the psychoanalytic concept of desire. Butler offers a robust critique of psychoanalysis, especially of the Oedipus complex, and draws upon the idea of desire in *Gender Trouble* (1990) and later, more directly, in *The Psychic Life of Power* (1997). Butler's work is not really psychosocial; it is not psychosocial as defined by most who work in the field, but it remains enormously influential and she deals with some of the same questions as psychosocial approaches address. Although she poses the question in the context of the conflict between Foucault's discursive approach and psychoanalytic theories, she is asking why people conform to oppressive regimes and where and how resistance can take place. One of the oppressive regimes is embedded in psychoanalysis, especially in the Freudian and Lacanian Oedipus complex, which Butler seeks to displace from its dominant position within psychoanalysis. She does use psychoanalytic theory in her own formulation of subjectivity, and although *The Psychic Life of Power* is the publication that deals most directly with the role of the psyche, psychoanalytic theory is really important in understanding Butler's critique of heteronormativity, and her conceptualization of subjectivity in *Gender Trouble* is largely where it starts.

Butler uses psychoanalysis to deconstruct the hegemony of heterosexuality, which she calls the heterosexual matrix through which heterosexual desire is reiterated and practised. Psychoanalysis, more than any other theoretical or ideological framework, focuses upon desire (Clough, 1994). At this point desire seems more practised and reiterated than a disruptive force within the psyche as might be more the case with in a psychoanalytic framework.

In *Gender Trouble*, Butler still follows Foucault and argues that psychoanalysis is a contributory factor in perpetuating the dominance of heterosexuality. Psychoanalytic therapies have been used to normalize heterosexual relationships by, for example, positioning same sex relationships as aberrant and perverse or deviant. For example, in 'Prohibition Psychoanalysis and the Production of the Heterosexual Matrix' she argues that psychoanalysis perpetuates heteronormativity (Butler, 1990). However, in later work Butler attempts to provide more substantial connections between psychoanalysis and social constructionist, discursive approaches.

The discussion that frames Butler's account of the interplay of the psyche and the social focuses on the question of the universality of Freud's concept of the Oedipus complex and the meaning of the phallus and, thus, of sexual difference in Lacan (Butler et al., 2000). Butler reverses Žižek's causal privileging of the psyche by claiming that the psyche is derived 'from prior social operations' (Butler, 1997:21). An important aspect of this reversal is her reinterpretation of the symbolic 'law of the father'. Butler reinterprets the symbolic law in terms of historical and social contingency as an aspect of power, and as a variable set of prohibitions, norms, threats, and idealizations.

She uses Foucault's concept of power but rejects the idea that the subject is only the product of disciplinary and normalizing power by arguing that Foucault reduces the psyche, or what Foucault calls the soul, to the social. For example, in *Discipline and Punish* (1977), Foucault explains his idea of technology of the self as part of the disciplinary power of institutions, such as the panoptic prison, which generates an inner agency of control and surveillance. The soul, which could be construed as the nearest Foucault gets to an inner self or psyche, is still an effect of the social and thus reducible to the social. Butler points out that the soul is not only not a very likely source of passionate attachment, but that it is also unclear what drives the subject to attach to power structures that are so constraining. Butler's emphasis upon iterative practices might suggest that the heterosexual matrix cannot be challenged and in effect, it works. However, she draws attention to the question of how 'psychic resistance to normalization' is possible (Butler, 1997:87). She suggests that it is the incommensurability between psyche and subject that enables psychic resistance to the compelling power of norms or to the normalizing power of the social (ibid.). Butler appears to allude to an unconscious psychic agency that is incommensurable with the conscious ego.

Her use of the term 'psyche' instead of the unconscious suggests a distancing from traditional psychoanalytical notions of the unconscious and an explicitly Lacanian unconscious. For example, she argues against the Lacanian 'Real', as unconscious, 'which resists symbolization absolutely' (Lacan, 1988:66), which 'is impossible to imagine, impossible to integrate into the symbolic order, and impossible to attain in any way' (Evans, 1996:160); the real appears to refer to an absolute outside, and that is precisely Butler's problem with the real. Whereas it constrains the symbolical and the imaginary from outside, the real itself is impossible to attain and cannot be assimilated into the social. The psyche as the unconscious *is* the social. Butler attempts to establish a middle position between Foucault and Lacan, between a soul that is social and an unconscious that constrains the social while being itself completely separate.

Butler indicates her distance from established psychoanalytical theory and, at the same time, establishes the cornerstones. Her account of the relation of the political and the psychic remains relatively unconvincing, but I have used it here to demonstrate one of her more explicit engagements, which endeavours to address, on the one hand, that the symbolic law is transformed into a changeable formation, the status and content of which depend on historical context and contingent power relations. For example, Butler argues that society is structured by the symbolic law of heterosexuality and a binary logic of gender, which triggers the foreclosure of early homosexual identifications and attachments to the same sex parent, producing a subject with a restricted sexual and gender identity. Without foreclosure, Butler loses the dimension of the psyche and the unconscious, and would be left with merely a Foucauldian subject. It is unclear what could constitute the unconscious (the psyche) in Butler's account. There is no persuasive account of resistance. If foreclosure is constitutive of the subject, then it is hard to see what psychic sources the subject will draw upon to resist the symbolic law.

Butler herself concedes that 'desire will aim at unravelling the subject, but be thwarted by precisely the subject in whose name it operates . . . for desire to triumph, the subject must be threatened with dissolution' (Butler, 1997:9).

Butler's work has been enormously influential, and whatever the difficulties there are in her specific attempts at reconciling psychoanalysis with Foucauldian social constructionism, her critique of sex and gender and her conceptualization of performativity as well as her later political, philosophical work make her a key player in the theoretical debates that are central to the psychosocial.

Another strand of psychoanalytic thinking that is more directly associated with the psychosocial draws upon object relations.

Object relations

Object relations offers explanations of the relationship between inner worlds and objects in the social world, between the developing ego and the objects, which include people and parts of people, encountered. From its very first arrival in the world the infant relates to the world outside itself, for example, in seeking out the mother's breast. This approach differs from Freud's assertion that the infant is motivated by drives to relate to others in order to satisfy those drives. Object relations reverses the order and suggests that human beings seek relationships first.

Object relations concentrates on the pre-Oedipal relationship between mother and child as a time before the revaluation of the father's place in the social order disrupts the symbiotic connections between mother and child. This is in opposition to the Freudian and Lacanian stress upon the Oedipal stage and the importance of the point at which the child recognizes paternal power and authority and enters into patriarchal culture. Object relations theories and practices, although embracing some diversity, offer a challenge to the male-dominated paradigms of Freud and Lacan (although both have been developed most productively by feminist critics, as was shown above).

In US object relations, for example, in the work of Nancy Chodorow and Dorothy Dinnerstein, there has been a foregrounding of the mother's subjectivity as an independent being with her own desires, and the sex of the child is seen as important in the mother–child relationship, rather than girls being construed negatively as 'not male' or as castrated.

Object relations theories, especially those based upon Melanie Klein's detailed observations and clinical work with young children, provide strong arguments for a conception of an inner world marked by conflicts. Inner life is not a simple reflection of or reaction to the society we live in; it is not psychodynamic nor is it structured according to principles of cognition, which are subject to rationality (Craib, 1998). As in all psychoanalytic theories, inner worlds are contradictory and fragmented, but object relations adds the importance of relationality to the psychoanalytic approaches of Freud and Lacan and offers a challenge to Freudian patriarchal assumptions and Lacanian phallocentricity.

There are particular features of object relations that have led to the influence of this school of thought in psychosocial studies. Firstly, object relations approaches offer a different approach to the operation of the unconscious, which emphasizes relationality, for example, between subject and object. Secondly, whilst retaining the centrality of the unconscious and the importance of sexual difference, these approaches challenge the Freudian and Lacanian stress on patriarchy and explore the mother–child relationship in the development of subjectivity. Thirdly, object relations present some diversity of approaches, for example, through alternatives to the pleasure-seeking libido and less emphasis upon sexuality and sex as the only object of desire. Kleinian psychoanalysis argues that there is an inner world that recognizes the necessity of conflicting phantasies that arise from the anxieties inherent in the intense intimacies of early dependency and love. This inner world is so complex that individuals unconsciously use aspects of the external world to represent aspects of their own internal world. These internal objects such as mental concepts or representations of others, which are not identical to the qualities of actual, are allowed a relative autonomy. These objects can be destructive or creative. They are destructive when **splitting** and **projection** overwhelm the capacity to distinguish between different realities of external and internal worlds.

Melanie Klein's work has been particularly influential within object relations and within psychosocial approaches. Klein developed an understanding of the pre-Oedipal psyche through play analysis, a technique for psychoanalyzing children that hugely influenced child analysis. Klein's model of mental structures established the life and death instincts as opposing principles. She focused upon defence mechanisms using the key concepts of the **paranoid schizoid position** and the **depressive position** as the major explanatory concepts in her work. These, she argued, were the mechanisms deployed by the rudimentary ego to deal with conflicts between the two drives. These are positions rather than developmental stages and as such can be found in the adult as well as the child psyche.

The paranoid schizoid position is dominated by persecutory mechanisms and those of splitting. Anxiety produces fear of annihilation and death so that splitting, projection, and **introjection** become strategies for defence of the ego and a means of organizing internal chaos in a self-preserving manner, albeit for the infant a relatively primitive one.

The depressive position signals the transition between seeing the mother as a part object and then as a whole object and understanding that feelings of love and hate are directed at the same person. When the infant realizes that feelings of hate are also being directed against the mother who is also loved, the child may experience guilt and the need to attempt reparation. Juliet Mitchell argues that Klein offers a rich descriptive phenomenology of the fluid experiences of nonverbal affect, which includes nonverbal communication, identifications, and merged relationships, all of which are elements of a successful clinical practice and relationship between therapist and patient.

Klein has been influential for a number of reasons. Her work opposes Freud's theorization of female sexuality based upon male norms and a single masculine model. Her emphasis upon the pre-Oedipal period (like Irigaray's, albeit from a different perspective and using very different methodologies) opens up the possibility of exploring this important period in the child's life and the relationship between the infant and the mother including the child's relationship to the mother's body. Also, in addressing the reparative aspects of the psyche, it becomes possible to think positively and creatively about change and social and psychic transformations.

Klein's work has been important for clinical therapeutic practice as well as work with children. Her work, like most of the approaches discussed so far, places considerable emphasis upon the psychic aspects of the interrelationship between inner and outer worlds and the possibilities of developing a psychosocial approach. Other very significant perspectives and theoretical frameworks have begun from very different starting points and with much greater emphasis upon the social, including, in the case of Marxism, the economic base of society.

Marxism

Marx's concern with social change and indeed with revolution, which demanded revolutionary collective action, required some understanding of the context in which revolution would occur and the processes through which, specifically in the case of capitalist societies, the proletariat would achieve a state of consciousness in which the overthrow of capitalism would become possible. Thus Marxism is attentive to states of consciousness and false consciousness and some of the complexities of the conditions in which collective action is motivated. Marxism has also been influential in the search for explanations of the interrelationship between the collective psyche and the social through its concerns with collective consciousness and collective action, and there have been several different attempts at reconciling agency and the personal with the inevitability of social conditions and the influence of socioeconomic forces upon action. For example, existentialist and phenomenological theoretical approaches have been explored in relation to those of economic determinism (Sartre, [1957]1963).

More recently in the second half of the twentieth century, specific engagements with the connecting or liminal spaces of the psychosocial have come from sociology, which draws upon the work of Karl Marx and Marxist materialist critiques such as the Frankfurt School and later Louis Althusser (1971) as well as developments in cultural studies, notably those of Stuart Hall (1992, 1997) and British cultural studies, especially as linked to the Birmingham Centre for Cultural Studies (BCCS).

Marxist materialism had been very critical of psychoanalysis, however, whatever the inclusion of some elements of psychoanalytic theory in developments of Marxism in the later twentieth century. As Raymond Williams pointed out in his *Keywords*, materialism has a long and complex history (Williams, 1976:163–7). Marxist materialism has always given priority to the economic base of society and the relations between people and production, especially in terms of ownership and control of capital. At its simplest, materialism is opposed to idealist, theological, or spiritual explanations for the material and physical origins and bases for causality in human and natural life. Social relations are shaped by material circumstance. The overarching emphasis of Marxism was to reject Hegel's idealism and the argument that ideas shaped social relations and historical change. As Marx and Engels wrote in *The German Ideology*, 'The ruling ideas are nothing more than the expression of the dominant material relations grasped as ideas' (Marx and Engels, 1976:59). Marx and Engels argue in relation to psychology that it is not consciousness which determines life, but life consciousnesses. Thus they rejected any philosophy which takes consciousness as its starting point. Historical materialism claims that the history of production is 'man's psychology present in tangible form' (Marx, 1975:354). This all looks pretty oppositional to any psychoanalytical or psychosocial approaches, and you may be wondering why Marxist materialism is here in this book. Historical materialism presents some difficulties in relation to the collective action, which is required to effect change, and Marx had to grapple with these problems.

For the purposes of this book, it is important to note that Marx argued for a recognition of human agency, albeit a freedom to act born of necessity, but none-theless a key motor for historical change. For revolutionary transformation to be effected under capitalism, the working class has to achieve a state of consciousness and recognize the possibility and the necessity of acting. This necessity also poses some troubling questions about the conditions in which, for example, revolution might take place. If resistance and revolution are in a sense inevitable, why do they not happen? Economic determinism is insufficient to explain action; the dialectic of historical change requires agency as well as social and cultural change. People react to those conditions and can bring about transformation. It is the concerns with the cultural components of the superstructure and the nature of consciousness and what conditions make it possible to act within Marxism that have made historical materialism relevant to the discussion of the psychosocial. The Marxist legacy is useful, firstly, because of its concerns with consciousness and action, and secondly, because of its concerns with inequality, which present a caveat for more individualized agentic accounts, which are insufficiently attentive to the material conditions in which subjects and selves are made and remade. Thirdly, the puzzles that historical materialism generates have been taken up with some enthusiasm by later theorists who have focused on the contributions of psychoanalysis in addressing questions about the relationship between the psychic and the social and exploring how inner worlds impact upon social and cultural practices and norms as well as the operation of the social within the psyche.

One such set of developments comes from the Frankfurt School's attempts to engage the relationship between Marxist materialism and psychoanalysis.

Frankfurt School

The work of the group of German left-wing intellectuals known as the Frankfurt School, Theodor Adorno, Erich Fromm, Max Horkheimer, Herbert Marcuse, and Wilhelm Reich's *The Mass Psychology of Fascism* (1970) has been influential in a number of ways. The Frankfurt School is not specifically psychosocial but is worth mentioning for two reasons. Firstly, the mixed and not always compatible social commentators and philosophers in this group addressed some of the questions that are the concern of contemporary psychosocial studies, especially in relation to irrationality, although issues are not expressed in the same language of passivity and distortion, but there are social and cultural questions about the seeming irrationality of individuals and groups in contemporary cultural life. Frankfurt School critical theorists questioned the apparent passivity of the mass of people in the face of the expansion of popular culture. The relationship between psycho-analysis and culture is a strong element in the genealogies of the psychosocial (Elliott and Frosh, 1995). Why do people accept mass-produced goods, values, and norms so uncritically and offer so little resistance or creative challenges? Secondly, some recent psychosocial theorists and research in this field have taken up some of the intellectual contributions of the Frankfurt School more directly in their own work.

The Frankfurt School is the collective term used to describe a group of critical thinkers associated with left-wing politics although not connected to any particular party and indeed critical of communism, which were associated with the Institute for Social Research set up in Frankfurt in 1923. The Frankfurt School used concepts of reification and alienation, taken from Marx, and were also greatly influenced by psychoanalytic theory in the exploration of the exploitative and insidious mechanisms of oppression, including the fast-developing mass media in contemporary society. These critical theories targeted the ways in which aesthetic and intellectual life could be seen as being downgraded by the public bureaucracies and commercial organizations that distort and manipulate public consciousness so that not only is the working class in a state of quiescent 'false consciousness' such that they fail to realize the conditions of their own oppression, but the public at large lacks critical awareness of social and political matters. Material wealth is presented as the key indicator of well-being and the greatest good in any society, even though large numbers of people who appear to collude with this statement are not themselves participating in any of the benefits of affluence.

Critical theory aimed to explore, analyze, and explain these phenomena including the extremes of what Max Weber called rationalization, which led to huge bureaucracies and market economies that prioritized money and profit at all costs: often at the cost of personal and collective well-being for a large number of people who nonetheless seemed oblivious to the extent to which they were being manipulated. A key concern was what could be seen as the oversimplified Marxist concept of false consciousness and the need to explore some of the complexities of the ways in which knowledge is produced and understood and the relationship between what is conscious and what is unconscious.

Frankfurt School theorists have been accused of excessive pessimism and over-determinism because they appear to be suggesting that the public passively and uncritically receives the outpourings of popular culture and the mass media. The Birmingham Centre of Cultural Studies later in the twentieth century was most actively engaged in challenging this overdeterminism whilst largely sharing the critical stance of the Frankfurt School (Hall, 1982). These issues remain, though, as well as some of the big questions about the reception of popular culture and its oppressive, exploitative, and stultifying, even soporific, qualities. There are still important questions. The third series of the reality television show, 'Big Brother', attracted huge numbers of votes to decide who should be expelled from the house, thus generating debate about the greater interest and enthusiasm, especially among young people, ages eighteen to twenty-four, for the democratic process in reality TV than the political process of the general election in the UK in 2005 (Coleman, 2006). How can the reception of popular culture be explained?

Max Horkheimer (1895–1973) and Theodor Adorno (1903–1969), two leading members of the School, were exiled to the US following the rise of Nazism and the Second World War but returned to Frankfurt in the late 1940s to continue their work. Other notable members of the School were Walter Benjamin (1892–1979), whose work has also been influential in psychosocial and psychoanalytic sociological work, and Herbert Marcuse (1898–1979), whose critique of the power structures of the establishment were seen as particularly significant in the late 1960s in student politics in the US and in Europe. This is illustrated in the UK, France, and Germany in revolutionary political activity, which also inspired the Marxist psychoanalytical work of Louis Althusser (1918–1990). The work of Eric Fromm (1900–1980), also part of the Frankfurt School, has also impacted upon more recent psychosocial approaches. In the second generation Jurgen Habermas (1929) has played a key role in revitalizing psychoanalysis within political philosophy and is probably the best-known political philosopher associated with the Frankfurt School. Habermas argued that self-reflection enables self-knowledge, which can provide freedom from ideological domination, for example, from dominant paradigms including the exclusivity of positivist science. For Habermas, psychoanalysis is a hermeneutic, interpretative science based upon self-reflection, which can yield understanding of conscious and unconscious thought.

The earlier work of Adorno, Benjamin, and Fromm has had a great deal of relevance for psychosocial studies. For example, Adorno, who was a musicologist, philosopher, and cultural critic, wrote a damning indictment of mass culture (Adorno, 2001a, 2001b) but nonetheless saw the possibilities of some agency and autonomy and even of resistance to the all-pervasive force of contemporary mass media in Schonberg's atonal music (Adorno, 1938).

Perhaps ironically, in light of the social forces that have shaped jazz as music of resistance to oppression and social inequalities, Adorno did not see such possibilities in jazz. Adorno also used a combination of sociological and psychoanalytical ideas to make sense of the personality traits of those who are attracted to fascism and, in particular in his own lifetime, Nazism (Adorno and Horkheimer, 1950). In Adorno's work, as with others of the Frankfurt School, what is relevant to the discussion in this book is the attempts made, often from different perspectives, to explore the relationship between levels of consciousness, inner worlds, and social and cultural forces and the question of the extent to which people are able to take responsibility for their own understanding and perception of culture. This is especially pertinent in light of social change, which led to the all-embracing ubiquitous forces of the mass media and popular culture.

Adorno and Horkheimer's work on anti-Semitism has contributed to more recent psychosocial work on extreme political ideologies and transnational expressions of hatred and violence, which also explore the processes through which racist and fascist politics are made and experienced in what could be seen as a psychosocial account. Their approach combines contingent political, social, and economic circumstances and emotional expressions of anger against particular social and ethnic groups. Victims and perpetrators are caught up in the dynamics of fascism, which brings together economic and social processes and affect.

Adorno and Horkheimer base their analysis upon a critique of capitalism and positivist rationality and develop an understanding of the formation of the self in relation to others using psychoanalytic concepts such as projection and sublimation.

Adorno is one of the most interesting members of the Frankfurt School because of his influence on later writers, such as Judith Butler, who uses his work on moral philosophy (Adorno, 2001a, 2001b) in the development of her own ideas about the ethics of the self and the question of responsibility, that is, taking responsibility for oneself. Adorno explores the extent to which being human involves being able to give an account of oneself within any particular social context.

The field is characterized by legacies from different disciplines, which also contributes to the interdisciplinarity of the developing field of psychosocial studies today. One of the conversations and productive relationships is that between psychology and sociology.

Psychology and the psychosocial

Stephen Frosh expresses the relationship between psychology and the psychosocial in terms of the problems of theorizing the relation between the individual and the social, which 'risks the Scylla of reducing one to the other (so that, for example, the social is seen as no more than the free interactions of individuals, or the individual is seen as fully constituted by her or his social class, or gender or "race" position), and the Charybdis of essentializing each element so that the social is "bracketed off" in discussions of the individual, or vice versa' (Frosh, 2003:1547). This ambiguous relationship is what the *psychosocial* seeks to explore. Nonetheless Frosh acknowledges the particularities of the relationship between the psychosocial and the discipline of psychology. Psychosocial work is sometimes based in departments of psychology rather than other social sciences disciplines, and the emphasis upon the psyche may lead to assumptions that this is the work of psychology as well as the use of concepts and approaches, which might seem more concerned with inner worlds of individuals. Psychoanalysis occupies a different space from psychology, however, and psychoanalysis has been particularly influential in sociology and other disciplines in the arts, humanities, and social sciences, including gender studies; feminist theory and feminist politics have also shared concerns with psychoanalytical theory (Benjamin, 1988).

Sociology has provided a welcoming home for psychosocial studies, though, because of the interdisciplinarity of the discipline and because sociology has generated some of the most interesting attempts at addressing ambivalence and disruption as well as seeking patterns. Sociology has also confronted the problem of why people do what they do and why; whatever the economic and social conditions, people do not do what might have been expected.

The term 'psychosocial' is often used to refer to relatively conventional articles and work dealing with social adjustment or interpersonal relations, for example, in therapeutic contexts or within health care and mental health and education. Explicit reference to 'psychosocial' has often been made in the context of counselling and psychotherapy, and, for example, in relation to health and well-being, the need to be attentive to the social and emotional dimensions of illness, as well as the emotional impact of problems of social welfare and social disadvantage. Within the health care literature there has been a move towards relating social conditions to mental health and to exploring the psychosocial determinants of health in social epidemiology. These trends are often in tension with pharmaceutical solutions to perceived health problems, but there is a significant move towards health and welfare services seeking to address the whole person, rather than an isolated set of symptoms. Psychosocial approaches also attribute agency and responsibility to participants and counter the passivity of the patient or client who is the recipient of expert intervention, but there are dangers if the personal and the social are still separate spheres if connected in the life experience because such separation can lead to blaming the victim and suggesting that vulnerable individuals have brought problems upon themselves. These could be health problems associated with lifestyle 'choices' such as overeating, lack of exercise, drinking alcohol to excess, or smoking, or they could be linked to mental health difficulties, which are also imbricated in contemporary patterns of social life with its emphasis upon success, pace, and individual responsibility. There is a growing literature in medical and health science as well as more widely in the application of therapeutic skills to everyday life.

It has, however, been rarer within the psychological literature to find attempts to examine the psychosocial as a seamless entity, as a space in which notions that are conventionally distinguished, such as individual and society, are thought of together and as intimately connected or possibly even the same thing. A possible reason for this separation is the difficulty of conceptualizing the 'psychosocial' as an intertwined entity, with all the puzzles and questions it raises: for example, in relation to conventional practices in separating these fields and in reconciling the two as co-constitutive.

The interdisciplinarity of psychosocial studies is one of its distinguishing features and major strengths and at the same time one of its contradictions. The discussion and the examples that follow in this book aim to demonstrate some of the creative possibilities of attempts to bring together the psychic and the social.

Conclusion

This chapter has set out some of the attempts that have been made to explore why people do what they do by linking psychic factors to those of social change. The chapter has suggested some of the conceptual tools that have been used and has looked at the links between different disciplines and, in particular, the role of psychoanalysis in shaping attempts to bring together inner and outer worlds. One of the problems that has been identified is the separation of the psychoanalytic and the social in most of the accounts, whatever the intentions of theorists who have worked in this field.

We are left with the puzzle of how to do this – how to integrate the psychic and the social and how to see them as entangled and not separate and distinct. We do have some conceptual tools with which to do this and even some success stories. Sociology has pointed to the need to disengage from oversocialized conceptualizations and the need to explore contradictions; people do not always act in their own best interests, nor do they act predictably, whatever the social conditions.

Psychoanalysis in various forms suggests some of the mechanisms through which a psychosocial approach might be developed, notably the idea of the unconscious with its disruptive energies and particular mechanisms such as those of defence, which open up so many possibilities for thinking about how collectively people feel threatened and might adopt defensive positions. Psychoanalysis suggests some possibilities for transferring some of the approaches of the consulting room and the therapeutic encounter but necessarily acknowledging that it is not enough simply to apply psychoanalytic concepts to social phenomena. The next step is thinking about how to go about it. What methodologies might be used in psychosocial studies? Why are the methods of finding out so important, and what is distinctly psychosocial about the links between theories and methods and how the ideas in this chapter are so closely connected to the methods in chapter 3?

Questions

1   What sort of things triggered the idea of a psychosocial approach?
2   Think of an example of a social phenomenon that is currently defined as a social issue, for example, in relation to health, such as smoking or being overweight. How are psychic and social factors connected in this example? Are feelings involved, and if so, how?
3   How can psychoanalysis explain social issues? Is it possible to apply a psychoanalytic approach to a social issue? Can you think of examples of where it might be useful to think about the unconscious in the context of a social rather than an individual issue?
4   What do you think are the main issues to think about in considering what are the key questions that the psychosocial addresses?
5   Can you think of any difficulties in combining psychological, psychoanalytic, and sociological approaches?

chapter 3

Methodologies

This chapter:

1   Explores some of the methodologies that have been and are being developed in psychosocial studies and the relationship between psychoanalysis and the psychosocial.
2   Highlights what could be seen as distinctly psychosocial about particular methodological approaches such as the use of different forms of narrative in a wide range of contexts, including film and literary texts as well as individual biographies.
3   Uses some particular examples of psychosocial methodologies and creative uses of psychoanalytic techniques to explore and evaluate the possibilities of psychosocial methods.
4   Examines some of the connections and disconnections between psychoanalysis and the research process through a focus upon the relationship between analyst and analysand in psychoanalysis in the clinical context and the researcher and the subjects of research more widely in psychosocial studies within the academy.

Methods are central to psychosocial studies, and one of the major contributions of psychosocial interdisciplinary contributions is the breakdown of boundaries between theory and practice; they become indistinguishable and inseparable. Alliances between sociological and psychoanalytic approaches have a relatively long history, for example, from work in the US from the 1920s to the 1950s, and within cultural studies in the UK and especially in feminist work in the UK, Europe, and Australia. Although sociology has taken on board psychoanalytic ideas, the emphasis has largely been upon theoretical material and modes of explanation:

more theory than practice (Clarke, 2006). Psychosocial researchers have more recently been developing different forms of practice and have worked with different forms of qualitative methodologies, which are becoming a key part of the field that can be identified as psychosocial studies. Contemporary approaches draw upon a range of methods as well as theoretical frameworks, which are widely enmeshed, and theory and practice are often indistinguishable in psychodynamic approaches.

There is a history of psychosocial practical interventions in the management of health care, for example, which has led to the idea of the correlation of psychic and social factors. Such approaches have led to the development of particular applied strategies in a wide range of particular situations based upon the correlates that have been identified. Psychosocial approaches have led to the identification of particular key elements in the defence mechanisms that people adopt in order to protect themselves against adversity and reduce the impact of risk in a variety of contexts but that operate at key points in people's lives (Rutter, 1987). This chapter is not so much about the practical applications as an engagement with the question of how these features are identified and what methodological approaches are available to the psychosocial researcher in order to access psychosocial processes in a wide range of fields. The psychosocial can be seen to embrace experience in diverse areas of experience and in different expressions of relationality.

The psychosocial presents possibilities for exploring processes that include inner and outer worlds and the operation of unconscious feelings, desires, and affects (Watts and Stenner, 2012). Any attempt at engaging with the unconscious also presents problems and some troubling issues. Is the role of the researcher akin to the analyst? How far does the process of interpretation take the researcher in imposing an understanding upon someone else's unconscious life, or on the collective unconscious, which might present different but equally challenging issues? The therapist's judgement in the clinical encounter is based on a somewhat different relationship in terms of the levels of trust and agreement between analyst and analysand from the researcher and the subjects of research (Billig, 1997; Wetherell, 2003), although as I shall argue in this chapter there are significant parallels and points of connection. Psychosocial researchers locate themselves within the process of research (Walkerdine, 1986). For example, although the relationship between the researcher and subjects of research is not the same as that of therapist or analyst and analysand, there is overlap in relationships, such as in the case of the process of **countertransference**, where feelings seemingly experienced by one person can be transferred to another, which is illustrated in some of Bion's work. Psychosocial practitioners acknowledge some of the difficulties and some of the criticisms (Frosh, 2011) as well as suggesting reinterpretations of Freud's work (Craib, 1998), which demonstrates that the unconscious, along with the id, ego, and superego are not entities, but themselves interpretations. Psychosocial research methods involve looking below the surface, and there are a variety of ways of doing this including exploring the potential of narrative. What can the stories of individuals, possibly related in the consulting room, deliver about psychosocial methods, and how can a personal narrative or even a collection of such narratives enhance our understanding of what might be seen as social processes?

Narrative and personal stories

Narratives and personal testimonies are important resources for psychosocial approaches. Stories are told in the clinic and in the therapy session, and these stories can have much wider application than the life of the individual concerned. Narrative is not necessarily a collection of individual stories either. Tom Wengraf explains this in more complex terms than simply the application of the personal to the political since the production of narrative is never entirely individual, but neither is it just a matter of collecting several individual stories. He argues that a methodological focus on 'biographic-narrative-based research does not mean it has to take the form of a collection of accounts of individual biographies or experiences' (Wengraf, 2004:58), although this may often be the approach taken. Exploring the particularity of individual experience and transforming subjectivity in particular historical and social locations and the processes through biography-based research lays the basis for systematic later wider social comparisons. The study of these narratives also lays a basis for comparisons of situated practices and processes of different interest to the researcher, thus enabling grounded description and theorization about very different objects of study.

> Narrative and biographical research methodologies are generating the kind of empirical data that can benefit from psychoanalytically informed analysis and provide fruitful sites of enquiry for those authors who are now posing the conceptual problem of linking the subjective, the social and the societal.
>
> (Froggett and Wengraf, 2004:95)

Hollway and Jefferson address some of the concerns that have been expressed about the use of psychoanalytical methods in the 2013 edition of their book on psychosocial methods. They acknowledge the particular ethical problems of interpreting another person's life and the possible lack of reliability of basing an argument upon a single life story. Qualitative researchers who seek rich, thick data through small-scale research projects, possibly with a single interview subject, run the risk of being accused of having insufficient evidence upon which to base their arguments. Similarly a single interview might be subject to an excess of interpretation with the scope tattoo that it can yield more than is feasible from one aspect of one life.

They summarize their approach as resting upon

> a psychoanalytic ontology of the non-unitary, defended subject – the psychoanalytic insistence on the importance of the dynamic unconscious – the idea

that subjects are constituted relationally and engage continuously in processes of identification, projection and introjection.

(Hollway and Jefferson, 2013:x)

They claim that this approach is attentive to both unconscious dynamics, which disrupt rationality, and to practices, identities, and **discourses**, which embrace the social as well as the inner worlds of the unconscious. Their methodologies particularly stress 'the importance of the individual's psychic conflict, ambivalence, loss and disappointment' (ibid:x).

This demonstrates what Hollway and Jefferson call the 'complex socio-cultural-historical-personal sphere of experience' (Hollway and Jefferson, 2013:xi).

In spite of some of the criticisms that their work on methodologies has received, in the second edition of their book they reiterate the claim that their approach to methods is polemical and defend their particular use of free association and narrative interview methodology. Their work is particularly useful for its detailed coverage of how to do it and guidance in working out how to approach a research project from a psychosocial perspective (Hollway and Jefferson, 2005b). They are also attentive to the relationship between researcher and subjects of research in a productive way, which alerts novice or inexperienced researchers to the dangerous waters they might be entering. Researchers are situated and also the bearer of a history and have their own biography and unconscious investments in the process; at least Hollway and Jefferson are aware of this.

Hollway and Jefferson provide some specific guidance that is both useful and practical and illustrative of a psychosocial approach to qualitative research. They describe the approach as Free Association and Narrative Interview (FANI) method, and I outline its key features below as illustration of a carefully worked through, explicitly psychosocial methodology.

Free association and narrative

Hollway and Jefferson summarize their approach in terms of four principles, each of which is designed to facilitate the process of in-depth open interviewing so that the interviewee is enabled in his or her production of a meaningful narrative, which the researcher can then interpret.

The first principle is open-ended questions, which is a well-known strategy in qualitative research methods in the social sciences. Rather than using a leading question, one starts with 'tell be about' and takes it from there, with more or less direction as required. Open questions are also a way of avoiding the yes or no response, which a more specific leading question might evoke.

The second principle of this biographical method is to elicit a story with a prompt such as 'tell me something about where you come from or about your background', which might leave more to the respondent than 'tell me about the place where you were born or brought up, or your first job'. Hollway and Jefferson argue that this approach resonates with the psychoanalytic strategy of free association: '[E]liciting stories has the virtue of indexicality, of anchoring people's accounts to events that have actually happened. . . . The characteristic of story-telling – to contain significance beyond the teller's intentions – is what it shares with the psychoanalytic method of free association' (Hollway and Jefferson 2013:32–3); thus the appropriate question would be more likely to be 'tell about your experiences of being frightened' rather than 'what do you most fear', which might elicit a single-word answer.

The third principle is the avoidance of 'why' questions. Hollway and Jefferson admit that this one is counterintuitive since asking respondents for their own explanation might seem to be the more democratic approach, leaving them to interpret their own experience, but they claim that this would be akin to using your own research questions and then posing the same questions to your interviewees. The researcher's frame of reference is not that of the person he or she is interviewing. The analyst may be there only to help the analysand take control of his or her life and understand his or her feelings, but whatever may be claimed to the contrary, a researcher has an agenda of producing knowledge and understanding inner and social worlds and of making sense of human experience and social relations. Hollway and Jefferson do cite examples of the failure of an approach that poses research questions to interviewees and asks them to make sense of their own lives and experience. One example relates to Roger, who is asked about his fear of crime, which he attributes to contemporary stories of murder and mayhem in spite of the relatively peaceful and mundane context in which he lives his own life. He compares the perceived contemporary breakdown of law and order with the 'golden age' of his strongly disciplined childhood. They claim that as researchers they are able to get under the empty clichés of Roger's own explanations to explore more directly his fears about loss of authority.

Fourthly, Hollway and Jefferson argue for following up responses by using the interviewees' own ordering and phrasing. Although follow-up questions should be as open as possible in order to elicit stories, they suggest that revisiting what respondents have said facilitates a fuller narrative and thus more material for the researcher.

Free association is seen as central to this approach for a number of reasons. In psychoanalysis, by 'asking the patient to say whatever comes to mind, the psychoanalyst is eliciting the kind of narrative that is not structured according to conscious logic; that is, the associations follow pathways defined by emotional motivations, rather than rational intentions. According to psychoanalysis, unconscious dynamics are a product of attempts to avoid or master anxiety ... free associations defy narrative conventions and enable the analyst to pick up on incoherences (for example contradictions, elisions, avoidances) and accord them due significance' (Hollway and Jefferson, 2013:34).

There are some limitations to these techniques, not least in the assumption that respondents have the same aims as the researcher and will comply with psychoanalytic techniques in a research project, but these are methods that endeavour to access unconscious manifestations of experience, emotions, and feelings, which might otherwise remain hidden in the research process. Narratives have more structure than free association and in telling a story the respondent will try to organize the narrative and be reminded of what comes next through the signposting of different stages in the story. The combination of methods can, however, be very productive and does enable the respondent to share thought processes and feelings that might otherwise be submerged. This discussion of methods does not indicate the relationship between gathering the data and the material from the interview and then conducting the interpretive process of analyzing the data. Free association and open-ended questioning does limit the extent to which the researcher can direct the interviewee and shape responses to fit into any pre-given framework, however, which does offer a more equal relationship.

Other psychosocial approaches also highlight the benefits of respondent-led narratives and are broadly within the same framework as Hollway and Jefferson's, especially in relation to their concerns with interviewee-led research and the use of psychoanalytical techniques and ways of making sense of interview data in a manner that can include some access to unconscious feelings and processes.

Biographic narrative interpretive method

This methodology for conducting and analyzing biographic narrative interviews has been used in a variety of European research projects (for example, Chamberlayne, Rustin, and Wengraf, 2012; Rosenthal, 1998). Other researchers have used modified versions of the approach. A basic tenet of the approach, as with other narrative methods in psychosocial studies, is that the narrative expression of research subjects is expressive both of conscious concerns and also of unconscious cultural, societal, and individual presuppositions and processes. In this sense, as Wengraf argues, it is psychoanalytic and socio-biographic and thus truly psychosocial (or perhaps, as Wengraf would argue, psycho-societal).

At a practical level the technique has much in common with Hollway and Jefferson's approach, as questions are as open ended as possible and the interviewee is invited to shape his or her own narrative. In each BNIM interview, there are three subsessions (Wengraf, 2001). In the first, the interviewer offers only a carefully constructed single narrative question, for example, 'Please tell me the story of your life, all the events and experiences that have been important to you personally'. The second session is a narrative follow-up in order to focus upon the key issues in the story. Finally there is a third session, which is optional and for clarification of narrative issues and if deemed necessary other contextual matters that the interviewer would like to pursue. Wengraf is very specific about the need for the interviewer to focus on what is required and not to deviate from the initial agenda. For example, in the case of the second interview, which should be recorded, he suggests, in his advice to students, that they ask only narrative-directed questions and not any others. Secondly, his advice is only to ask about *the topics raised* by the interviewee and not any others that might interest you more. Thirdly, ask about the topics raised using the interviewee's own words and do not combine different topics or go back to what has been said (Wengraf, 2004).

This kind of detailed guidance is useful because in establishing a relationship with an interviewee, it is very tempting to interject with your own experience or get diverted into particular topics that interest you. The aim here is to retain the narrative structure of the interviewee and not to shape the story through one's own interventions. This requires discipline because in order to gain the confidence of the interviewee, the researcher may well want to establish points of connection.

Another important element in this guidance is about the researcher's own use of language. As many experienced ethnographers and qualitative researchers will aver, when you talk to people who have already been the subjects of a research project, or have become familiar with social interventions, such as antiracism projects in sport, in the case of my own work, you can find that they already use the language of analysis. In my work at football clubs in particular (Woodward, 2009) I have found fans immersed in the discourse of diversity and social inclusion, albeit with actions and feelings that might well belie their familiarity with this language. Boxers in the gym are more likely to use the language of sports psychology or of community (Woodward, 2006, 2014), but the issue being addressed by biographical narrative methods is really important if as researchers we are seeking to go beyond what is said and to access deeper meanings including those feelings of which the respondent may not even be aware.

The approach assumes that narrative expression is expressive both of conscious concerns and also of unconscious cultural, social, and individual presuppositions and processes. BNIM supports research into the lived experience of individuals and collectives. It facilitates understanding both the 'inner' and the 'outer' worlds of 'historically evolving persons in historically evolving situations', and particularly the *interactivity* of inner and outer world dynamics. As such, BNIM lends itself particularly to both psycho-dynamic *and* socio-dynamic approaches, serving specialists of both the 'psycho' and the 'societal', but *especially* those researchers wanting a tool that supports a fully psycho-societal understanding in which neither sociological nor psychological dynamics and structures are neglected or privileged, and in which both are understood not statically but as situated historically.

BNIM is a methodology for exploring lived experiences through biographic narrative interviews has been used over the past fifteen or more years in a variety of collective research projects, either more or less directly (for example, Rosenthal 1998; Chamberlayne et al., 2002; Froggett et al., 2005). This approach is in many ways similar to Hollway and Jefferson's Free Association narrative interviews.

Creative thinking

Psychosocial studies have been concerned with ensuring that the vitality of the voices of those who are the subjects of research is retained whilst presenting well-supported and demonstrably robust academic claims. Whilst seeking to avoid the pitfalls of positivist approaches as well as the dangers of overinterpretation in analyzing narrative interviews, some researchers have developed a range of other techniques that build on psychoanalytic ideas of free association and creativity, including the idea of reverie and of dreaming. Alfred Lorenzer, the German cultural psychoanalyst, used the concepts of *scene* to describe the strategy of setting the interviewee in a scene, describing him or her as a character, which is closer to tacit and intuitive knowledge, which Hollway explored in her work on mothers and motherhood (Hollway, 2010, 2011b). Thus an interviewee is introduced through a description of the person rather like a character in a play. Wendy Hollway uses the example of a young woman whom she first described using conventional social categories:

> Jenny is black British of African heritage and lives with her parents and three younger brothers in a council flat. When she discovered that she was pregnant she was 17 and studying social sciences at a sixth form college.
>
> (Hollway, 2011a:93)

Hollway's second version of an introduction to Jenny framed by Lorenzer's notion of the scene is as follows:

> Jenny sits in her bedroom, on the bunk bed. Clothes bulge from hangers on the top rail. Around the room are various soft toys and on the wall a couple of Bob Marley posters. She waits while her family's social worker, who she has known all her life, tells her parents the news that she is pregnant.
>
> (ibid.:93)

Hollway suggests that this poses questions (why does the family have a social worker?) rather than closing down the situation by using traditional categories. She quotes Lorenzer as follows: 'the scenic animates our experience, rendering it subjectively meaningful and more alive' (quoted in Hollway, 2011a:94).

What such a technique might facilitate is the amassing of feelings and social context at the same time, although the scene itself is still informed by social categories, and the researcher has to select what they include. Hollway suggests that such techniques might be used to avoid the reification of data and to capture the vitality of experience.

More creative techniques such as recording and listening rather than transcribing and exploring reverie through dream workshops are all ways of endeavouring to capture experience and to explore the trans-subjective and the qualities of reverie, which the psychosocial seeks to develop.

Applying narrative techniques

Personal narratives and those that emerge in the clinical or therapeutic encounter also capture some of the most powerful intensities of relationships and enable the researcher, like the analyst, to go beyond the surface and explore some of the complicated and contradictory elements that make up not only the self but emotions, which motivate political expressions and even political and social movements of exclusion and marginalization. Simon Clarke suggests that psychosocial approaches lend themselves particularly well to research into the fear and anxiety that gives rise to social exclusion and marginalization of particular groups (Clarke, 2006).

Franz Fanon drew upon his own clinical experience the social and cultural phenomenon of racism, thus demonstrating how the social institution of racism and racialization works. In his book *Black Skins White Masks*, Fanon explains how the colonial subject experiences feelings of inadequacy, for example, in the case of an Antillean patient who comes to live in Paris and is immersed in a white world of colonial power and white privilege. Fanon argues that it is migration that confronts the Antillean not only with racism but also with feelings that may manifest themselves as neuroses (as in the case of his patient). He has not thought of himself as black, but as Antillean, until he arrives in France. At the point of arriving in the colonial, white place the Antillean has no resources with which to combat the phobia he experiences; his previous feelings of inadequacy and experience of inequality, for example, through the privileging of white people and white culture, have all been conscious. It is only when he arrives in France that the Antillean has to confront the new identity of, in Fanon's terms, being Negro. Fanon identifies the particular mechanisms of projection onto the black man as deriving from corporeal, mostly genital fixations. Fanon draws upon Freud's notion of this person as representing the repressed, often incestuous desires of the white man, or, as Fanon also argues in the discussion of his own case studies, the white woman.

Far from individualizing racism and the racist person, approaches such as Fanon's have been developed to explore how racism works through a combination of psychoanalytic methods. For example, Michael Rustin has used a Kleinian approach to explore the ways in which the mechanisms of psychotic thought fit into racial categorizations (Rustin, 1991). What, in the consulting room, is pathological is manifest in systems of thought and ways of being that express intense hatred against groups so classified that have had and continue to have considerable support particularly in the political parties of the far right historically but also in some routine everyday practices of racism, which are far from infrequent in many societies. Rustin focuses upon the stories that reveal the inner world of the individual racist in order to demonstrate some of the issues that antiracist groups and policymakers need to confront.

Rustin suggests that the exploration of individual stories in which defence mechanisms can be understood can be productive in countering the oversimplification of racism, for example, as an expression of conscious hatred or the inevitable outcome in economic recession. By understanding what the individual needs to expel and resist, it is possible to extend an understanding of processes by which powerful transitive communications take place between imaginary groups in the wider society, for example, through prejudice, racism, and xenophobia as empty categories waiting to contain those feelings. Current expressions of hostility to migrants and the success of extreme right-wing parties, for example, in the European Parliament elections in 2014, often mask the projective identifications of white communities against migrant groups, many of whom are also white, of course, in the context of European migration. In France the right-wing Front National (FN), led by Marine le Pen, the daughter of Jean-Marie le Pen, was successful in securing seats in the European Parliament in Strasberg in 2014. In the UK, somewhat ironically the party that was most hostile to UK membership of the European Community (EU), the UK Independence Party (UKIP), won twenty-four seats, and the most pro-European party, the Liberal Democrats, won only one seat. UKIP's situation was different from the FN, with whom the UKIP leader, Nigel Farage, denied any connections, not least because of the more extreme right-wing policies of the FN, but there is an interesting and disturbing phenomenon taking place in this example, which could be a really useful psychosocial research project. Some understanding of the contradictory processes of the contradictory workings of **social unconscious** processes might help to make sense of this. It cannot simply be read off from demographic change. Firstly, there is the trend towards separation and disassociation from the wider (European) community, for example, which is expressed in both the UK and France as the desire to take control of the country's own national identity and its people's social life. Secondly, there is the fear of outsiders and the 'othering' of those who have rights of citizenship within the EU. Thirdly, there are contradictory emotions being expressed and suppressed. For example, UKIP had no members of the UK parliament in 2014, and the pro-European Liberal Democrats were part of the coalition government with the Conservative party. There is often a backlash at midterm elections, so some expression of disapproval of the government in office is to be expected, but why did this opposition take the form of voting into the European Parliament a party with no interest in being part of the EU or its parliament except to take the UK out of the EU?

Xenophobia, ethnocentrism, and racism involve projective identification in which hated and despised self-attributes, for example, those borne of economic failure and the impact of socioeconomic downturns, of members of the group overwhelmed by prejudice, are phantacized to be present in the stigmatized group. When migrant people appear to be economically active and leading productive lives, at particular historic moments, especially those that have been marked by economic crises and transitions in modes of production and forms of employment as well as social change in family and community life, prejudice, social exclusion, and even racism offer containers for those feelings of anxiety and fear as well as projective identification. These processes are understood through the personal narratives and even clinical encounters in which these psychoanalytic terms have been developed.

The extension of understanding of social phenomena through personal stories and through analysis and therapy also requires crossing the boundaries of normality and abnormality and pathology and a breakdown of the barrier between personal, individual and social, and political.

Narrative: Literary texts

Another way of making sense of the unconscious is by exploring its manifestations and representations in the social world, for example, within cultural forms such as film and literature. Freud argued that sublimation was the source of creativity, for example, by the conversion of repressed desires and sexual energy into works of art or socially valued artefacts, objects, or texts. Klein saw creative works as reparation for damage that has been done. Either way sublimation compels psychoanalysis into the social world of culture and historical institutions and values. Thus it can be argued that cultural forms present important and valuable sites for psychosocial exploration.

Film studies have been greatly influenced by psychoanalytic approaches. Even if psychoanalysis has not always been a welcome guest at the feast of social research, it has been enormously influential in the study of film and in exploring seeing, looking, and being looked at in the context of art and film (Berger, 1972). Berger argued that men were privileged in how they look. Men are able to look actively and critically without their look being returned with equal scrutiny by women.

Berger wrote of the privileged male **gaze** in a way that has led to significant developments in exploring ways of looking and the politics of the visual. The concept of gaze has offered a powerful explanation of the politics of looking, which has been very influential – the notion of 'the gaze' especially as developed by Laura Mulvey, in her seminal work on visual narrative (1975). Mulvey's initial understanding of the gaze was framed by a Lacanian explanation, which she used to explain the ways in which women look through the male gaze and how their images of themselves are mediated by the signification of the phallus.

In her 1975 work, Mulvey demonstrated the objectification of women in film through male ways of looking. Firstly, the camera and the process of imaging are voyeuristic and part of the male gaze. Secondly, women characters are seen through the gaze of male characters in the film, and thirdly, there is the gaze of the spectator who watches the film. By exploring some of the apparatuses linking the inner world of subjectivity and the processes through which representations are taken in, Mulvey was also able to provide some of the tools with which to challenge the male gaze. In the world of art criticism there has been extensive exploration of the female gaze and of a wide range of democratizing strategies in the reconfiguration of sexual difference and subjectivity (Betterton, 1987; Edholm, 1992; King, 1992).

This seems a long way from the psychosocial in its explanation, although it does provide a focus upon the ways in which representations are internalized. The gaze, and especially Mulvey's later work (1989), has led to more recent, more democratic developments of the concept to provide some mechanisms through which visual images and subjectivities can be explored in combination. A democracy of the gaze can only be achieved if there is equality between the kinds of people who represent and those who are represented (Kappeler, 1986). Freedom of representation is itself ethnocentric and speaks of privilege, but challenges are only possible through an exploration of how the process works at an intersubjective level as well as through deconstructing images.

Some of the more overtly psychosocial claims made in relation to narrative interviews can be seen to resonate with the critiques subjectivities and intersubjectivities in the field of visual culture. The aim of the psychosocial is to

> [u]ncover the mediating links between social norms, family dynamics and psychic life. Understanding more about normative, unconscious processes that are repeatedly enacted in everyday social situations, processes that derive from social inequities and the ideologies that sustain them, might provide one such link.
>
> (Layton, 2004:48)

An analysis of the gaze also demonstrates silences and absences, including absent presences (Woodward, 1997; Kaplan, 1992). Kaplan describes the absent presence of motherhood in film echoing Luce Irigaray's claims about the death of the mother in western culture (Irigaray, 1991). Maternal subjectivity has been unrepresented and, made visible, it has mediated through a patriarchal gaze, which denies the desiring sexual subjectivity of mothers, for example, in the asexual figure of the Madonna. The gaze provides a concept that can be deployed to explore the challenges to silence as well as uncovering the source of silence and absence.

The gaze brings together the inner world of the unconscious, intersubjectivities, and the social world in which sexual desires are so closely imbricated. The gaze is intersubjective, and although the initial development of the concept was largely framed by the desire to use psychoanalytical concepts to explain the power of looking and indeed *scopophilia*, which has largely lost its popularity in critiques of popular culture (Miklitsch, 2012), but which nonetheless offers a useful and interesting way of exploring the making of subjectivity and the processes through which images and representations are taken in.

Other representational forms perform similar functions and are part of the similar processes through which inner worlds are made and the unconscious operates with the social world. Thus they offer an appropriate site for psychosocial research, which requires somewhat different methods from the interview techniques discussed above but remains based upon the same principles that integrate theory and practice, albeit in very different ways.

Textual analysis stories and novels

A variety of interdisciplinary and transdisciplinary approaches that incorporate psychoanalytic methods into social and cultural research have been developed, especially in the US. These methods take on board emotions as integral to social and cultural processes. In this section I discuss in some detail an example of the application of psychosocial, or perhaps more especially, psychoanalytical cultural analysis of texts. The approach remains within the parameters of the psychosocial and fits in with psychosocial aims at exploring the interstices between the psychic and the social and combining the social and psychic.

Esther Rashkin's approach to literary criticism brings together the concerns of character analysis with those of psychoanalysis. She draws upon the work of French psychoanalysts Nicholas Abraham and Maria Torokt (see Rashkin, 1988) to explore different works of short fiction: Joseph Conrad's 'The Secret Sharer', Auguste Comte de Villiers de l'Isle-Adam's *L'Intersigne* and Honoré de Balzac's *Facino Cane*, Henry James's 'The Jolly Corner', and Edgar Allan Poe's 'The Fall of the House of Usher'. Rashkin seeks the inscription of a particular kind of secret in each text. She is interested in the literary presence of the clinical configuration, which relates to the phantom as an unspeakable secret that is associated with a shameful family drama, which has been silently transmitted to someone else, in whom it subsequently lodges, rather in the manner of the intersubjective unconscious. In the case of this reworking of Freud the symptoms do not arise from the individual's own experience but from someone else's trauma or the secrets that are part of someone else's life.

Using theories of the phantom that is created by trauma and cryptonomy, which is a reconfiguration of the Freudian unconscious as the shrouding of lexical relationships, provides a way of reading that enables the exploration of long-departed spirits and silences (Rashkin, 1988). Cryptonomy involves the retracing of displaced symbol fragments, trauma, as an ego-threatening event that compels the individual simultaneously to hide and reveal the source of the threat and *anasemia*, which is the analytic methodology that entails moving back towards sources of signification that are increasingly beyond perception.

Rashkin rereads an entire genre usually associated with the uncanny from the perspective of what she calls a transgenerational haunting. The secrets uncovered include murder, adultery, illegitimacy, a father's Judaism, and rape; each text conceals within itself its own secret life, that is, the veiled event that constitutes the text's generative force.

Rashkin's method involves a rhetorical deciphering of Balzac's story of Facino Cane who has a passion for gold, which he inherited from his mother. This generational reference builds up connections to the past and to a familial genealogy. The analysis suggests the potential presence of a phantom in the text, a presence further supported by an allusion to the *Livre d'or*, which is a book of noble genealogy in which the names of Cane's ancestors are inscribed. There is also a linguistic genealogy that makes up some of the ambivalence of haunting. For example, there are several allusions to different languages throughout the text, which suggest that it is possible to reread the key word *or*, which is 'gold' in French, as the identical-sounding Hebrew OR, which means light, a word first used in the book of Genesis, the first book in the Torah and in the Old Testament, which describes the birth of world, its origins, and its genealogy. Other references to the riches of the Rothschilds, a banking family whose name has become synonymous with wealth, and to the biblical psalm that includes reference to the Jews' captivity in Babylon suggest, Rashkin argues, that the secret concerns Judaism, including the passion for gold (in French), which is reconceptualized as search for light, for enlightenment. Therefore the inherited desire for gold may be reinterpreted as a quest for origins merely couched in a passion for gold. It is in this context that Facino Cane's eventual blindness must be understood, Rashkin contends; his origins must remain in the dark because of the intense shame attached to his birth. The secret, Rashkin suggests, is that his biological father was a Jew. This secret is demonstrated through a complex linguistic trace through wordplay and a psycho-analytic quest for meaning, which outlines the key features of this methodology, which incorporates a number of different methods such as: its various structuralist deconstruction and rhetorical and psychoanalytic processes, as well as narrative. This textual analysis suggests the desirability and even the necessity of intertextual corroboration and expansion, which can be embraced by a critical, cultural psychoanalysis.

The purpose of this example is to demonstrate some of the range of methods and material that can be the subject of psychosocial research and the diverse sites at which expressions of emotions are evident.

The role of the researcher

Psychosocial methods are interpretative; they involve the search for underlying meanings and the translation and organization of what is being researched. There are clearly parallels between the researcher and the analyst in some of the examples that have been discussed in this chapter. The use of psychoanalytic concepts that are available to the researcher but are unlikely to be quite so familiar to the subjects of research might suggest an unequal relationship, although, as with good practice in therapy and clinical work, the aim of the professional is to facilitate the understanding of the person in therapy and to engage in a collaborative practice that is subject to ethical guidelines, as of course is academic research. There remain some considerations, though, and some caveats. The researcher has to be attentive to the collaborative process in the co-production of knowledge and understanding.

One lesson that has been learned from psychoanalysis and especially from object relations, however, is the relationship between the analyst and the analysand. This has been the subject of considerable discussion and reflection (for example, reflec-tions on clinical practice; see Bion, [1961]1991, [1962]2004; and more widely on research methods; see Hollway, 1989; Hollway and Jefferson, 2001, [2000]2013) and raises issues about emotional connections as well as the **transference** of unconscious feelings between researcher and interviewee, as between analyst and analysand.

Valerie Walkerdine expresses well this aspect of the relationship; the researcher's feelings in relation to the interview. The researcher's feelings can also be part of the research process. They can

> [t]ell us about how a researcher comes to produce such an account and opens it up to the possibility of different readings of the same material. It tells us that the process of reading itself is not all in the text, but is produced out of a complex interaction between reader and text. But perhaps it tells us more about this: as a researcher, I am no more, no different from the subjects of my research.

(Walkerdine, 1997:73)

Walkerdine has used this kind of reflection upon her own situation as a researcher by reflecting on watching the boxing film *Rocky* (1986). Her purpose is not really to think about boxing but rather about her co-viewing with a particular working-class family. This work is relevant to reflecting of the role of the researcher and has had resonance with my own work on boxing because I am acutely conscious both of the brutality of boxing and its shocking qualities and by positioning within the field with the subjects of my research, for example, in the gym, where I hang about and have never participated (Woodward, 2008). When Walkerdine is watching the *Rocky* film she is shocked at the violence and realizes that she is an outsider. Mr Cole, the father in the co-viewing family, understands boxing and its heroic narratives of masculinity (Woodward, 2006), but Walkerdine does not, although as time progresses, she gets drawn into the narrative. She argues that for identification to take place there have to be associations; 'meanings in the film meant something to the viewer because of the other places in which those meanings were constituted in their lives' (Walkerdine, 1997:54). She uses the idea of intertexuality to show how she is able to draw upon her own working-class background, to get caught up in the narrative. The researcher is part of the process. As Walkerdine explains, 'My own feelings and fantasies must, I felt, have some bearing on my, and therefore anybody's, interpretation and explanation' (1997:54). The strength of her reflection lies in its psychosocial placing of an analysis of **phantasy** in the social terrain in which phantasies also circulate.

Boxing demands a particular acknowledgement of the intersubjective and unconscious processes that are in play, not least because of its tensions and its physicality. Reflection upon the relationship between the researcher and the subject of research or the field of research is not limited to a relationship between people, and as this section has demonstrated, texts and images are also bearers of phantasy and expressions of the unconscious.

The relationship between researcher and the field and the reflection this relationship requires can be productive in many ways. In working on *Sporting Times* (Woodward, 2012a) my immersion in the field, writing in the 'real time' of the Olympic Games in 2012 provided a particularly instructive version of the process, which Walkerdine records at rather more leisure. My aim was to capture something of temporality and 'being in time' through a personal experience, of watching the Olympics, but by starting with the experience and allowing the experience to generate the findings rather than establishing any prior set of theoretical understanding of temporality. The process has to be open, insofar as this is possible in an area of social life so shaped by hyperbole and the spectacular. Nonetheless, it was time I was interested in and not the specificities of the competitions. I watched the television for the recordings and wrote on my iPad: it was very difficult in the 100m, a race in which the record is 9.58 seconds:

> "Now" on 4 August 2012 are the quarter finals of the 100m at 12.30 BST. I want Usain Bolt, the Jamaican world champion to win, as do many of those watching, and I also wonder if he will break a record. I want him to qualify. I know he will, but it is still a tense moment. I hold my breath at the start. Bolt is not known for being quick out of the blocks. Anxiety is increased because the race, spectators and fans are haunted by the memory of Bolt's disqualification at the World Athletics Championships in 2011. . . . No! He's out of the blocks, not fast . . . but I know he can win because he decelerates more slowly than anyone else. This is counter-intuitive as I am convinced he is speeding up at the end of the race. I have the knowledge but I cannot believe it as I watch. What we want to see and what we think is Bolt is going faster than everyone else in the last segment of the race.
>
> (Woodward, 2012a:16)

The perception of time and the passage of clock time are not synchronized; perception and the object of perception, experience of time and its measurement are absorbed into the collective emotion of the 'real time' moment. The present includes past fears and future hopes in this mix.

This project is illustrative of a psychosocial auto-ethnographic engagement with emotion and subjectivity, which, using the particular field of sporting spectacle, provides a powerful expression of the psychic in the social and the social in the psychic. This is greatly intensified within the particular context of the real time of the present, which calls upon the past and reconstructs memory, whilst iteratively invoking the future. The inequalities are embedded in the present with its expression of competition, but there is always the promise of, and the aspirations for, the future. Temporality and the experience of time bring together external quantitative measurement, which is recorded in extremely precise and sophisticated detail, especially in sport, and the internal experience, which might be of timelessness or of time that is immeasurable because the experience, even as expressed by athletes in the 100m, is timeless (Woodward, 2012a). This is an interdisciplinary field to which neuroscience and various forms of 'technoscience' (Haraway, [1985]2000), are also implicated in psychosocial approaches.

Writing the psychosocial

As has been argued in this chapter, psychosocial techniques and methods address the relationality of inner, personal worlds and social worlds through the use of techniques such as narrative. This involves the subjects using the first person to locate themselves and tell their stories. It also involves reflection upon the process of listening and the situated researcher who also speaks in the first person. Luce Irigaray distinguishes between the first-person locutor who speaks and the relationship that person has with the person he or she is addressing (Irigaray, 1993, 2004). In her work on language she focuses upon gender difference, but at the root of her argument is the entanglement of social and psychic forces in the biography of the person and the specific relationship between the speaker and the person who listens, or maybe fails to listen or at least to hear, because of the failure to acknowledge different positions. She argues that sexual difference is generated through speech, for example, because

> men and women do not generate language and structure discourses in the same way. And they cannot understand one another, nor even listen to the one in the other without first becoming conscious about such difference.
>
> (Irigaray, 2004:36)

Irigaray's discussion is instructive for a number of reasons. Firstly, she draws attention to the specific processes that are involved when people speak as 'I'. Secondly, she draws attention to the relationship between speaking and listening, which is at the heart of the psychosocial research process, often on a one-to-one basis. Thirdly, Irigaray makes the case for consideration for speech as part of the psychosocial process through which sexual difference is made, embodied, and experienced. The making of sexual difference involves a relationship between 'I', 'you', and 'us' (Irigaray, 1993).

The use of the first-person pronoun as the speaking subject provides an acknowledgement of experience; it does not necessarily privilege experience at the expense of interpretation or any other mechanism for the exploration of social life. Such accounts provide a means of capturing what Bev Skeggs, in the case of gender difference, calls a way of 'understanding how women occupy the category "women", a category which is classed and raced and produced through power relations and through struggles across different sites in space and time' (Skeggs, 1997:27).

As Toni Morrison said in 1989:

> We are the subjects of our own narratives, witnesses to and participants in our own experience, and, in no way coincidentally, in the experiences of those with whom we have come in contact. . . . And you read imaginative literature by and about us to choose to examine centers of the self and to

have the opportunity to compare these centers with the 'raceless' one with whom we are all familiar.

(1989:9)

Toni Morrison's first person is a collective subject; her 'we' is not a complacent privileged author but a first-person plural that demonstrates the power of claiming the right to speak as a woman, which incorporates the lived experience of social circumstances and exploitation and marginalization.

An acknowledgement of the subject position permits its location. Thinking in terms of a speaking subject of enunciation allows the possibility of making clear the choices available to individual speakers and writers and reveals the position they take up in what Julia Kristeva calls 'the operating consciousness' of representation (Kristeva, 1982).

This discussion draws attention to the productive use of the first person but also the importance of acknowledging the situatedness of the person who speaks as 'I' and who may incorporate a collectivity of 'we', which is expressive of unconscious as well as conscious identifications. Feminist writers have adopted different strategies for incorporating an understanding of these differences (Stanley, 1990). Stanley suggests the use of the third-person 'she', but this loses the location of the self and the unconscious and inner subjectivity of the researcher.

Another strategy involves incorporating relationality into the subject, and the psychic dynamic of the self in relation to the world is to name the subject as a particular 'I'. In writing a book about generational feminist conversations, which involved cross-generational dialogues with my younger daughter, we decided to use the first person and name, I-Kath and I-Sophie, with third-person agreement for verbs that followed because the 'I' embraces subjectivity and the possibilities of **intersubjectivity**, and the name and the third-person agreement made this speaking, writing subject both specifically situated and located within a political, social terrain (Woodward and Woodward, 2009).

The adoption of I-Sophie and I-Kath was both a practical device in order to accommodate a book written by two people and also important theoretically and politically in terms of the book as a conversation. This strategy links in closely to the writings of Luce Irigaray in *Je, Tous, Nous*, where she discusses the need to create a space for mothers and daughters that valorizes the relationship and does not subsume it to the patriarchal imaginary. One aspect of this she suggests as useful is when women talk to 'create sentences in which I-woman (*je-femme*) talks to you-woman (*tu-femme*)' ([1990]2007:43–4). The device we have suggested is an instance of this where we are given an individual identity from which to speak, which validates a distance between us and a specificity of our identities and positioning. This also involves an awareness of the fact that we were both speaking and writing as women and thus there is both a commonality and also a difference allowed within this. The strategy aimed to create a shared voice, yet not one that overruled the possibility for the articulation of difference between us.

methodologies

Conclusion

In psychosocial studies theory and methods are inextricably interconnected. This is one of the distinguishing features of psychosocial studies. Although there is a diverse range of methods and methodologies in the field, they all share a concern with uncovering underlying meanings and offering some interpretation of what is going on. The organizing principles of research analysis are largely those of psychoanalysis, although the psychosocial is appropriating them to ensure that psychoanalysis is not added on to social phenomena. Again this is also a distinguishing feature of the psychosocial in that the expressions of inner worlds, feelings, and emotions are never outside the society and its social and cultural meanings. Hauntings and memories and the manifestations of the unconscious, which might be accessed through narrative psychosocial methods, are never purely psychic but are located within and associated with relations with other people and a biographic history, which is made and makes social relations too.

Psychosocial researchers are attentive to the risks of the privileging of the researcher in what might be called the 'white coat syndrome' of expert knowledge, perhaps more so than some ethnographers (Woodward, 2008), although there remain some questions about the parallels between psychoanalysis and research. Psychosocial researchers have developed strategies in order to address these issues. The use of narrative can be seen as maximizing the participation of the subject of research in the process and of avoiding the tendency of many researchers to set their own agendas and to lead their subjects along a prejudged trajectory.

I have included some detailed discussion of narrative methods that are based upon avowedly psychosocial principles and seek to go beyond the application of psychoanalysis to explanations of the social. Narrative techniques are based upon unstructured interviews with individuals and the use of open-ended questions, which permit the exploration of meanings in relation to the interviewee's own life experience. Biography can deliver a great deal about people's life history, their sense of who they are, and the identifications that they have made, including childhood experience. Free association has been stressed as a means of enabling the respondent to organize the interview and thus facilitate insight into unconscious motivations and anxieties. Researchers who work with these methods also show some of the social and dynamic processes through which inner and outer worlds are connected, not least in relation to privilege and hierarchy and notions of 'othering'. Psychosocial narrative methods can access some of the unconscious mediation between social norms and psychic life, which might appear to be personal and individual but nonetheless have much wider application especially into policy in relation to racism and other forms of prejudice and discrimination.

Psychosocial methodologies are also particularly attentive to the role of the researcher especially in conducting psychosocial interviews. There are always subjective elements to the research process (Walkerdine et al., 2001). We have to be aware of them (Woodward, 2008), but as I have argued, this reflection can be immensely productive; it is not only a caveat against overinterpretation on the part of the researcher, although closing down or overinfluencing respondents in interviews can severely restrict what it is possible to understand. The extent of self-reflexivity in the process of conducting research is a central question within the methodologies of psychosocial studies. As Simon Clarke argues, '[T]here is no doubt that we bring our own baggage and agenda to the research interview' (Clarke, 2006:1165). As Clarke points out, if research is grant funded, there are obligations to stick to an agenda and to deliver the promised outcomes, although the content of these outcomes is not pre-given. The strength of psychoanalysis is the possibilities it offers for the conceptualization of the dynamic interplay between the inner world and the psyche of the interviewee and the social world, which can enable us to understand something of how the external world is represented and internalized.

Approaches to conducting psychosocial research have much in common with the processes of analysis, but there are also developments within cultural psycho-analysis, some of which resonate with earlier cultural studies work, which could also be seen as psychosocial. The field is relatively open, especially given that the imagination and the creative and destructive forces and energies of the unconscious are recognized as elements in the process. More recent textual work has taken on board some of the criticisms of psychoanalytic deconstruction, for example, in film studies associated with the *Screen* approach (Merck et al., 1992) and Mulvey's seminal work on the *gaze* (1975). Mulvey's conceptualization of the male gaze has been taken up in a variety of ways, which expand its explanatory remit and demonstrate how internal structures and processes shape as well as are shaped bicultural and social relations (Mulvey, 1989).

Narrative with the intense detailed work of analysis that it requires remains central to many studies but has become increasingly recognized as a key resource and one that psychosocial researchers are developing in innovative ways.

What these approaches have in common, even if they apply to vastly diverse fields, is concern with the combination of the psychic and the social and the desire to bring together internal and external processes and inner and social worlds in order to explore the psychic in the social and the social in the psychic. In conducting interviews, or in exploring texts, the psychosocial requires an open-minded approach to the subject of research. In the case of interviewing this includes an awareness of the emotional life of the researcher as well as the subject of research as part of what is being explored and analyzed. Critical self-reflection is central to psychosocial methods in order to attempt to ensure that the subject speaks rather than starting with a paradigm or even a theoretical framework into which the subject must fit. This is why methods and methodologies are so important. We do start with some assumptions, for example, about the existence of the unconscious, but the unconscious is only accessible if the subject speaks and tells his or her story.

Questions

1   What are the strengths and weaknesses of research based on individual narratives? How would you defend the findings of a research project based on a single interview?

2   How reflexive does the researcher have to be in thinking about how the researcher affects the research process and the research findings? Can you think of any examples from your own experience? Did you have a preset agenda? How far did you feel that you might have influenced responses?

3   How would you explore a contradiction in social life, for example, of people doing something that is seen as unhealthy such as overeating or eating unhealthy foods or continuing to smoke in spite of all the health warnings, using a psychosocial approach?

4   Can you think of an example of a current social issue of prejudice that could be explored by psychosocial methods? How would you set about conducting research into this subject?

chapter 4

Selves

> **This chapter:**
>
> 1 Looks at conceptualizations of self, subject, and identity as of central importance to psychosocial studies.
> 2 Maps the field selecting accounts that have been particularly pertinent or relevant to the key questions of psychosocial studies.
> 3 Traces the important ideas rather than following a strict chronological narrative.
> 4 Suggests some of the gaps in theories of the self and some of the problems that have been encountered in exploring the constitution of selves, subjects, and identities.

Introduction

This chapter focuses upon the self and some of the ways in which research across the social sciences and humanities has engaged with the puzzle, not only of how selves are constituted but also what is the relationship between the notion of a self and the wider social world that self inhabits and in which that self is made. Questions about identity, the self, and subjectivity are central to psychosocial studies and to the interrelationships between self, psyche, and the society. Inner worlds require some conceptualization of the self, albeit one that is always connected (and disconnected) and interrelated in some ways so its social situation. As Judith Butler states in her discussion of the self and the ethical life, '[T]here is no "I" that can fully stand apart from the social conditions of its emergence, no "I" that is not implicated in a set of conditioning moral norms, which being norms have social character that exceed s a purely personal or idiosyncratic meaning' (Butler, 2005:7). Butler's intervention is relatively recent, however: where do the ideas about this 'I' or the self, subject, or of identity come from? What are the ideas that shape contemporary engagements with the psychosocial? The self is not neutral, as Butler says, in theoretical frameworks either in spite of the tendency of most philosophical writing and social theory to refer to a human being as 'man' with the use of a male third-person pronoun. I gave up using the Latin adverb *sic* to show that 'man' and 'he' were used in the original of the following texts where I have quoted from the sources because it is so ubiquitous. I make the comment here to alert the reader to such assumptions and to show that although common practice at the time, the use of 'man' has political significance too. For example, in the some of the sociological accounts of changing versions of the self in US society in the second half of the twentieth century, such as Riesman's study of the American character, he really does mean men in the workplace, but the use of a male norm eliminates the possibilities of gender difference.

Many developments in the field have grown out of research into the self, the subject, and identity, with the emphasis upon different terms to describe that self at different times. In the latter part of the twentieth century such concerns drew upon work in a number of different disciplinary areas. *Who am I?* is the sort of question that immediately suggests some reference to you, us, and them, to all the people with whom 'I' have contact and to how I am seen by others as well as how I see myself. *Who am I?* leads to *Where do I fit in?* Who I am is closely interwoven with ideas about the society in which I live. In the 1980s especially, the concept of identity was invoked and deployed as a way of thinking about the links between the personal and the social, as 'a meeting place of the psychological and the social, of the psyche and society; it is the embodiment and the location of the psycho-social' (Woodward, 1997:vii). Some of the accounts that follow in this chapter set the scene for what has emerged as an identifiable field of psychosocial studies, even if earlier theoretical frameworks would not have adopted the label. Zygmunt Bauman distinguishes between self, identity, and agent, as different labels that have emerged and changed over time, but he argues that the differences have more limited significance in contemporary debates than might have been thought (Bauman, 1991, 1992). Bauman, along with Giddens (1991), suggests that the idea of an autonomous self is largely based upon producing accounts of oneself; this could be telling stories about oneself or reflecting upon that self in order to make sense of who you are within an explanatory framework such as that afforded by psychoanalysis. Giddens explains some of the social transformations of the latter part of the twentieth century that remain into the twenty-first, in relation to people's perception of risk and anxiety, which have nonetheless heightened people's awareness of the possibilities of creatively reinventing themselves. Risk generates anxiety but also the associated possibility of acting and of taking some control over those fears.

> Where large areas of a person's life are no longer set by pre-existing patterns and habits, the individual is continually obliged to negotiate life-style options.

Moreover – and this is crucial – such choices are not just 'internal' or marginal aspects of the individual's attitudes, but define who the 'individual' is. In other words, life-style choices are constitutive of a reflective self.

(Giddens, 1992:75)

This is further developed in Anthony Elliott's work on reinvention in the twenty-first century (Elliott, 2013) and the specific area of risk is the subject of chapter 7, but this account is included here as symptomatic of historical change and the particularities of the self in late modernity. The self that can be reinvented is also a self who has the capacity to act and to initiate action as well as respond to social conditions. Such accounts are also implicated in attempts to refute Wrong's notion of an 'oversocialized' concept of the self. The promise of reinvention, and even just of self-reflection, suggest that this is not a self that is only socially constructed. Thus there is a distinction between the self as agent and the subject of social forces. Subject and subjectivity, however, carry contradictory meanings and include a sense of agency in that the subject, the first person who speaks, can initiate action as an agent. The language has changed, but many of the debates are still about the extent to which action is shaped and even determined by social forces.

Who am I?

One of the most frequently used activities in teaching about the self, the subject, and identity is to ask people to think about ten statements starting with 'I am'. What would you include, just thinking of ten statements that you could make about yourself? Most people who try the exercise pick things like gender, age, work, ethnicity (although it is not often that white people identify as such), and physical appearance, which might include any disabilities, which may be visible or not.

Bodies are central to the I who speaks and the I who is recognized by others, and embodied characteristics are likely to appear on the list. Some aspects of the body only appear important to us when things change or go wrong (there's nothing like a physical impairment to make you think about the bit of your body that cannot do what you want to do or the environment in which you live that does not support you with this disability). Some corporeal attributes are more central than others; gender – whether you fit into one of the two categories that are on most forms or not – is usually an important part of who we are for most people. Other attributes are the ones that are important, such as a relationship, as a mother or father or related to your place in the world such as the paid (or voluntary) work you do being a student or a teacher.

What does this list tell us about a psychosocial view of the self? The list could be read discursively, as likely to include the distinguishing features of subjectivity and identity in any particular society or culture. In the twenty-first century bureaucratic demands and form filling require each of us to identity who we are and to be identified, by sex, age, nationality, and, increasingly, physical character-istics, like fingerprinting and retina screening. If you are given free choice, however, what else might the list reveal? This is a list of attributes, qualities, and capacities that are identified as making up the self who selects them, but none is unique or totally disassociated from the social and cultural context in which the subject speaks. Some are particularly socially inflected. Women often allude to body size, thus reflecting anxieties, which may well be unfounded by actual measurements and be more indicative of anxiety, which can also be indicated by absences and silences: what you don't include. The subject's identification of body size is not simply a reflection of a society that values the very slim body. What does your list suggest about what matters to you and the relationship between your percep-tion of yourself and the social and cultural world in which you situate yourself and are situated?

Self, subject, identity

The idea of a bounded self and the degree to which that self takes responsibility for actions has a long history in philosophical, cultural, and theological debates as well as being central to the relatively more modern discipline of psychology. The claim that there is a reflective self with a self-identity is more recent histori-cally, with its associations with rationalism and Enlightenment. This version of the self may demonstrate more about contemporary western discourses of reflection (Frosh, 2002) than psychoanalytic theories would accept. Some more critical analyses have expressed the idea of reflexivity more negatively, for example, as being expressive of excessive introspection, which could even be construed as self-indulgence, albeit within a discourse that encourages attentiveness to the self, which Nikolas Rose as characterized as 'psy discourse', which characterized the growth of psychiatric and psychoanalytic discourse in the twentieth century (Rose, 1987, 1990). Discussions of self, subject, and identity are heavily weighted by cultural and ethical values as well as part of a chronology of contributions to the field. Concerns with 'knowing the self' do, however, have a significant genealogy, and what is of some significance is the deployment of particular terms and con-cepts within specific historical circumstances, both temporally and spatially.

The concept of identity has become less central in the academy although claims to identities retain enormous purchase in politics, whether global political conflicts about national identities, for example, in the Ukraine, or in sexual politics where Facebook in 2014 decided to allow users to classify themselves according to one of more than fifty gender identities. Identity may appear to be to restricting and fixed, but claims to and protection of a recognized identity that can be classified remains a powerful component of political and everyday life. What is happening when Facebook changes its registration page so that you no longer have to log on as female or male but can register as gender, androgynous, various permuta-tions of trans or bi or a whole range of alternatives? The social media site explains the policy shift in the language of equal opportunities as promoting diversity and of providing Facebook users with the possibility of expressing their 'true, authentic self' (Cambridge Facebook Diversity, 2014).

This example raises several issues, not only about terminology. There is the appeal to a 'true self', which gives voice to the desire for authenticity and unity. There is also the matter of agency and the notion that people are the gender they say they are.

In some instances self, subject, and identity are interchangeable, although identity has been particularly strongly associated with latter part of the twentieth-century social movements and 'identity politics' (Woodward, 1997). The subject has powerful connections to psychoanalysis. What might be most important in thinking about the subject is the distinction between a subject that is produced and regulated by social institutions and made through discursive regimes as in Foucault's work (1971), and a self with desires, anxieties, and needs that is part of the psychoanalytical framework that has been so influential in psychosocial studies, but of which Foucault was so critical, seeing psychoanalysis as another discursive regime that produces its own subjects. Michel Foucault uses 'subject' to suggest someone who is subject to other forces, as in the subject of the state, although his later work posits a notion of self forged through self-knowledge and self-regulation (Foucault, 1998).

There are clearly overlaps between the different terms and concepts that are deployed to describe and locate the possibilities of a bounded self, whether entirely socially constructed or exercising some control over what happens to a person, or the set of embodied attributes, feelings, desires, needs, and energies, which is an identifiable and recognizable, ethical human self. Identity has been preferred at some points because of its accommodation of the interrelationship between the personal and the social and the complex possibilities of interplay between agency and social construction or even constraint. In thinking about the self, one of the key tensions and relationships that has to be negotiated is the interrelationship between personal responsibility and social, cultural, or other constraints. The concept of identity has been seen to take into account the extent to which individuals or groups participate actively in shaping selves who have responsibility for their own actions.

Some sociological approaches such as those of Anthony Giddens have framed the debate as one of structure and agency. Giddens (1991) has stressed the extent to which the self has become so transformed in what he calls late modernity that external influences and constraints embedded in cultural and religious norms, and notions of obligation and duty have been replaced by the reflexive project of managing the self. Consequently high priority is afforded to the self-constructing self. The projects with which the self engages are transformative and reflexive and largely individual, although Giddens also maps out the social and cultural shifts that have been both conducive to such changes in the making and remaking of the self and have resulted from these changes.

Although there is a legacy of binary thinking with agency and structure set in opposition to each other, the debate does not have to be so configured, and psychosocial developments have contributed enormously to alternative conceptualizations, notably which include the political and social dimensions of the self, which nonetheless retain an understanding of responsibility and reflexivity.

Many early twentieth-century engagements with self, subject, and identity, more specifically in the language of the time, with the self, involved a conversation with instincts and what could be termed human nature. Some of this debate is more concerned with determinism and reductionism, that is, that the self can be reduced to a set of biological and genetic characteristics that determine that self. This is a different challenge to the unitary coherent self that psychoanalytic theory suggests. This self is a determined, rather than a contradictory, fragmented self. Natural forces were always in the mix, especially post-Darwinian evolutionary theory, as they continue to be in the twenty-first century, albeit reconfigured and sometimes translated into the language of neuroscience. For example, the tension between a view of the self as governed entirely by biological, genetic forces where selfhood and independence is an illusion, as argued by evolutionary biologist Richard Dawkins, the author of the best-selling book *The Selfish Gene* (Dawkins ([1976]2006) and philosophers Thomas Nagel and Mary Midgely (Midgely, 2010, 2014). The language of science may be more sophisticated than that of the nineteenth century, but the tensions remain and Charles Darwin and the selfish gene are still invoked in the debate (Midgely, 2010, 2014). In the making of the self, the interrelationships between psychic and social always include some of these elements of genetic inheritance and the enfleshed capacities and limitations of the body. The body has been increasingly acknowledged in more recent work following the 'corporeal turn' (Howson, 2005; Woodward, 2009, 2012b, 2014) and in feminist critiques, for example, which build on Freudian and Lacanian psychoanalytic theory but challenge its patriarchal approaches (Grosz, 1994; Irigaray, 1984, [1977]1985, 2004) as will be considered below.

Before looking at some of the psychoanalytic legacy and offering some explanation of the centrality of psychoanalytic thinking in psychosocial studies, I am going to outline some of the earlier engagements with the issues raised by the psychosocial, even if the label was not used. The main puzzles in this chapter relate to the interrelationships between inner and social worlds, how they are connected or disconnected, and what happens when individuals are, or are not, recruited into subject positions. What earlier attempts have there been to grapple with these issues linking self and society?

The looking glass self

One early twentieth-century exploration of the connections between personal and social worlds, which includes the biological elements of selfhood, is Charles Horton Cooley's idea of the 'looking glass self' developed in his 1902 *Human*

Nature and the Social Order. The looking glass self starts with interaction and is an example of an approach to identity that focuses upon everyday practices and the routine encounters between the personal and the social, the psychic and the social. Cooley's version of the self is rooted in everyday practices and the language of personal pronouns. This is a self who can be known through observation rather than metaphysical inquiry. Cooley drew upon the ideas of William James ([1882]1961) who, in stressing the reflective nature of the self and the situation whereby whenever I am thinking, I am aware that I am thinking. It is a consciousness of the process of thinking and not just an awareness of the content of my thoughts. This idea is resonant of Descartes's *cogito*. James, however, stressed the empirical features of this process. Cooley's approach was pragmatic rather than transcendental like that of Descartes. As Cooley said, '[I]t is well to say at the outset that by the word "self" in this discussion is meant simply that which us designated in common speech by the pronouns of the first person singular' (1964:168). Cooley identifies what he means by the self and goes on to stress that this is an empirical self who has to be observed in the social context. These are actual people who acknowledge and appropriate their own actions and their presence in the world. Even if this is a self who is specifically human in a Darwinian sense, it is still a self who is made and remade in the context of social interaction. This is a commonsense, familiar, everyday view of the self in keeping with Cooley's pragmatist approach.

Cooley's version of the self operates through imagination and what he calls the 'looking glass self'. We imagine how we appear to others and also imagine the other person's assessment of us. The third element of this self is the feeling or emotion that a person has, which Cooley describes as 'some sort of self-feeling, such as pride or mortification' (1964:184). This dimension of self-hood is central to social life, to the adjustment of the self to others. Cooley's work also focuses upon the idea of the internalization of collective norms by individuals. It is interesting that although the starting point for the development of Cooley's theory of the looking glass self is the individual self, the main contribution lies in the entanglement of social and psychic elements.

This perspective on the self, however, not only stresses the importance of how we think about ourselves and about how we imagine others see us, but it also retains a strong emphasis upon instinct and a shared human legacy. In the work of the social philosopher George Herbert Mead, the self becomes more socially interactive and less instinctive. Mead's work also offers an engagement with the kind of debates that now inform psychosocial studies.

The 'I' and the 'me'

Mead prioritizes social interaction and to the intellectual life in his work. '[T]he internalization and inner dramatization by the individual, of what is happening outside which constitute . . . [the] chief mode of interaction with other individuals living in the same society' (1934:173). This is a self who is made during the process of interaction, rather than a self who exists prior to communication; interaction is integral to the whole process of self-making. This self reflects upon itself:

> The essence of the self, as we have said is cognitive; it lies in the internalization of gestures which constitute thinking, or in terms of which thought or reflection proceeds. And hence the origins and foundations of the self, like those of thinking are social.
>
> (Mead, 1934:173)

There is considerable emphasis upon the social dimensions of the making of the self in Mead's account, which is nonetheless subject to assertions of origins and foundations. This suggests that social processes are involved, that the self does not exist prior to social interaction, but that there are origins that can be traced and some basis upon which the self is constructed. Mead, like James and Cooley, uses language as a key component in his understanding of the self. Mead is probably most well known for his development of the idea of the 'I' and the 'me': 'The "I" reacts to the self which arises through the taking of the attitudes of others.

> Through taking those attitudes we have introduced the "me" and we react to it as an "I". . . . The "I" is the response of the organism to others: the "me" is the organised set of attitudes, of others which one himself assumes.
>
> (Mead, 1934:174–5)

Thus Mead's self is self-conscious, although consciousness alone is not enough to explain the ways in which selves are made. We have to be conscious of something. The process that links the 'I' to the 'me' and produces the self involves connections between inner and outer worlds. Within this theoretical framework, 'I' understand myself through imaging how I am understood by others, as 'me'. Mead's interactive reflective self is a part of the society that provides the meaning, based upon experience, which is the substance of reflection as well as providing the possibilities of diversity and difference among and between people.

Social circumstances demand different responses, whether in the multiple selves that constitute daily life or across time and space within different historical and social contexts. Selves are produced through the process of imagining. For example, children go through the process of making selves through play. Mead suggests that when children play, for example, by creating imaginary others and acting out adult roles they practice selves that are later adopted and become an 'I'. Whilst Mead's approach draws upon experience and could thus have been included within pragmatism, his emphasis upon the imagination and the possibilities of creativity added an important dimension to understanding the self relationally. Mead's self is a social self who is constituted through processes of imagination, which connect the personal and the social. This is a self that through reflexivity is capable to exercising some agency. It is also a self that allows some exploration of internal processes and the dialectic between inner and outer worlds; even if Mead's social world appears rather too consensual, there is more limited investigation of outer worlds, which remain somewhat separate and distinct from the internal processes through which selves are made.

Performing the self

One of the most important strands in sociological thinking about the relationship between inner and outer worlds in the making of the self is that of Erving Goffman. Judith Butler draws on his work in making the transition from performance to performativity and in trying to negotiate the relationship between a possibly oversocialized, excessively social constructionist, discursive approach and psychoanalytic theory.

Mead's symbolic interactionist focus was on taking up a role, as in those cases when children development an understanding of the self by imaginatively taking on the roles of others such as teachers or parents or characters in stories. Goffman developed some of these ideas by using the idea that people go on taking on roles throughout their lives in order to work out their sense of self and to relate to others in the social world. If Mead underplayed the social world, Goffman gave it his full attention. Each role involves interaction with others so that people modify their roles in relation to the expectations of others. Goffman, like Mead, concentrated on the importance of the **symbolic** but extended the concept of a role to explore how roles are performed.

In the dramaturgical model, which Goffman explores (1959), the self is not only a social self, it is also a self that takes account of the social situation, in the everyday drama of social interaction and in routine encounters; this self develops from and responds to those social situations.

> The perspective employed in this report is that of theatrical performance; the principles delivered are dramaturgical ones. I shall consider the way in which the individual in ordinary work situations presents himself [sic] and his activity to others, the ways in which he guides and controls, the impression they form of him, and the kinds of things he may not do while sustaining his performance before them.
>
> (Goffman, 1959:xi)

Although this self is analogous to the actor who plays a part, there is scope for negotiation, choice, interpretation, and even some improvisation, which is where inner worlds and the psyche are implicated. This self has to be presented, but this entails active engagement in the performance. Everyday encounters and interactions involve what Goffman calls impression management (1961). The success of such performances is not guaranteed, and there is more uncertainty in Goffman's approach than Mead's. For Goffman public displays of the self involve information that is 'given' and intentional and supplied directly and that which is revealed or indicated inadvertently, in Goffman's words, 'given off'. Such mistakes are resonant of Freudian slips, whereby as Freud suggested people often reveal more about who they are when they say what they do not mean to say than those words that are expressed with intention (Freud, [1905]2000). Although there are contradictions and insecurities that are implicated in this version of the self, it still suggests that there is some authentic 'real' self who delivers the performance, occasionally revealing more than was intended.

Goffman's work using analogies of theatre and film with everyday life, for example, in his work on frames Goffman (1974), opened up possibilities for incorporating inner and social worlds into an understanding of the self and made possible more recent work, which integrates the two spheres more effectively and recognizes the complexity and fragmentation of subjectivity such as Butler's use of the concept of performativity, which endeavours to combine psychoanalytic and discursive critiques (Butler, 1990, 1993).

Conforming selves

Some of the sociological accounts of the self that attempted to take on board the interrelationship between social and internal processes, or at least sociology and psychology, were particularly concerned with the nature of conformity. How did people fit into a particular sort of society? The society in question that produced some of the most relevant work in this context was the US. For example, David Riesman developed the idea of national character types in his famous book exploring the North American personality, *The Lonely Crowd* (Riesman, 1950). Riesman suggested that with ever more dominant and pervasive techniques of industrialization and urbanization, people, who for Riesman were decidedly social and 'made by society' (ibid.:3) became more inner directed. Riesman writes about personality rather than the self as such, but his argument is based on attempting to explore some of the connections between a changing society and the inner worlds of individuals. The self, even if not so called in *The Lonely Crowd*, is largely socially constructed but retains some elements of inherited characteristics, although what mattered most for Riesman was character, which incorporates the specificities of history and is contingent but also reflects inner desires. Character is 'the more or less permanent, socially and historically conditioned organization of an individual's drives and satisfactions' (Riesman, 1950:4). He draws on psychoanalytic ideas such as those of Erich Fromm in order to incorporate the desiring subject into his analysis. As Fromm argues, individuals are not simply socialized into a character type but have to desire its qualities and properties (Fromm, 1940).

Riesman's main thesis concerned the shift from inner-directed industrialization and a production-focused economy to other-directed character types in postindustrialized consumer societies. The prevalence of inner-directed character types receded in the face of postindustrial other directedness, for example, especially among the North American middle classes. This was of course a highly contested argument; others claimed that the self was increasingly turning inward not outward. For example, Richard Sennett in *The Fall of the Public Man* (1974) and Robert Bellah in *Habits of the Heart* ([1985]1996) challenged Riesman's thesis. Rather than passively responding to social imperatives and simply reflecting social values, Sennett claims that people are becoming increasingly self-directed and self-absorbed (Sennett, 1974) and that radical individualism was what plagued the self in the latter part of the twentieth century (Bellah, [1985]1996). Riesman has a definition of the process whereby values and qualities are taken into the self.

> What is common to all the other-directed people is that their contemporaries are the source of direction for the individual – either those known to him or those with whom he is indirectly acquainted, through friends and through the mass media. This source is of course 'internalized' in the sense that depending on it for guidance: it is only the process of striving itself and the process of paying close attention to the signals of others that remain unaltered through life.
> (1950:21)

Riesman was writing about populations and population as well as culture change, which seems a long way from psychosocial studies, but his attempt to engage with psychological aspects of change as well as societal ones and to engage with the interface between individuals and their characters and the broad sweep of social change clearly demonstrate that there are different routes into psychosocial debates.

Riesman's exploration of conformity presents a depressing scenario of internalized characteristics making a self that is relatively untroubled and clearly nonresistant or disruptive. In spite of Riesman's acknowledgement of internalization processes, however, his version of the self remains somewhat oversocialized, although the historical specificity does suggest more plasticity and mobility to the subject than universalist theories might suggest. Although there are different positions, all of these attempts to engage with the interconnections between the personal and the social remain largely dependent on the social arena and set up distinctions between inner and outer worlds. Nonetheless, the making of the self as an internal process is recognized and connections between inner and outer worlds are addressed.

In psychoanalytic thought, especially as developed by Freud, it is drives that motivate the subject, as was shown in chapter 2. Psychoanalysis offers a much more specific and complex account of inner worlds in the making of the self than many, if not most, other approaches. Because of its enormous influence on psychosocial studies, this chapter considers the role of the unconscious in the working of the inner world of the self.

The subject and the unconscious

Freud's conceptualization of the unconscious provides a good starting point for exploring the self and in particular how inner and outer worlds not only connect but are entangled inseparably. Psychoanalytic theory has been frequently invoked in theories of identity (Butler, 1990, 1993, 2000, 2005; Butler et al., 2000; Hall, 1992; Kaplan, 1992, 2005), especially in approaches to identity as the intersection of the personal and the social (Woodward, 1997). Psychoanalytic theory has also infiltrated into commonsense and everyday understandings of subjectivity. Michele Barrett argues that 'the insights of psychoanalysis with regard to the unconscious, repression, fantasy, sexuality and so on are not merely "within the true" of psychoanalytic discourse but play an important part in the way in which people in contemporary western societies now understand themselves . . . psychoanalytic concepts are rooted in culture' (Barrett, 1991:115).

Psychoanalytic theories address the internal psychic processes and engage with that inner space that constitutes the psyche. Freud's work, although clearly undertaken at times of enormous social and political upheaval including the First World War, can be seen to concentrate on the psychic processes of individual patients. It is through an understanding of the workings of the unconscious that psychoanalytic theories are able to contribute to an understanding of the self in relation to the wider society and to the processes of **identification**. Identification involves 'a psychological process whereby the subject assimilates an aspect, property or attribute of the other and is transformed, wholly or partly, after the model the other provides' (Laplanche and Pontalis, 1973:203). The subject is thus constituted through a range of identifications.

The Freudian model of the psyche with its interrelated components of id, ego, and superego provides a means of accessing and making sense of the processes and systems of the inner world of the psyche in order to resolve the conflicts between personal needs and desires of the id and the social elements expressed in the superego. The unconscious thus comprises repressed desires, feelings, and ideas that may be unacceptable because they threaten either the individual or others and the wider society. The id is the source of such desires, which demand attention and satisfaction. The unconscious is made up of powerful desires, often unmet, which have been created because of the intrusion of the father into the child's relationship with its mother. Lacan, following Freud, also gives primacy to this notion of the unconscious in the shaping of the self, although Lacan's radical reworking of Freud accords much greater emphasis to the symbolic and the role of representational systems, especially language in the formation of the subject. Lacan's approach is more to develop a linguistic model of reflexivity. '[I]t is not a question of knowing whether I speak of myself in a way that conforms to what I am, but rather of knowing whether I am the same as that which I speak' (Lacan, 1977:165). Lacan offers some explanation of why people invest in some subject positions and come to be 'spoken' by the versions of the self that are available within a particular culture. Consequently the pronoun 'I' is used, and although each person claims it as their own, the pronoun in language is separate from the 'I' who speaks. In a sense the first-person pronoun in a language like English or French, is secondhand; it exists in language before I use it and there is a gap between the 'I' who speaks and the 'I' of language.

In Lacan's version of the subject, the self is never fixed or stable because there is a gap and a sense that something is missing, which haunts the speaker and the subject, as a desire that can never quite be fulfilled or satisfied.

The unconscious operates according to its own laws and to a different logic from the conscious thought processes of the rational mind. Whereas the conscious mind demands intelligibility, coherence, and unity, these are not characteristics of the more troubled and disrupted unconscious. The unconscious may be troubled, but it also has creative capacities, which can be accessed through therapy or through spontaneous eruptions into consciousness. For example, the unconscious, which makes up the subject, can be revealed through a dream, 'which is not more careless, more irrational, more incomplete than waking thought; it is completely different from it qualitatively and for that reason is not immediately comparable with it. It does not think, calculate or judge in any way at all; it restricts itself to giving things a new form . . . in the attention that is paid to the logical relationships between thoughts' (Freud, [1900]1965:545).

Conscious thought on the other hand is powered by what Freud called the secondary process, which involves the imposition of inflexible logical structures that are both calculating and judgemental. The unconscious, by contrast, is expressed through the fluidity of dreams and a free-flowing psychic energy. The unconscious is ambivalent and contradictory with very different temporalities and spatialities, which counter the pursuit of clarity and meaningful precision of the primary process of consciousness. The unconscious not only has its own logic, but it also has its own temporality. If you think about the dreams that you may recall and then try to relate to someone else, what happened in the dream on reporting seems absurd and incomprehensible although at the time of dreaming it was unquestioned. The ego attempts to resolve the conflict between the unconscious and consciousness and to gain some sort of control over inner and outer worlds in order to achieve some stability. This tension is resonant of the desire for certainty and stability in the securing of identity and the self, especially within a world perceived to be characterized by risk, danger, change, and insecurity.

Psychoanalytic theories provide not only the possibilities of therapy for the individual but also explanatory frameworks through which to make sense of the contradiction and irrationality of the self. For example, individuals and collectives, even nations, may invest identifications that are unacceptable to themselves. Individuals may get involved with sexual partners who are clearly unsuitable for all sorts of reasons; they may fall in love with someone and have a relationship that is not in their best interests and may even be detrimental to their well-being. They may appear to be unconsciously committed to a relationship that they may even be consciously aware is damaging. The unconscious has its own conflicts and its own dynamic. Freudian psychoanalysis provides a focus upon ambivalence and conflict by tracing irrational investment in subject positions back to the repression of unconscious needs and desires. The self is not a unified whole. The psyche comprises the unconscious id; the superego, which acts like a social conscience;

and the ego, which attempts resolution of conflict. The self is thus in a state of flux and never quite fixed or unified.

The subject, however, desires a unitary safety and the security of knowing itself. This desire may be expressed through identification, which goes beyond imitation and is the expression of a deep longing for unity. According to Lacan (1988), the first step in the formation of the self is the moment when the infant realizes its separateness from its mother. The child realizes the disruption of the primary and primitive union with its mother, at the point of entry into language. The mirror stage is used by Lacan to describe the moment when the infant constructs a self, which is based upon a reflection, either actually as seen in a mirror or mirrored through the eyes of others. This is a perception of a bounded self, as seen in the mirror, which sets the scene for future identification. The infant lacks bodily coordination and a developed sense of what is inside and what is outside itself in the first few months of life, but at about the age of eighteen months the infant is said to identify with its own mirror image. The image is beguiling especially in the sense of wholeness it evokes, which counteracts the anxiety of the actual experience of chaos and disunity. Each person has a sense of who they are, through seeing the self, reflected in an illusion of unity. Identity and a notion of the self depend upon something outside itself, and its unity is consequently an expression of lack based upon identification, which is aimed at establishing a unified sense of self. In Lacanian psychoanalysis, the mirror is the first point at which the infant consciously recognizes the distinction between its own body and the outside world. This is the first image of unity and wholeness. It is, however, as Lacan points out, a unity base upon illusion, which is 'imaginary'. There is a gap between the ideal of the image and the infant's fragmented psychic state. The mirror, which could be seen as the reflection of the child in the mother's eyes, is metaphorical, but it provides a point outside the self through which the self is recognized (or mis-recognized as a unity). This means that the imaginary has its origins outside and comes from the infant's misrecognition of itself and misapprehension of unity. As a result, for Lacan, although his focus appears to be upon internal processes and the psyche, the source of meaning is external and lies outside the individual. The mirror also provides the first experience of unity, however illusory this may be. This is the stage just before that at which the infant begins to be introduced to symbolic representations and when the infant is given the experience of what it would be like to be whole.

Whatever the obvious limitations of Lacan's prescriptions about child develop-ment, which are clearly not based on observation or any involvement with mothers and babies, the metaphor of the mirror has enormous resonance across a wide range of cultural experiences. Lacan's focus on the psychic experience of identi-fication expressed through such a powerful desire for unity facilitates an explana-tion of the making of the self, which is more complex as well as drawing upon and reconstituting deeply held feelings as well as those that arise from social processes and influences.

The mirror phase marks the beginning of the process through which the self is formed within the Lacanian paradigm. As has been pointed out by later critics within the psychoanalytic tradition, such as Luce Irigaray (1991) or followers of Melanie Klein's object relations approach (1986), this misses out on the close relationship between mother and child in the phase prior to the beginning of the process of recognition of the self and later the entry into language. It does, however, have relevance to the psychosocial project and has been influential at different times, especially in textual analysis of film, for example.

The process started in the mirror phase is completed in Lacanian thinking by the entry into the symbolic order, initially construed as language, although this has been expanded to embrace a wider range of symbolic and representational systems. At this point the infant is compelled to abandon the illusion of unity and to identify with the subject positions made available within the symbolic order. The cultural forms that make up the symbolic order exist outside the self and thus appear not to present a route into the true nature of the self. They are 'borrowed' from culture and are not fixed or innate. Thus we (this is a universal concept; we is all of us) are recruited into the symbolic order and take up subject positions that are already there.

These subject positions are gender inflected in very specific ways in Freudian and Lacanian psychoanalytic thinking. Sex/gender is the basis of the making of the subject in these accounts. Sexual differentiation, whereby infants come to identify as either female or male, is crucial to Lacan's approach, with a strong emphasis upon male authority and masculine supremacy in the symbolic order. There are clearly problems with so phallocentric and patriarchal a version of the making of the subject; Lacan's account does accord primacy to cultural factors in the making of men's power. As Juliet Mitchell argued (1971), the Lacanian account does offer some explanation of how patriarchy works as well as justifying its inequalities in his own version. Mitchell's *Psychoanalysis and Feminism* (1974) was an important attempt at using psychoanalytic theory to explain unconscious attachments to and investments in systems of gender and sexuality. Mitchell suggested that using Lacanian psychoanalytic theory could rescue Freud from biological reductionism and open up new ways of explaining how women internalize a set of cultural practices that are oppressive. The unconscious is a route into understanding why people do not always act in their own best interests. For Mitchell, psychoanalysis does not justify patriarchy and heterosexual oppression, but rather it can be used to show how patriarchy works; psychoanalysis is a description of not a prescription for patriarchy.

Jacqueline Rose offers a different challenge and stresses a different aspect of the unconscious. For Rose the internalization of gender does *not* work. The unconscious constantly reveals the 'failure' of identity. Because there is no continuity in psychic life, so there is no stability of sexual identity, no position for women (or for men) which is ever simply achieved. . . . '[F]ailure' is something endlessly repeated and relived moment by moment. . . . It appears not only in the symptom but also in dreams, in slips of the tongue and in forms of sexual pleasure that are pushed to the sidelines of the norm.

(Mitchell, 1974:187)

Psychoanalytic theories have the advantage of putting sex and gender onto the agenda and demonstrating the centrality of sex, whatever the challenges to psychoanalysis's rigid binaries and phallocentrism. Critics of the patriarchal assumptions of Freud and Lacan have stressed the disruptive potential of the unconscious. Also crucial to psychoanalytic engagements is the inseparable entanglement of psychic and social forces, which accounts for the importance of psychoanalytic thinking in psychosocial studies. Freud and especially Lacan have been challenged within psychoanalytic theory and by those who largely reject its insights and application, for example, following Foucault and then Deleuze. The most productive challenges, however, come from objects relations theories and feminist critiques, which seek to retain the concept of the unconscious whilst rejecting its phallocentricity and the way in which in Lacan's work the phallus is the key signifier of cultural meaning. Psychoanalytic theories, as chapter 2 showed, are central to psychosocial studies, and as this chapter suggests they play an important part in thinking about the interrelationship between the self and the social in relation to psychic as well as social forces.

Psychoanalytic approaches start but definitely do not finish with Freud – or Lacan – as has been demonstrated above and in chapter 2. Freud's notion of the unconscious in the making of the subject, however, is a very good place to start because the unconscious opens up all sorts of possibilities for the unexpected and the disruptive, as critics of Freudian and especially Lacanian patriarchy have been keen to point out. One such critic whose work continues to challenge heterosexist and phallocentric claims but with different emphases and whose work has particular resonance to some contemporary debates is the French feminist Luce Irigaray.

Luce Irigaray

Irigaray has been very productive across a wide range, but my purpose here is to identify some particular challenges to gendered subjects as presented in Freudian and Lacanian psychoanalytic theories. One aspect of the gendered subject that Irigaray has put onto the agenda is that of the mother. She has argued that patriarchal systems exclude the mother from culture, thus not only diminishing and marginalizing maternal subjects but also making this identification impossible. She challenges Freud's insistence upon the power of the Oedipal myth as the definitive means of the making of the gendered subject by arguing that

[w]hen Freud describes and theorizes, notably in *Totem and Taboo*, the murder of the father as founding the primal horde, he forgets a more archaic murder,

that of the mother, necessitated by the establishment of a certain order of polis.

Give or take a few additions and retractions, our imaginary still functions in accordance with the schema established through Greek mythologies and tragedies.

(Irigaray, 1985:36)

It is the father-son relationship that dominates the drama and creates the desiring subject.

Mothers are particularly hidden from history and absent from culture: an absent presence (Woodward, 1997), since, as Irigaray argues, 'It remains in the shadow of our culture. But men no more or rather less do without it than can women' (in Whitford, 1991:35). The mother is the ghost at the feast of culture and in particular within Freudian and Lacanian psychoanalytic theories. Irigaray's is not a biologist view, although she has been criticized for biological reductionism because of her focus upon the sexed body and the maternal body because she is writing about a cultural silence and the impact this has on everyone, especially women, who are the ones silenced.

She suggests that the silence enjoined on the mother perpetuates fears and fantasies such as that of the woman as devouring monster, which arise out of 'the unanalysed hatred from which women as a group suffer culturally' (in Whitford, 1991:25). Irigaray suggests that Freudian and Lacanian psychoanalytic theories are particularly responsible for the exclusion of women – all women, not only those who are mothers – because she seeks to avoid reducing women to the maternal function and her point is about cultural silencing and the marginalization of women's embodied relationships of which the maternal is one. One way of redressing the balance is to recognize and value the mother-daughter relationship and to put the mother relationship into the symbolic.

The reason for the inclusion of this strand of Irigaray's work is threefold. Firstly, she is offering a critique of Freud and Lacan from within a psychoanalytic framework by arguing for an alternative approach and by pointing out the social and cultural specificities of Freud's and Lacan's universalist claims about the workings of the psyche and its relationship to culture. Secondly, she suggests that psychoanalysis itself is governed by unconscious fantasies that it cannot analyze. This is an important counterargument to the universalism and authority of psychoanalysis about which some contemporary critics have expressed concern (for example, Wetherell, 2003; Billig, 1997). Thirdly, Irigaray's critique highlights the particularly patriarchal characteristics of psychoanalysis, which involves the transmission of culture from father to son, with the priority of identification with the father and compliance with his law.

Irigaray, like other feminist critics, points to the patriarchal bias of Freud and Lacan and seeks an alternative by an exploration of what and who is silenced and excluded, which demonstrates most clearly the absence of the mother as a cultural figure and the huge importance of the child's relationship with the mother in the making of the self. Object relations theory has been of particular interest to feminists because this approach too highlights the maternal relationship in the process of making the subject.

Melanie Klein's object relations offer a particularly productive challenge to the patriarchal imbalances of Freud and Lacan in this context. Klein's work has been extensively used in psychosocial studies, as is apparent from the discussion in chapter 2 and in many of the examples that follow in later chapters, but object relations deserves some particular discussion in the context of challenges to the Freudian and Lacanian versions of gendered selves.

Object relations and the self

Object relations offer a very different analysis of subjectivity from both Freud and Lacan, whilst remaining a psychoanalytic approach that focuses upon early childhood experience in the making of the self. This post-Freudian approach concentrates on the preverbal infant experience and upon the child's relationship with the mother and provides much greater recognition of the mother and especially the maternal relationship than Freud, who accords primacy to the father and the Oedipus complex. Klein proposed a primary femininity and identification with the mother for all infants. As an alternative to Freud's claim that little girls were 'little men', Klein challenged the status given to the penis by Freud and suggested that a more realistic envy in male development would be womb envy. The father has a very small part to play in Klein's object relations approach to subjectivity, as, historically, have actual fathers in most infants' lives.

Object relations is a system of explanations based upon the premise that mental processes comprise elements taken in from outside. The object is the thing, or most likely for the infant, the person, its mother, or part of a person, the breast through which an instinctual drive is able to achieve its aim. Klein redefined Freud's drives by foregrounding destructive impulses and their attachment to objects, most significantly the breast, as an object that can be a good object for the infant, or, when withdrawn, the breast becomes a bad object, through the process of splitting. In infancy objects are split into good and bad because the primitive ego cannot cope with the instinctual drives that consume the infant.

Those who followed in the school of British object relations, such as W. R. D. Fairburn (1952), Harry Guntrip (1961), and D. W. Winnicott (1953, 1960a, 1960b, 1965, 1967, 1971a, 1971b) redefined the mother–child relationship by stressing the actual environment and the nature of maternal care in shaping the developing self, by distinguishing between internal and external worlds rather than, as Klein had, between phantasy and reality.

What is particularly important about object relations in the discussion of self, subject, and identity in this chapter is that this approach offers a psychoanalytic theory, which gives status to the mother and recognizes mothers as significant figures in the development of the child, rather than relegating those who are empirically the infant's primary carer to a subordinate role subjugated by patriarchy, men's bodies, and the law of the father. Object relations, although subject to significant criticisms in some quarters, opens up more egalitarian and realistic possibilities for understanding the making of the self. The emphasis upon the mother, of course, also opens up the idea of blaming mothers for whatever goes wrong, as feminists who took up the object relations approach, such as Dorothy Dinnerstein in her book *The Mermaid and the Minotaur* (1976) and Nancy Chodorow in *The Reproduction of Mothering* (1978) in the US were keen to argue. Both, albeit making with some entrenched heterosexist assumptions at the time about 'normal' families, made the case for joint parenting to disrupt the historical propagation of women's oppression.

Melanie Klein's object relations approach was based on observation of children and on the infant's development of the self in relation to its mother. Klein's approach is of methodological significance, as her observations are based upon empirical field-work and not hypothetical deduction or interpretation from a particular perspective, as might be said of Freud's consulting room. The mother–child relationship, rather than that with the father, is the basis of Kleinian object relations. This work has also been most productive in generating the specific aspects of that relationship – firstly, in demonstrating the relationality of human beings; the development of the self is always relational. Secondly, Klein's work generated ideas about the nature of that relationality, for example, in the object relations and defence mechanisms, which inform later experiences and relationships.

Within psychosocial studies, object relations offers very different weighted understandings of early childhood relationships from those of Freud and to a greater extent Lacan. Nancy Chodorow, like many feminist critics of Freud, challenged the patriarchal assumptions of psychoanalysis and instead used an object relations approach. Chodorow, like Irigaray, focused on the mother–child relationship and the impact of the mother figure on women's subjectivities. Chodorow focused upon the child's pre-Oedipal relationship with the mother where the self is understood as developed through relations with others, rather than through Freudian drives. Thus the mother occupies a central place in the child's formation of the self. Chodorow presented what could fairly be described as a psychosocial analysis of how women, mainly as compensation for men's failure to support them, make extensive psychic and emotional investments in desiring and nurturing children. Women long for children not so much because of innate drives but because of the inadequacies of men's nurturing skills in their relationship with women. What could be described as feminine and masculine personality traits or female and male selves are outcomes of how children are parented. Mothering and fathering in turn are the products of gendered structures produced in the now-parents' own childhoods. As a result women mother daughters who value attachment and connection and thus in their turn want to be mothers themselves. Men, on the other hand, fear connectedness and attachment, and the cycle of heterosexual lack of nurturing and connectiveness persists and is repeated.

Conclusion

Some conceptualization of the self or the subject is central to psychosocial studies, not least because the self is always part of the processes of entanglement between personal and social, and theories of subjectivity have to be able to accommodate an understanding of relationality between self and society and inner worlds and social worlds.

The idea of the self has also been important in sociological engagements with psychosocial issues, which have endeavoured to redress the imbalances of the social in the personal social relationship, for example, as expressed in Wrong's oversocialization thesis (Wrong, 1961). The subject is also a good starting point for the exploration of inner worlds, which may appear less accessible at the level of the social, especially in oversocialized models. The discussion in this chapter has demonstrated some of the connections and also the importance of psychoanalytic insights and concepts, in particular the potential offered by the concept of the unconscious from crossing some of the boundaries and, in particular, for engaging with relationality.

This chapter has shown the importance of conceptualizations of self, subject, and identity in relation to the psychosocial and provided some explanation of why conceptualizations of the self, the subject, and identity are so important. In order to achieve this, the chapter has explored some earlier attempts at engaging with the relationship between the personal and the social in the making and the remaking of the self.

I have demonstrated the relevance of psychoanalytic approaches that have also been deployed to challenge the oversocialization of the self, whilst acknowledging some of the weaknesses and the strengths of psychoanalytic theories, and suggested some possibilities for alternative, psychosocial strategies and approaches.

Questions

1   What is the role of psychoanalytic theory in discussions of the subject and subjectivity?
2   What sort of relationship between the psychic and the social emerges from these discussions of the self, the subject, and identity?
3   What problems can you see with approaches that see inner and outer worlds as two separate spaces that are connected and disconnected?
4   How have theorists attempted to deal with the problem of 'oversocialization'?

chapter 5

Affect

> **This chapter:**
>
> 1   Maps out some of the ideas that form the 'turn to affect' to locate psychosocial ideas.
> 2   Explores the relevance of the concept of affect to an understanding of the relationship between the psychic and the social.
> 3   Considers the relationship among affect, emotion, and feeling within psychosocial studies.
> 4   Explores the concept of affective transmission in psychosocial studies.
> 5   Uses a psychosocial approach to explore the liminal space of 'being in the zone'.

Introduction

There has been a great deal of discussion about **affect** in recent years, but what is affect? Recently affect has been understood to refer to the communication of emotions, or feelings. Some approaches position affect within a wider framework. One thing is affected by another, which suggests movement, impact, and possibly change; when something is affected by something else or someone else, it becomes transformed in some way. People are affected by other people and by their experiences. This chapter focuses upon human experience, rather than exploring the possibilities of affective objects, which has also been a significant development in the 'turn to affect' (Harvey et al., 2014). This chapter explores the processes through which feelings and emotions are transmitted, even when what is happening is not immediately obvious and cannot be understood from an observation of behaviour.

What is psychosocial about affect, and where does this 'affective turn' fit into psychosocial studies? What can a psychosocial approach tell us about how affect works? One of the major questions addressed by psychosocial approaches to affect is how feelings and emotions might be transmitted from one person to another or among large groups of people without anyone being conscious of what is happening. What happens when affects are not immediately obvious or when affect may operate at the level of the unconscious? What is taking place can be described in Christopher Bollas's terms as an 'unthought known', which is a state characteristic of the preverbal, pre-Oedipal stage when the experience of the object (whether the mother or father or another object or part of the person) precedes the knowing of the object:

> The infant has a prolonged sense of the uncanny, as he dwells with a spirit of place the creation of which is not identifiable.
>
> > (Bollas, 1987:39)

The shadow of this state remains, and the 'unthought known' can be creatively used to refer to those moments and feelings in adult life when we come to realize something and feel that we have always known it even though this was not a conscious or stated knowledge to which we could lay claim. In everyday experience we might refer to those occasions of recognition as 'uncanny'. The notion of something being uncanny is not the only description of affect, but the unthought known provides one route into understanding the role of memory and haunting in moments of recognition, which may appear to be uncanny. It is one way of explaining the interplay of affect where past and present combine in the present.

The turn to affect

In recent years affect has become the focus of a whole range of studies across the social sciences, so much so that all of this interest has been classified as the 'affective turn' (Clough, with Halley, 2008; Clough, 2008a, 2008b, 2009; Hoggett, 2012; Maxwell and Aggleton, 2013; Wetherell, 2012). There has been a growth in contributions to the study of affect, which can also be called the 'sensualist turn' (Berlant, 2003:1), incorporating feelings and sensation into the discussion in a concerted critique of poststructuralism's focus on discourse (Wetherell, 2012).

The turn to affect has taken a number of different routes. An immediate response to talk of affect might be to assume that this is about emotions and feelings. Affect could include both feelings and emotions in all their manifestations including perturbations of mind and body and their psychosomatic outcomes. Affect raises all sorts of questions about how it works and the links between bodies, emotions, and feelings. How do you control emotion – collective or individual? How do you exercise any control over the corporeal effects of emotion – crying, blushing, fainting, or even fitting (for example, experiencing an epileptic fit, when the incident takes over one's body)?

Contemporary life, especially within the context of late modernity, in neoliberal democracies has become increasingly concerned with emotion and feeling as aspects of well-being (Frosh, 2011; Giddens, 1991, 1992; Hochschild, 1983; Sclater, Jones, Price, and Yates, 2009). Emotion might have corporeal and biological sources, but as Arlie Hochschild argues in *The Managed Heart* (1983), social factors influence what we expect and thus what feelings signal. Hochschild examined two groups of public-contact workers: flight attendants and bill collectors. The flight attendant's job is to deliver a service and to generate further demand for the service, to enhance the status of the customer and to be 'nicer than natural'. The bill collector's job is, if necessary, to deflate the status of the customer by being 'nastier than natural'. Between these extremes, roughly one-third of American men and one-half of American women hold jobs that call for substantial emotional labour. In many of these jobs, they are trained to accept feeling rules and techniques of emotion management that serve the company's commercial purpose. Just as we have seldom recognized or understood emotional labour, we have not appreciated its cost to those who do it for a living. Like a manual labourer who becomes alienated from what he or she makes, an emotional laborer, such as a flight attendant, can become alienated not only from his or her own expressions of feeling so that his or her smile is not his or her own but also from what he or she actually feels. Hochschild's work, although not explicitly psychosocial, has been important in demonstrating the inseparability of inner and social worlds and the centrality of emotion in contemporary society, so much so that feeling and emotion have become commodities.

Emotional distress is increasingly recognized as inhibiting well-being as well as having physical affects. For example, following trauma, whether the result of accidents including environmental disasters or occasions when individuals are victims of criminal offences, people are frequently offered counselling in order to restore their capacity to cope with everyday life. In neoliberal democracies, professional soldiers can be offered therapeutic assistance to overcome some of the trauma of armed combat, which is in many ways contradictory given the purpose of the military, but does demonstrate an increasing cultural awareness of the impact of emotional distress on well-being and performance. Emotion is central to social life and not an individualized peripheral concern. The turn to affect is one of the ways in which there has been a move towards trying to understand some of these processes of influence and movement when something changes something else – when something or someone affects and is affected by something or someone else.

Margie Wetherell suggests two main strands in the 'turn to affect' (Wetherell, 2012). Firstly, there is the more familiar psychological notion that focuses on the emotions. This is broadly where the psychosocial can be placed, although, as this chapter shows, the psychosocial approach to affect is much more complex in its diverse engagements with processes than might be suggested by the idea that affect is another term for feelings and, especially, emotions. Secondly, there is a more broad-based wide-ranging concept that embraces difference, process, and force and is more likely to be associated with Deleuzian approaches (Deleuze and Guattari, 1977). The latter approach reflects an ontological shift from an empirical focus upon the emotions to a particular theoretical position, which does not prioritize human beings and their emotions or attribute agency only to people. There are some connections, but these are polarized positions, not least because of their very different accommodations of human subjectivity. One example of a link is in the work of Patricia Clough who focuses upon a particular route into studying affect, which derives from her work on the connections and disconnections with psychoanalytic theory, but arrives at a Deleuzian approach, which emphasizes the dynamic nature of the process of the interrelationship between objects, subjects, and events (Clough, 2008a, 2008b).

Wetherell maps out some of the arguments about different versions and approaches to affect, which acknowledge the explicit contributions of the psychosocial, but also demonstrates the differences between theoretical perspectives (Wetherell, 2012). She argues for a pragmatic approach, which redresses the imbalances of conventional psychological approaches to affect as emotion and Deleuzian ideas about affect as force that operates between objects. Wetherell bemoans the lack of understanding of the contribution of a discursive approach to affect and the ways in which a focus upon the uncanny, as if affect were a mysterious phenomenon, blocks pragmatic approaches to affect such as her own.

Whilst Wetherell's pragmatic discursive approach would not come under the umbrella term of the psychosocial in any of its recognized forms, she still acknowledges the importance of psychosocial contributions. She is also concerned with similar puzzles about the processes involved in the intersections of the personal and the political and especially the social and cultural processes and the energy that constitutes the self. What is missing in her account is a psychoanalytical incorporation of the unconscious.

There are clear distinctions especially between the Deleuzian conceptualization of affect and that which is deployed in psychosocial approaches, not least the rejection of the inner world in which the unconscious of the human subject operates. Such approaches take a very different view of autonomy from psychosocial studies. Approaches that draw upon the Deleuzian legacy, such as Brian Massumi's, appeal to a preconscious inner world, which is 'beyond consciousness' (Massumi, 2005). In this space, emotion is relegated to 'the tawdry status of the private' (Massumi, 2002:219). Massumi's engagement with affect does address the problems of explaining what seems to be outside consciousness and difficult to explain; what is, in his terms, beyond discourse (Massumi, 2002), but his appeal is to a preconscious world and not to the psychoanalytical unconscious. Massumi's discussion of affect as being beyond consciousness is appealing although his solution to the puzzle is to reject psychoanalytical explanations in favour of Deleuzian notions of unmediated sensation, which involves a disavowal of both the unconscious and of any particularities of human agency. I mention this here for two reasons: firstly, because this is one distinctive strand in the turn to affect, and secondly, because the issues identified are very similar to those that are the focus of psychosocial studies in that affect is not immediately detectable or explicable.

The Deleuzian approach does, however, explore the processes and suggest a middle space of affect, which lies between the objects that affect and are affected by each other (Woodward, 2014). Affect involves a dynamic relationship that can be theorized in different ways. The to and fro of affect suggests a space in the middle between what affects and what is affected, however affect is theorized. This approach does not prioritize emotion, or human beings, however, but sees affect as relational. Although there are some attempts to combine a Deleuzian approach with some of the insights of psychoanalysis (Clough, 2008a, 2008b; Gregg and Seigworth, 2010), it seems largely incompatible with a psychosocial approach. There are a range of approaches that seek to take on board the turn to affect, however, with varying emphases upon inner worlds of feeling and social and cultural worlds. Each engages with the circulation or transmission of affect and the movement of affect.

Cultural theorist Lawrence Grossberg argues that affect describes complex articulation among imagination, bodies, and experiences. Affect makes visible the multiplicity of cultural apparatuses in effective ties (Grossberg, 2010). Affect, according to Grossberg, refuses the position of culture as the necessary third term of a dialectic between subject and object, between the particular and the universal – a position in which culture has established itself as the very being of mediation, which Grossberg refers to as a third space. Affect proposes constructionism, mediation, and the 'ideal'. Culture has been about conflicts between intellect and creativity, rationality and emotion, significance and signification – affect challenges these tensions because it includes different elements (Grossberg, 2013).

This approach is nearer the Deleuzian (Deleuze, 1988, 1992) in its understanding of mediation as problematic, but what is interesting is the positing of a third space in the relationship. For Grossberg, affect proposes constructionism, mediation, and the 'ideal' because he also argues that culture has been about conflicts between intellect and creativity, rationality and emotion, significance and signification, and affect challenges these tensions (Grossberg, 2010).

Sarah Ahmed also stresses the importance of cultural values and practices in the circulation of affect, which range from face-to-face and corporeal encounters in which affect is transmitted (Ahmed, 2004a, 2004b). She uses the particular example of happiness as a contradictory affect, especially in the context of political struggles, for example, against racialized and ethnicized oppression and exclusion (Ahmed, 2010). What is particularly relevant about Ahmed's innovative discussion is her incorporation of emotion into a two-way relationship with the social and cultural terrain. This approach also suggests connections between the affective states of individuals and the cultural times they inhabit. There are also scientific arguments that suggest that the nervous systems of human beings are designed to be 'captured by the nervous systems of others' (Stern, 2004:76). Human beings are social in that personally, deeply felt emotions are more widely interlinked to others and the society in which they live through a highly developed affective intersubjectivity.

Psychosocial affects; affective transmission

How is affect transmitted from one person to another, or even among large groups of people? Is it simply a matter of contagion, as at the sports stadium, of joy and happiness for those whose team is winning and deep gloom and frustration for those whose team is losing? I am writing this book in 2014 in the year of the men's Football World Cup in Brazil when the excesses of sporting emotion are all too evident. Much of the work that has been undertaken in sport has been focused upon regulation and control, and affect is translated as excess, or more specifically hooliganism – superfluous emotion leading to aggression that has to be controlled and suppressed (Giulianotti, 1999, 2002, 2005) in the civilizing march of human societies (Elias, [1939]1982). Nonetheless, sport offers an interesting site for exploration of processes of identification and for the idea of transmission, which are more complex than regulatory discourses suggest. For example, the spontaneous expression of chants at football stadia (Schoonderwoerd, 2011; Warner, 2011) suggest a two-way process of affect between spectators and players. Even the feelings and expressions of spectators at a football match are not simply a crude, contagious outcome of the activities on the pitch or the score (Woodward and Goldblatt, 2011) but present some of the ambivalences of the processes of affect.

What do we mean by transmission? Teresa Brennan suggests that affective transmission takes place when one person's feelings and emotions are taken up by another, or by a whole group of people (Brennan, 2004). This could be relatively unproblematic and obvious, as in the case when your lead striker scores a brilliant goal, which secures promotion for your team, or at an everyday level, when in conversation with a friend, for example, walking along the road you sense and experience your friend's fear that a car is approaching too fast. There are, however, many other instances in which why one person, or group of people, should feel the emotion of another is not at all obvious, and there are connections to be disentangled.

Christopher Bollas argues that Freud's understanding of affective transmission from the patient to the analyst is akin to a radio transmission (Bollas, 1995).

> He must turn his own unconscious like a receptive organ toward the transmitting unconscious of the patient. He must adjust himself to the patient as a telephone receiver is adjusted to the transmitting microphones. Just as the

receiver converts back into sound waves the electric oscillations in the telephone line which were set up by the sound waves, so the doctor's unconscious is able from the derivatives of the unconscious which will be communicated to him to reconstruct that unconscious, which has determined the patient free associations.

(Freud, 1921:115–116)

Freud might have been trying to explain this intersubjective phenomenon in technical terms, which might have been more remarkable at the time than it appears now, but it does suggest something of the process of transmission, which assumes receptivity on the part of the analyst, which is not unreasonable. Psychosocial approaches to affect also draw upon psychoanalytic engagements with the interpersonal transmission of affect from one person to another or within small group interactions. Approaches informed by object relations focus upon the operation of particular processes such as transference, projection, and projective identification. In object relations, following Melanie Klein, when transference involves the successful transmission of affect, it is projective identification. For example, an emotion or affective relation is transferred from one person to another so that in analysis, the analyst may unconsciously experience emotions and feelings that have been transmitted by the patient so that the analyst feels as if it is coming from inside, from themselves. Ian Craib relates a story to illustrate this, when a patient insists that therapy is of no use so insistently and repeatedly that ultimately the analyst feels useless and despairs of being able to conduct any kind of effective therapy (Craib, 2001). The patient is not making an evaluation of the therapy *per se* but transferring his or her own feelings of despair to the therapist. This is a process of the transference of the affective state of hopelessness so that the other person takes it on board in a successful projective identification. This explanation of what is happening within the therapeutic encounter has wider application.

For example, within a small group transference might be used to explain how the circulation of affect might lead to the eruption of strong feelings, apparently without obvious cause. This might be a very large group. The mood can change, even in a crowd, such as sports fans at a football stadium, when performance on the pitch does not offer a simple causal explanation of crowd behaviour. Even those not present can pick up on the affective circulation within the stadium; baseball rivalries between the Red Sox and the Yankees extend far beyond the stadium not only in outcomes, which can be measured and described, but also in the transmission of affect. One process through which affect circulates is projective identification.

Projective identification

The psychoanalyst Thomas Ogden suggests a new approach to understanding affective transmission through projective identification, which supports the claim of psychosocial approaches that affect and the transmission of affect among people is not only multifaceted with different social and cultural elements contributing to the complexity of the processes. There is also more going on than can be understood by describing what is visible and audible and what can be discursively analyzed. There are unconscious forces in play too. Sometimes – often – we are uncertain about the feelings and emotions we have and cannot quite locate their source or even identify quite what these feelings are. Physical sensations such as feelings of nausea or palpitations may derive from affective transmission and projective identifications.

Ogden describes an occasion with a patient in therapy. He has been treating the woman for some time, but he finds that he begins to feel anxious and unwell with her. He describes a particular occasion with Mrs. B, when he realizes what is happening and uses the concept of projective identification to explain the process of affective transmission.

> I felt thirsty and leaned over in my chair to take a sip from a glass of water that I keep on the floor next to my chair (I had on many occasions done the same thing during Mrs. B's hours, as well as with other patients). Just as I was reaching for the glass, Mrs. B startled me by abruptly (and for the first time in analysis) turning around on the couch to look at me. She had a look of panic on her face and said, 'I'm sorry I didn't know what was happening to you'.
>
> It was only the intensity of this moment, in which there was a feeling of terror that something catastrophic was happening to me, that I was able to name for myself the terror that I had been carrying around with me for some time. I became aware of the anxiety that I had been feeling and the . . . dread of the meetings with Mrs. B (as reflected in my procrastinating behaviour) had been directly connected with an unconscious sensation/fantasy that my somatic symptoms of malaise, nausea and vertigo were caused by Mrs. B and that she was killing me.
>
> (Ogden, 1994:14–5)

This might seem an extreme reaction on the part of Ogden as the therapist, but Peter Redman (2009) argues that Ogden's explanation of the scenario offers significant insights into the process of projective identification as part of the transmission of affect. Redman argues that Mrs. B was projecting experiences from her own childhood when she felt her parents made her feel like a monster, onto the therapist, making him feel significantly threatened. For Ogden his patient was a dangerous destructive threat. Ogden admits that he was particularly receptive to Mrs. B's projection because of his own experiences. He actually felt that he might be seriously threatened to the point of fearing for his life.

Redman argues that there is more happening here than 'the overt social and discursive dimensions of the interaction alone' (Redman, 2009:58). This is more than a combination of different social and cultural elements that make up emotional life. For Redman, it is the unconscious that is 'a register in process – a flow . . . and things, even as these (particularly in the case of other people) are changed by it' (Redman, 2009:63). This is thus an illustration of agentic affective meaning making, which, in the present moment combines past emotions and circumstances with the current relational situation. Past associations and feelings make sense of new experience and enable us to make and shape new experiences. This is thus a truly relational unconscious. Mrs. B's panic is not just the product of the workings of her own unconscious; it is part of a relational pattern. Ogden too has been projecting feelings, emotions, and experience onto his patient; it is not a one-way process but a co-production of two intersecting unconscious structures. This relational unconscious can also be seen as a form of 'third space', as an unacknowledged relational bond, which infuses 'the expression and constriction of each partner's subjectivity and individual unconscious within that particular relation' (Gerson, 2004:72). For Redman, following Hollway (2004, 2010), the unconscious is dynamic; it is more than something that cannot be articulated. The unconscious may be 'unthought' and 'unthinkable', but it still informs practice, experience, and action. Not only does the unconscious repress disturbed feelings, it also transmits feeling to the unconscious of others.

Although the examples discussed in this section relate largely to therapeutic encounters, as does much of the psychosocial work on the third space of affective transmission, which attempts to engage with some seemingly inexplicable aspects of affect, they do have much wider application. The transmission of affect and projective transmission suggest a third space between that which affects and that which is affected, as well as the possibilities of the relational unconscious, which is indeed beyond discourse as well as being subject to discursive, social, and cultural influences.

Although Wetherell, for example, argues against the associations of affect with what is uncanny (Wetherell, 2012) and unknowable – or at least in Bollas's terms 'unthought', the concept of a third space and of the role of the relational unconscious has a great deal to offer in exploring those instances of affect that are not immediately comprehensible through discourse analysis or explanation by social and cultural interactions. Not all such experiences are uncanny or even mysterious, though. The concept of 'being in the zone', which is discussed in the next section, refers to something that is both exceptional in its associations with peak performance and mundane in the possibilities it offers for those who are not elite performers in any particular way but who nonetheless experience a sense of everything coming together and of harmony.

The discussion of the zone that follows in this chapter uses an approach that is psychosocial, not least because of its emphasis upon relationality, and demonstrates some of the strengths of the psychosocial over some more narrowly psychological accounts. The example that follows is one that relates to an experience that can be personal and collective. 'Being in the zone' is also an excellent

affect

illustration of the possibilities of a third space and of relationality, which lends itself particularly well to a psychosocial approach.

Being in the zone

'Being in the groove. It just takes you away. You're not even in the world'.

Bootsy Collins

'I was in the zone . . . executing my shots . . . staying in the moment'.

Victoria Azarenka

'Sometimes I think I have multiple personality disorder, my personalities are "me in the zone" and "me not in the zone"'.

Jacques, programmer

'Once I pick up those bamboo knitting needles and start with a simple knit or purl, I'm hooked. As an athlete would say, I'm in the zone'.

Carla, knitter
(in Banks, 2014:3)

A dripping wet canvas covered entire floor. There was complete silence. . . . Pollock looked at the painting. Then, unexpectedly, he picked up can and paint brush and started to move around the canvas. It was as if he suddenly realized the painting was not finished. His movements, slow at first, gradually became faster and more dance like as he flung black, white, and rust colored paint onto the canvas. He completely forgot that Lee and I were there; he did not seem to hear the click of the camera shutter. . . . My photography sessions lasted as long as he kept painting, perhaps half an hour. In all time, Pollock did not stop. How could he keep up this level of activity? Finally, he said 'That is it'.

(Hans Namuth, Jackson Pollock Painting, On: Number 31, 1950, in Chevalley and Woodward, 2014:27)

These are all examples of 'being in the zone'. In different areas of life the experience has different labels, but the zone has particular characteristics, whether it is called the zone or the groove or, as in psychology, 'flow'. 'Being in the zone' suggests heightened experience in which everything comes together: a state of harmony. When you are in the zone, you are not aware of time passing; the zone may be experienced as timeless, but it is moving and becoming and not fixed or finite and closed. Being in the zone is something that is experienced in the 'real time' of the moment too (Woodward, 2012a). Being in the zone is corporeal and often relates to a physical experience of intense sensation and can transcend the everyday, although the zone has mundane dimensions too (Woodward, forthcoming). It can be possible as one of the more routine, 'ordinary affects' of everyday life (Stewart, 2007). The zone is personal and political. People often refer to an individual experience, although, for example, in music, it is also collective with boundaries between individuals being crossed. Is it individual or collective or both?

The idea of 'being in the zone' offers a puzzle, especially because of the possibilities the zone offers for a third space – somewhere between the psyche and the social but that nonetheless involves both. The zone refers to a place beyond discourse (Massumi, 2002). In French it is a state of grace that is difficult to define and hard to access, but you know if you have been there (Woodward, forthcoming). It is not confined to elite performers, and although you need a reasonable level of competence to 'be in the zone', it is not only record-breaking athletes or virtuoso musicians who experience the zone. The expression 'being in the zone' is commonly used in sports to denote peak performance and a sense of harmony, which is often described as timeless, being outside time, and not conscious of time passing. It is when you really get your eye in and you are not aware of the passage of time or of levels of skill, competence, and the specific aspects of performance. In music the zone is a state of synergy when everything comes together, as in being in the groove in jazz where musicians improvise together in a seemingly effortless state (Bitz, 2014; Bitz film, 2014). Computer programmers talk of the elegance of the zone where they are on a roll and it all works perfectly. There are even apps that promise access to the zone (Banks, 2014), and the zone has entered the realm of corporate culture as a motivating tool for ambitious employees and managers seeking optimum performance from the workforce.

Theorizing the zone

Attempts to theorize this state, which is not confined to individuals, or to particular activities, has in the past been largely the subject of psychological investigation. For example, the work of Mihaly Csikszentmihalyi (1975, 1997, 2003) has been particularly influential in developing the idea of flow, which is used to describe a mental state of complete immersion that characterizes some activities such as a musician's or an artist's intense engagement with creative work. Those who are 'in the zone', according to Csikszentmihalyi, are so intensely focused upon the moment that consciousness merges with action such that awareness of the passing of time is halted or distorted. Each of the aspects of flow identified by Csikszentmihalyi constitute aspects of the individual's mental state, although he argues that flow has social implications and outcomes, not least in the promotion of optimum performance and in greater satisfaction and well-being, for example, in the workplace or in an educational establishment. Csikszentmihalyi suggests the idea of 'flow' to capture the feeling of 'going with the flow', which many of his respondents use to describe the feeling of being swept along as if in a river (Csikszentmihalyi, 1975). He suggests that it is possible to achieve the optimal experience of flow through setting clear targets and goals. Others have used Csikszentmihalyi's work to develop more detailed analysis of the stages of recognition of flow, for example, in exploring the mental states that precede as well as follow the state of flow, but the focus remains upon individual mental states, which are largely separate from the social world.

The concept of being in the zone, however, lends itself particularly well to a psychosocial explanation, and one example of this I want to use here is Paul Stenner's development of the concept of liminal spaces (Stenner, 2014) to explore the psychosocial processes that are implicated in the experience of 'being in the zone' and that have much wider application as part of a psychosocial approach.

Stenner takes some of Csikszentmihalyi's discussion of the key features of flow as a starting point for exploring how in this state the self dissolves and the zone becomes a zone of affectivity that is characterized by a state of transition from one state to another. However, as a liminal space the zone is more than the state in the middle; as Victor Turner (1977) suggests, it is betwixt and between, but in some sense both: before and after. Being in the zone does not require a point of departure and another of arrival; it is a state in itself but one that involves a transformation of consciousness and, importantly for the discussion here, it is a state of affectivity.

The zone involves a free play of feelings in what Stenner describes as a liminal state.

Stenner draws upon the work of the cultural anthropologist Victor Turner in exploring the psychosocial dimensions of liminality (Turner, 1977). Turner developed Arnold van Gennep's (1960) exploration of rites and rituals including, in particular, rites of passage, all of which van Gennep argued were marked by sequential stages, one of which was a liminal transitional stage of rites. The liminal stage is the transitional stage when individuals or groups move through the threshold that marks the separation of the other two stages, for example, from childhood to adulthood when the person being initiated is incorporated into a new identity. Turner developed van Gennep's ideas to suggest the transition from one culturally defined state to another as involving a preliminal, liminal, and postliminal stage (Turner, 1977). Twilight can be seen as a temporal liminal stage, between day and night and between daylight and darkness.

Liminality, according to Stenner, involves transitions associated with the suspension and removal of limits, which include the normative limits to everyday conduct. Thus liminality opens up new ways of exploring and understanding social order and disorder and the relationship between affectivity and events and between inner worlds and social, cultural worlds from a psychosocial perspective (Brown and Stenner, 2009). The zone is an affective state in the distinctive emotions and feelings that characterize it. It is also a state that is marked by distinctive experiences of temporality, notably of timelessness, of not noticing the passage of time or of being lost in time, which the temporality of liminality can accommodate better than the psychological notion of flow. Liminality also offers the possibility of collective experience and does not limit 'being in the zone' to the individual who reports having experienced it.

Given the heightened experience of 'being in the zone' and the desirability of this state, when everything fits and comes together, Stenner suggests that this liminal state is one marked by positive emotion and the features of happiness, demonstrating the relationship between affect and the liminal state (Stenner, 2014). The liminal space is one in which the to and fro of affect operates, connecting what has been with what will be but occupying its own state and time. This liminal space is also one in which affect as feeling and emotion is transmitted, but the emphasis in Stenner's approach is on the specificities of liminality, which incorporates social and psychic elements in complex ways.

Liminality clearly applies to other situations and relationships, but the example of 'being in the zone' uses an experience that lacks the formality of ritual and, whilst clearly involving some preparation and reasonable level of competence, is not an experience that can be planned with any degree of certainty. Nonetheless the zone offers an experience, albeit much sought after by practitioners, which seems to occupy a third space, which the concept of liminality goes some way towards explaining.

Conclusion

Psychosocial approaches are part of the 'turn to affect' in distinctive ways, but they are also part of attempts to engage actively with the ways in which affect results in change. Psychosocial approaches are particularly interested in the third space between affects, for example, in what is happening when one person takes on the emotion and feeling of another without necessarily being consciously aware of what is happening and why they feel as they do. Thus, some psychosocial approaches draw upon clinical experiences of intersubjectivity, for example, in affective transmission between therapist and patient, which are then used to theorize the possibilities of a third space in which affective transmission takes place. This chapter has cited a few particular examples that demonstrate the psychosocial possibilities of the turn to affect. Emotions and feelings are central to these approaches, but the emphasis is upon the processes of affective transmission and projective identification, not only on what constitutes emotion.

The unconscious, and especially the relational unconscious, is an important component of psychosocial approaches to affect that offer a route into understanding some experiences, for example, of anxiety or fear, which are otherwise incomprehensible. It is not possible, for example, in the case of Thomas Ogden and his patient cited in this chapter, to explore or understand Ogden's feelings of being threatened without grasping the relationality between his unconscious and that of his patient and the complex set of experiences that make up each in relation to each other in the particular context.

Other psychosocial approaches have focused more specifically upon the nature of the liminal of space affective transmission and the transformative aspects of affect. Again feelings and emotions are part of the process, but the major contribution of a psychosocial approach is the theoretical conceptualization of liminality and the possibilities it affords for understanding the nature of affect.

Affect is much more than emotion and is a particularly good example of the relationality of psychosocial approaches.

Questions

1   How would you define affect? What makes affect different from emotion and feeling, or is affect another word for emotion?
2   What do you understand by liminality? How can the concept of liminality contribute to an explanation of particular mental states, such as 'being in the zone'?
3   Can you think of examples of times when affect is banal and ordinary and when affect might be difficult to explain and even mysterious?
4   What can a psychosocial approach contribute to an understanding of affect and in particular affective transmission?
5   Can you think of an example of an experience of peak performance or of being in harmony that could be described as 'being in the zone'? How would you describe this state?

chapter 6

Intimacies

This chapter:

1   Looks at why intimacies are so important in psychosocial studies and asks what intimacy is.
2   Outlines current debates in terms of the different strands of thought from which they have emerged including theories of individualization and psychoanalytic approaches upon which psychosocial work draws.
3   Focuses upon the example of maternal relations and early childhood development to consider how psychosocial concepts can be used to understand and explain these relationships and how they impact upon social relations.
4   Explores the contributions of psychosocial approaches to sexualities within the context of social change.
5   Highlights the issues that are raised by specifically psychosocial approaches to the processes through which intimate relations are made and experienced.

Introduction

This chapter explores some of the ways in which psychosocial approaches address intimate relations and explores psychosocial responses to changes in this area of experience, which is not confined to the personal. Intimacies cover a whole range of relationships of family and friendship as well as sexual relationships. Psychosocial approaches have had considerable impact in this field, both in challenging the perceived certainties of intimate relations as well as contributing to new ways of thinking about intimacy (Brown, 2006; Roseneil, 2000, 2013). Intimate life has been seen as created through individualization and reflexive modernization (for example, Giddens 1992; Beck and Beck-Gernsheim, 1995, 2002; Bauman, 2001). Intimacy and the extended emphasis, for example, with popular culture upon the need for successful intimate relations, albeit at a time when there is more and more relationship breakdown and more anxiety about the perceived failure of establishing enduring love (Enduring Love, 2014; Gabb, 2008). Relationships may be short term, couples may live apart (an estimated 10 percent do in the UK according to the Enduring Love 2014 project), and relationships are varied and diverse, with formal recognition of contracted same sex relationships in some parts of the world, if total rejection in others to the extent of persecution, but persistent homophobia even in those places where there is legislative acceptance, such as the UK. Sexual relations and sexuality continue to present contradictions and tensions and irrationality ranging from personal ambivalence and falling for the wrong person and staying with unsuitable partners to social and political contradictions in legal systems, which enable same sex relationships and expressions of transgressive sexual preferences but do nothing to protect individuals who make choices that fall outside traditional cultural norms. The contemporary climate is both highly polarized across the globe and deeply contradictory. Attitudes remain entrenched in many social and cultural contexts as well as in the psyche of individuals.

More recently, work on gendered practices of interdependency and care have been included within the study of intimate relations (Brown, 2010, 2012; Finch and Mason, 1993; Jamieson, 1998; Smart, 2000; Ribbens-McCarthy and Edwards, 2003; Tee et al., 2012), which have been influenced by the work of Teresa Brennan (1993), Jane Flax (1993), Jessica Benjamin (1995), Judith Butler (1997), and Nancy Chodorow (1999). Such approaches build on Butler's view of the psyche as a source of resistance to constraining social identities. In the making of the self in these areas of life that matter so much, but that can be so conflictual that individuals have to do emotional work in reconciling different conflicts (Craib, 1998), sometimes this emotional work takes place in the more public sphere of policy-directed social care.

What sort of relationships would you think of as intimate? Sexual relations, those of family members, friendship groups, and the relationship people have with professional carers might all be included. Intimate relations often include body contact and the senses, including touch, which carries ambivalent connotations of transgression in that some touching is forbidden and culturally proscribed whereas intimate caring practices require physical contact. Intimacies involve contact and relationships with others, and within ourselves, in relations to feelings and emotions. Intimacies include close relationships in which the people involved often have intense affective investment as well as, on occasion, strong feelings of antipathy and even anger, hatred, and disgust. Intimacy implies care, often in terms of affection, although, as the example cited at the opening to this book showed, care can involve the intimate work of looking after someone's personal, physical needs, which can be described as intimate because of the nature of the work, which is nonetheless a professional practice – a job and not necessarily a labour of love. People do of course perform intimate caring for the people they love, not least babies and children or a person we love who has experienced illness or some impairment. All of us, as infants, have had to be cared for during a period that lasts some time among human beings, whereas, in spite of increased longevity in many parts of the world, it is not necessarily the case that everyone has to have extended periods of care in adulthood or even at the end of life. Being cared for as infants is a time of dependency and the nature of that care and the relationship we have with the people (most likely in the west, a person and most likely a woman everywhere), is what is central to psychosocial approaches to intimacy. Bodies are changing, for example, in relation to motherhood where it is now possible to have a host mother, a donor egg, and a donor sperm (Nordquist and Smart, 2014). Intimate relationships of very different kinds have connections to our earliest relationships, and we can find out a great deal about intimacy in very many different forms in adult life by understanding some of the psychosocial processes through which people come in their earliest experience of intimacy with another person. Given that this is a relational experience, in, for example, the mother–child relationship, intimacies are intersubjective. Thus intimacy provides a productive area of experience, not only for exploring the psychosocial, but also for understanding relationality in an area of life that is intense and ambivalent and invokes a range of contradictory and often conflictual emotions, which emerge in a huge range of different social contexts. Intimacy is not only about the personal and the private. 'The sphere of personal life-intimacy, sexuality, love, friendship, parenthood – is *both* socially patterned and constructed, varying cross-culturally and historically, *and* that it has a life of its own, that it is experienced beyond the control of reason, as inherently individual, internal and as particular to specific relationships' (Roseneil in Hollway and Jefferson, [2000]2013:x–xi).

Intimate relationships can be construed as those that involve often intense feelings of dependency, and powerful emotions including love matter enormously in everyday life, but why are they so important in psychosocial studies, and what can a focus upon these intimate relations tell us about the relationship between inner and outer worlds and wider social issues? Do intimate relations belong to the private and personal?

Intimacy as a site of research and practice

Intimacy as a broad term that embraces a whole range of relationships of family and friendship as well as sexual relationships and the issue of sexualities is the main concern of this chapter. This is an expanding field, and the concept of intimacy has been used partly to avoid the constraints of traditional terminology, which restricted the field covered to family or (largely heterosexual) familial relationships and opened up ways of conceptualizing different forms of relationships and of domestic living to incorporate friendship as well as the range of sexualities, which are given expression in people's lives in the twenty-first century. How does the development of theories of **intersectionality**, which explore the intersection and relationship between different social processes and inequalities, provide a means of reimagining affective and intimate relations? The exploration of intimacies in changing times is a field in which psychosocial approaches have had considerable impact, both in challenging the perceived certainties of intimate relations as well as contributing to new ways of thinking about intimacy (Brown, 2006; Roseneil, 2013). Different approaches can be seen as occupying positions between those that saw intimate life as created through individualization and reflexive modernization such as those of Anthony Giddens (1992), Ulrich Beck and Elizabeth Beck-Gernsheim (1995, 2002), and Zygmunt Bauman (2001). Late modernity has been characterized as a time of individualization when people are alienated or separated from others, for example, more people live alone, outside conventional family relationships. Individualization values characteristics such as independence, self-reliance, and autonomy, which might also involve disconnection and distancing from others rather than recognition of interdependence. Individualization is strongly linked to competition and the celebration of success and the denial of failure and weakness and the need for others. The acknowledgement of personal weaknesses is seen as an individual project to be addressed through self-help and strategies of self-improvement (Beck and Beck-Gernsheim, 1995, 2002; Rose, 1990, 1996, 1999). Within this framework, on the one hand, individualization attributes weakness and failure to individuals, and on the other, those individuals, many of whom may need the most support because of social and cultural processes of marginalization and deprivation that impact upon them, have to take responsibility for their own difficulties.

Psychosocial approaches such as Joanne Brown (2010, 2012), Janet Finch and Jennifer Mason (1993), Lyn Jamieson (1998), Carol Smart (2000), and Jane Ribbens-McCarthy, Jeanette Edwards (2003) and Stephen Tee et al. (2012) have focused more upon gendered practices of interdependency and care, which demonstrate the interconnections between the experience of individuals and their social worlds. Recent work, much of which is presented from feminist perspectives, is attentive to the entanglements of the personal experiences of caring and being cared for and the gendered systems that permeate the wider society. Such approaches have been influenced by the work of Teresa Brennan (1993), Jane Flax (1993), Jessica Benjamin (1995), Judith Butler (1997), and Nancy Chodorow (1999), all of whom offer routes into exploring fluidity and change and the transformative possibilities of intimate relations. Intimate relations, for example, those based upon romantic love can be seen as changing. Joanne Brown uses biographical and narrative interviews to explore how people in different generations understand love and weighs up the increasing impossibilities of romantic love in the contemporary world from a psychosocial perspective, which considers the possibilities of a Kleinian reparative love and a Freudian transference love.

Brennan's work has been particularly important in engaging with the intersubjectivity of affect and the processes through which emotions and feelings can be transferred between people. She argues that these processes are constitutive and reflective of change, for example, in the ways in which shared feeling and anxieties can be pathologized. Brenan focuses upon psychogenic illness and contemporary concerns about mental illness to explain some of these processes (Brennan, 2004). This body of work engages with the ways in which people relate to each other and the connections between the individual and the social world they inhabit and that inhabits them, however discourses of individualization in particular societies deny dependency.

Psychosocial approaches stress the importance of intersubjectivity and relationality. As Christopher Bollas notes, '[I]ndividuals regularly project parts of themselves into their others, shaping their relational world according to the idiom of their internal world, creating a village of friends who constitute a secret culture of the subject's desire' (1987:50). Whilst psychosocial approaches draw upon the psychoanalytic, they are nonetheless different in their inclusion of the social world as well as the personal biography of individuals and their own stories. As Sasha Roseneil argues,

> A psycho-social analysis that seeks to theorize the mutual imbrications of the psychic and the social must move beyond this [personal biography] to consider how subjectivity and a person's sense of their relational world are related to wider historicized configurations of social relations and to their power dynamics.
>
> (2009:416)

Judith Butler's view of the psyche as a source of resistance to constraining social identities has also been very influential in the rethinking of intimacy in ways that engage with the psychic as well as the social dimensions and seek to explore what is psychosocial about intimacy. Emotional work, far from being the concern of the private arena and intimate personal relationships, can be central to the public arena, for example, of paid work, which brings together psychic investments and social forces. As Ian Craib argued, individuals have to do emotional work to reconcile different conflicts (Craib, 1995). Sometimes the emotional work occupies the field of policy-directed social care.

This chapter explores intimacies in relation to the psychosocial central concern with familial, especially maternal relationships and the importance of early childhood development and sexualities as an example of intimate relationships in adult life as well as the more dispersed area of caring for as well as caring about.

Locating the psychosocial

Psychosocial approaches to intimacy draw substantially upon psychoanalytic ideas, concepts, and practices. Psychoanalysis, through therapy and analysis, has focused upon subjectivity and the possibility of unravelling inner conflicts and thereby seeking resolution to distress by unpacking some of the contradictions of the unconscious and repressed feelings that are seen as part of early childhood experience. As one of the most intimate relations in most people's lives and certainly the most dependent, infancy and early childhood and the relationship with parents, especially the mother as primary carer, are central to understanding later experience and subsequent relations. Mothers are still the people who give birth, and the vast majority of primary carers across the world are women who may or may not be the child's birth mother, but it still makes sense to talk about the gendered nature of mothering and the care of infants. Not everyone breastfeeds their children, but only women have the ability to do so, and the mother–child relationship is not only corporeal and enfleshed because it involves the mother providing physical care of the infant. The mother's body too is implicated in this relationship, and separation applies to the mother who has given birth to the child as well as to the baby who leaves the womb. Much less attention has been paid to mothers beyond evaluation of their competency, although Winnicott (1955, 1960a, 1965, 1967) at least accepts the qualities of 'good enough mothering'. Good enough mothering is the acceptable end product of the mother who starts by endeavouring to adapt completely to the new infant. This discussion is designed to locate the centrality of maternal subjectivities in the psychosocial debate about intimacies and to offer a caveat to the overemphasis upon the mother leading to the attribution of guilt and the phenomenon of blaming mothers.

Mothering and intimacy are thus connected through social practices, cultural norms, and powerful, if ambivalent, feelings and emotions (Parker, 1996; Rich, 1975; Woodward, 1997; Woodward and Woodward, 2009). The ubiquity and fragility of human dependence and the shared experience of mothering, whoever occupies the role, makes the mother–child relationship one that is central to an understanding of inner worlds as well as social practices and culture. The strength and intensities of mothers' feelings as well as the child's vulnerability has only more recently been acknowledged and explored as part of this relationality. In terms of the exploration of intimacy, it is object relations theories and practices that have drawn attention to the mother–child relationship.

Mothers and the maternal

Psychoanalytic theories, especially those that have been developed out of object relations, are centrally concerned with intersubjective relating especially between mother and child, as Melanie Klein argued in her original work in 1946 (Melanie Klein Trust, 1997). Kleinian approaches to intimate relations as a major concern of psychoanalytic approaches, especially those that challenge Freud's patriarchal assumptions and Lacan's phallocentricity, place more emphasis upon the maternal than the paternal and focus upon the affective intersubjective relationship of the mother and child and upon the practice that incorporates theory. For D.W. Winnicott the external mother is the target of the infant's projected feelings of distress and of joy (1958). Wilfred Bion (1967, [1962]1991, [1962]2004) also uses the concepts of **containment** and the container-contained relationship as connected to the formation of a thinking mind, which Rozika Parker (1996) later explores as the ambivalence of the mother's relationship with the child as part of the process of separation-individuation. Jessica Benjamin (1988, 1995) suggests that mutual recognition between mother and child is central to the quality of intersubjective relationships arising from the mother–child relationship, which nonetheless can succumb to an inequitable balance of power between doer and done-to.

Maternal subjectivity is central to object relations accounts. Motherhood and especially the subjective relationship between mother and woman are major concerns of feminist work, which seeks to challenge Freud's patriarchal emphasis upon the father and Lacan's phallocentricity as well as the, albeit illusory, primacy of the phallus as the key signifier of culture, whilst retaining a psychoanalytical perspective. In many psychoanalytical studies the child has been the object of study, even in Klein's work, although this is changing with more recent work on the mother–child relationship (Hollway, 2010).

The major contributions of the discussion of maternal subjectivities and the mother–child relationship in exploring intimate relations is not to attribute blame or responsibility to individuals but rather to use a study of the infant's experience to explore later life and the experience of other, subsequent intimate relations. The study of the mother–child relationship by object relations theorists and practitioners has yielded a number of useful conceptualizations that demonstrate the relationality of social practice and cultural norms and unconscious experience and inner worlds. This understanding applies both to therapy and to a wider understanding of social relations and the social unconscious. For example, the concept of containment does not only apply to the individual whose anger and distress have not been taken in and returned in a palatable form. There are myriad examples throughout this book and in psychosocial studies of instances when the concept of containment and the container contained can be more widely applied to an understanding of social care and health care, for example. This is particularly relevant to the field of mental health (Young, 1994).

Whilst the mother–child relationship is clearly of particular importance in the exploration of intimate relations, another aspect of intimacy that is not unrelated and that has been a major concern of psychoanalysis is sexuality and sexual relations.

Sex and sexualities

Sex and sexuality are key aspects of intimate relations that are of crucial importance, for example, sex and gender are central to subjectivity: how we see ourselves and how we are seen by others and how we relate to others. Sexuality, although not, of course, the same as sex, is also intensely implicated in the self and in the expression of sexual feelings and those of love and affection. Psychoanalysis gives a high profile to sex, gender, and sexuality in psychic and social life (Rose, 1986). Thus it is hardly surprising that in the turmoil of contemporary debates about sexual identities, sexual difference, and sexualities, many of which are located within political contestation about human rights, that these are big issues and highly contentious. There is the volubility that Foucault argued characterized modern neoliberal societies (Foucault, 1981) in which sex has become so pervasive and dominant as part of the common currency of daily life. We are confronted with sexualized . images and representations in all aspects of our lives (Levy, 2005). In the world in the twenty-first century sex is a commodity, but how do these public, visible, audible obsessions with sex and sexuality relate to personal lives and intersubjectivity? Why is sex so powerful? Sex and sexuality are central to personal experience and to intersubjective relationships as well as to the making of selves. The aspect of intimacy, which is expressed in sexual relations among people, is probably one of the most contradictory. People make choices that are inappropriate as well as those that can lead to long-term happiness and contentment. Social forces and mixed up with feelings of guilt, lust, excitement, affection, and passion.

Sexual difference is reinstated through a binary logic in areas of everyday life. These can be as diverse as children's toys and paid employment where wage differentials persist into the twenty-first century. Similarly, in spite of significant advances in equality legislation in some parts of the world and even the recognition on social networking sites like Facebook that there is a diverse range of possible sexualities, mechanisms of heternormativity operate, either to enforce conformity through techniques of compulsion or through more subtle entreaties. All of this evidence suggests that the Freudian psychoanalytic emphasis upon sexual difference remains a powerful explanatory tool in exploring intimate relations as experienced in the psyche as well as through psychic investments that are made in the perpetuation of sex differences. Freudian psychoanalysis suggests that sex difference was not biologically determined, although it is difficult to disentangle Freud's own emphasis upon innate drives from the social and cultural imperatives of normativity. He did acknowledge the diversity and the perversity of sexual desires, however. Sex and sexuality are contested terrains marked by conflict and ambiguity, however strong Freud's association of activity with masculinity and passivity with femininity reinstates gender polarity as do his normative assumptions about adult heterosexuality.

There are other theoretical endeavours to combine the feelings and desires of the unconscious with those of the social world. Butler attempts to reconcile a Foucauldian version of sex as socially constructed and a psychoanalytic perspective. She argues,

> Sex is, from the start normative; it is what Foucault has called a 'regulatory ideal'. In this sense, then, sex not only functions as a norm, but is part of a regulatory practice that produces (through the repetition or iteration of a norm which is without origin) the bodies it governs, that is, whose regulatory

force is made clear as a kind of productive power, the power to produce – demarcate, circulate, differentiate – the bodies it controls . . . 'sex' is an ideal construct, which is forcibly materialized through time.

(Butler, 1993:1)

Psychoanalytic approaches demonstrate more acceptance of inner drives rather than socially constructed energies and imposed cultural normativities, which remain a powerful factor in Butler's account. Butler's analysis is presented within a theoretical framework (not surprisingly for a professor of rhetoric). Nonetheless Butler provides some of the most useful, and radical, conceptual tools for exploring the interconnections between personal and social life and the manifestations of the psychic in the social, as well as the social forces, for example, of heternormativity, which are lived in personal, inner worlds of the psyche.

One strategy for exploring sexuality is through a study of personal life in which sexuality and sexual relations are part of intimate life.

The following example is a case study in which Sasha Roseneil (2006) presents a psychosocial approach to the conditions of personal life in the twenty-first century. I cite the example of this case study because Roseneil's aim is to explore the complex intertwining of psychic and social factors in intimate relations, and she uses psychosocial methods to do so.

A case study

Roseneil uses the example of Angel, a forty-six-year-old heterosexual white man living in a northern city of the UK to demonstrate how patterns of intimate relations are changing and in particular, the relationship between feelings and emotions and the unconscious and social and cultural norms and practices. (It might be worth saying that the pronunciation of the name that Angel has adopted for the research project would be pronounced with a Spanish accent if, as Roseneil suggests, he has taken the name of the retired Spanish footballer, Angel Morales. In Spanish the name doesn't sound quite so angelic and unlikely). This study is set against a background of social transformation in intimate relations, for example, in the increase in the number of relationship breakdowns, decline in marriage, greater diversity in relationships such as same sex relationships, more people living alone, and more relationships conducted at a distance and the increased importance of friendship networks in many people's lives. Relationship breakdown is not just a statistical piece of evidence; it is the source of loss, pain, and feelings of failure and disappointment. A psychosocial analysis endeavours to connect the social trends and the existential pain of loss and internal conflict. This example is not the conventional sociological account of social change in personal lives but an engagement with what may be unstated and unacknowledged. A psychosocial approach aims to go further than the accounts people give of their own lives as well as the evidence of change; it seeks to uncover deeper meanings that nonetheless contribute to the social changes, which can be observed, recorded, and measured.

Roseneil sets out to explore Angel's life from the psychoanalytic perspective of subjectivity as nonunitary and defended and uses the concept of the dynamic unconscious (Hollway and Jefferson, [2000]2013). Methodologically the case study is based upon a single interview (conducted by a young woman working on the project) from a larger research project on adults who do not live with a sexual partner (and might thus be seen as individualized in Giddens's terminology [1992]). This example is cited here because it illustrates the approach discussed in chapter 3, especially in terms of eliciting a story and of open-ended interviewing (Hollway and Jefferson, [2000]2013).

Angel's story is not that atypical in the neoliberal, postindustrialized world of the twenty-first century. Following the end of his fifteen-year marriage, his next relationship broke down, and following a period of unemployment he moved out of London. Roseneil constructs a diagram of Angel's relationships, with his friends and neighbours as well as sexual relationships, to demonstrate the complexity of intimate connections. He describes his friendship network, but this too, it transpires, is a source of disappointment because friends were lost following the breakdown of his marriage. Friendships are lost through mobility too as Angel moved from one place to another (Roseneil, 2006:856). He presents himself as sociable as a defence against his feelings of loss. He also refers to feeling angry and 'rampaging about' (856). Roseneil suggests that this too could be a reversion to childhood states of loss, which is also consistent with a version of masculinity through which he is able to express himself and try to make sense of his experience.

By asking open-ended narrative questions, the life story emerges along with moments of distress, of 'being in a right state' and feeling that the walls were closing in after the breakup of the relationship that followed the end of his marriage (855). Loss of friendships and dislocation are experienced personally but are also part of social processes. Friendships within the heterosexual matrix are organized around the primary sexual relationship that a person has (often in the form of coupledom). Angel's distress is described as what Butler calls 'heterosexual melancholia' (Butler, 1997).

Roseneil describes Angel's 'arrangement' with a woman, which he does not see as a relationship but rather a 'non-conventional partnership (848), which he enthusiastically describes as an arrangement largely based on sex. 'We both like films. We both like the same authors, so we are capable of speaking about other things apart from just sex, but that's effectively what it's based on' (859). He also attributes this form of relationship to the woman's eagerness to participate and his own capacity to satisfy her demand for sex although there is a tension between macho bravado and cozy domesticity in the relationship at times. Telling the story brings out the tensions and contradictions, and Roseneil offers some interpretations of the narrative and of Angel's presentation of himself in order to develop a psychosocial critique.

I have only picked out a few moments in the interview to illustrate the more general points about the nature of an exploration of intimacy in late modernity, using psychosocial methods.

As a sociologist, Roseneil is probably more conscious than most of the risks of overinterpretation and the limits to a psychosocial approach. I say as a sociologist because qualitative sociologists usually do have to present a robust defence of their methodologies and to support their claims with some quantitative data (Hammersley and Atkinson, 2007), but there are particular sensitivities in relation to psychosocial methods because of the links to psychoanalysis and the connections between the researcher and the analyst that might situate the subject of research as the analysand, which is probably not what they signed up for, however much interviewees might enjoy talking about their own lives. Roseneil states very clearly, 'This is a psychoanalytically oriented, psychosocial analysis of an interview, not psychoanalysis of Angel' (864).

The interview is contingent and is a co-production. Social life is not motivated by rational choices, and people cannot always articulate the contradictions they are experiencing, but these feelings and defence mechanisms do have impact not only on individuals but in the wider context of social and cultural life. What matters in spite of some of the possible anxieties about interpretation is that the subject remains anonymous and what the project delivers is a deeper understanding of intimate relations, especially in the context of social change, which has implications for social policy and an understanding of how people live their lives and the things that matter to them.

Conclusion

Intimacy has assumed considerable importance in relation to social policy and understanding sociocultural change in the twenty-first century as a way of focusing upon particular aspects of psychosocial life. Intimacies are the concern of the private arena and impact upon and are influenced by policy decisions and wider social trends. The concept of intimacy is influenced by psychoanalytic and psychosocial concerns and is in many ways vastly preferable to earlier classification of personal relations under the category of family or sexuality. Intimacy permits the combination of the personal and deeply held feelings and emotions that are lived and experienced within social worlds where policies and practices impact upon what is possible.

Psychoanalysis has the advantage of concentrating on interpersonal and caring relationships in people's lives starting with the early stages of development as well as of addressing the importance of sex and sexuality in people's lives and in the making of subjectivities.

Although psychosocial approaches draw substantially upon psychoanalytic theories, there are clearly several points at which psychoanalytic theories and practices cannot deliver the understanding of relationality, which the psychosocial seeks to explore and understand. Freudian and Lacanian psychoanalysis, although prioritizing sex differences and sexuality in relation to subjectivity, remain relatively entrenched in the binary logic of unequal sex difference and based upon heteronormativity, however extensive the developments of, for example, Lacan's work by feminist critics.

Objects relations offers more democratic and egalitarian possibilities for an understanding of intimate relations in the context of caring, although there are still some problems associated with the relocation of the spotlight from patriarchal power to maternal responsibility and guilt in the context of the mother–child relationship.

However, as this chapter has shown, psychosocial work on intimacies has been able to redress some of the difficulties with psychoanalytic approaches and build upon their strengths, not least through the use of key concepts and to offer a route into rethinking intimacies in order to demonstrate their social and their psychic relations.

Questions

1   What do you understand intimacy to mean? What do psychosocial approaches suggest are the key features?
2   What can psychosocial approaches contribute to a development of psychoanalytic explanations of intimacy? How do they draw upon early childhood experiences?
3   Why are sex and sexuality so central to accounts of intimate relations?
4   How do psychosocial approaches present a relational account of sexuality that connects inner and outer worlds?
5   What is the relevance of maternal subjectivities to the relational experience of caring, and what are the dangers in stressing the connections between mothering and caring?

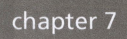

Risk

This chapter:

1 Explores some of the different meanings of the 'risk society'.
2 Looks at some different ways in which risk is manifest in the world today and at how risk might be psychosocial.
3 Looks at what contributions a psychosocial approach can make towards an understanding of the implications of risk.
4 Explores the concept of anxiety and the relationship between psychic and social anxieties.

Introduction

This chapter explores the extent to which risk and anxiety are central to contemporary societies (Beck, 1992) as well as part of the human condition. Risk generates anxieties about security and about the self in particular ways at particular times. Exploring the processes involved in risk raises questions about how anxiety and fear operate within social as well as individual, inner worlds. Risk is strongly linked to anxiety and the management of anxiety in which social systems increasingly play an important part as has been recognized for some time (Menzies Lyth, 1960) and as was demonstrated in chapter 6.

Physical and existential dangers threaten the confidence with which nations assert their identity and the security of their boundaries as well as the boundaries of the self and well-being. Risk is particularly interesting because the fear generated by risk is real and motivates collective and individual action, often of an extreme nature, but the perception of risk is also discursive and could constitute a regime of truth or a moral panic in its manifestations in the contemporary world. Risk ranges from concerns about food additives and obesity and routine engagement with risk assessment techniques in most corporations and public organizations to fear of terrorist attack (Seidler, 2013).

Risk is a major concern in the contemporary world, even though life expectancy has been extended in most parts of the world and morbidity rates have fallen. Risk and anxiety cannot be explained adequately without being attentive to the psychodynamics of anxiety and the perception of risk as well as its socially quantifiable dimensions. This chapter explores the connections between risk and the making and remaking of the self and especially between the personal, the psychic, and the social, which leads into the next chapter's focus upon a particular manifestation and outcome of the risk society, trauma.

The risk society?

Do we live in societies characterized by risk? Is the world in the twenty-first century a riskier place than it has ever been? At one level it seems an absurd suggestion. Could everyday life be riskier in the societies of late modernity than at times when mortality rates were high and expected age of death rarely exceeded forty for the vast majority of people and neonatal death rates were exceptionally high compared with those in modern, developed societies? It has become commonplace to claim that 'we live in a risk society' (Beck, 1992) in spite of the evidence that the contemporary world is clearly a much safer place than most previous societies. Mortality and morbidity rates have decreased significantly, and there are routine injunctions to care for ourselves because such care is possible in a culture where risk seems to be both avoidable and increasingly a personal responsibility. In some sense it is bizarre that these are the times when we talk about risk, danger, and insecurity, especially in those parts of the world where a longer and healthy lifespan seems most assured. The debate has intensified in light of the fear of terrorist attacks following the attack on the World Trade Center and the Pentagon in the US on 11 September, 2001, as chapter 8 shows. Risk has become associated with trauma even though most risk assessment seems relatively anodyne, and, whilst the idea of risk might be linked to danger and incite fear and anxiety, sometimes risk assessment is about evaluating relatively low levels and certainly not life-threatening risk and danger. The discussion of risk and a preoccupation with the threat of risk is, ironically, more a feature of the language and everyday discourse of the privileged west and global north than those parts of the world where life expectancy is short. When life expectancy is in the forties, people have to deal with the materialities of risk and the exigencies of ill health and the dangers of poverty, rather than engaging with a narrative of anxiety.

Ulrich Beck argues that late modernity is characterized by individualization and a shift from structure to agency whereby meaning and identity are based upon the individual rather than the institution or the community (Beck, 1992). Late modernity involves technological rationalization and enormous transformations in social and personal relations as well as changes in the structures of power and influence. Uncertainty is generated through changing patterns of employment, not least the rise of the so-called knowledge society and the decline, if not the complete disappearance in parts of the UK, for example, of traditional heavy manufacturing industry. Anthony Giddens has argued that what is important is the response of western societies to risk and the management of futures (Giddens, 1999) in societies that both celebrate risk taking, for example, in the management of markets and of career paths, where no longer is it very likely or even possible that an employee will remain in exactly the same kind of employment in which he or she started out for life, and express the need to control the myriad dangers that beset us such as environmental risk. The management of contemporary life in western societies involves considerable responsibility for exercising control over the multiple risks that are present on a daily basis, within the home as well as in the workplace and when travelling.

Risk and perception of risk extends to all areas of experience and individual and collective life. In affluent countries and neoliberal democracies people are warned of the dangers of obesity and of eating particular foods; the recommendations and the dangers seem to change daily. Almost daily we receive contradictory advice; fruit is good for us, liquidized fruit is as dangerous as sweet fizzy drinks and even cocaine; statins limit the production of cholesterol and should be prescribed for everyone over the age of fifty to reduce the risk of heart attack and stroke; statins have serious side effects and make no impact upon those not already suffering from heart disease; we need at least eight hours of sleep each night; as we get older we need less sleep; childbirth is a medical event that must take place in hospital; home birth is safer. Childrearing is a minefield of conflicting information and within health and social care there are conflicting and contradictory and fast-changing recommendations about care of the elderly and the management of mental health.

The threat of terrorist attack is probably the most prevalent perception of risk and danger at the global level in the west, although western 'defence' mechanisms vastly increase the risk of those living in targeted parts of the world, like Iraq and Afghanistan. Is the risk society a matter of perception allied to an explosion of techno-scientific apparatuses of intervention and scientific knowledge, for example, in medicine and nutrition and the vast quantity of 'big data' that is now available to fuel our fears? Those fears, however they are linked to transformations in knowledge production and dissemination, are no less real. Risk is part of everyday life and international relations and is a manifestation of the psychic reality of those fears in the social worlds of the twenty-first century, which is why risk has become of particular interest to those involved in psychosocial studies. Risk and the management of the proliferation of discourses about risk present fertile ground for the exploration of the interconnectedness of personal fears and social anxieties.

Anxiety

A major outcome of the experience of living in a risk society is the anxiety that is thus invoked. Anxiety, whether initiated by the unconscious or resulting from external forces or both, is central to psychoanalytic explorations of human relations and of being human. Anxiety serves a purpose in inciting defence mechanisms and acts as a warning so that defence mechanisms can ward off the overwhelming sense of helplessness that can be created by anxiety. Anxiety might take the form of total annihilation of the ego as in the primitive and primary anxiety, which arises from a traumatic experience. Such anxiety involves being completely taken over by instinctive tensions and feelings. In such cases of automatic anxiety the individual is confronted by a force of excitations, whether internal or external, which he or she cannot control or overcome (Laplanche and Pontalis, 1985).

In the case of risk as described in the discussion above it is more likely to be Freud's second version of anxiety as signal anxiety that is implicated in the subject's response. In such instances the individual is confronted with a warning, which is not the direct outcome of instinctual tension but a signal that something that might be overwhelming is about to happen. These feelings are related to the trauma of birth in Freud's writings (Freud, 1926).

Signal anxiety is a combination of the external source that generates feelings of helplessness in the case of the social recommendations of risk avoidance and the human condition of which anxiety plays so large a part because of the helplessness and dependency of the human infant.

Anxiety and the defence mechanisms that surround it and that are deployed to deal with it can lead to neuroses, which are now more commonly called anxiety disorders, and which psychoanalysis can address by exploring some of the unconscious conflicts that give rise to those anxieties. In the case of risk this includes exploring the external factors and the processes through which social factors become psychic and become part of a person's inner world as well as identifying what is particular about the ways in which external factors express as well as are expressed by internal fears and anxieties.

Anxiety plays a crucial part in our lives because it preserves us from physical and psychic danger. It is through the operation of psychic anxiety that we are able to avoid danger and even total disintegration, according to psychoanalytic theory. The ego has to institute defence mechanisms in order to avoid automatic anxiety and primary breakdown. Anxiety can be traced back to childhood experience, for example, in Kleinian terms, the capacity of the primary carer to contain the infant's fears and the possibility that the child has to develop defence mechanisms.

How does psychoanalysis or, more importantly for our purposes in this book, how do psychosocial approaches enable us to make sense of risk and people's management of risk, especially given the contradictory nature of some of the discourse of risk in contemporary societies? In the twenty-first century in neo-liberal democracies people are constantly reminded of the risks they take on a daily basis and are provided with enormous amounts of information about those risks, but it is individuals who are given the responsibility of minimizing risk and anxiety. Anxiety is generated in part by external factors, but the reason it works and we are so concerned with risk is because anxiety is part of the human condition and the risk society with its reiteration of injunctions to avoid risk both incites anxiety and provokes the signal anxiety and our defence mechanisms.

The following example illustrates one of the more routine iterations of risk avoidance in contemporary societies. Whereas the workplace used to be a potentially very dangerous place, health and safety measures and legislation have gone some way towards rendering the workplace a safer place. Fewer people in the 'risk societies' of the west (but not in many other parts of the world) are now employed in hazardous labour underground in mining or perilous industrial work, and if they do work with chemicals, for example, there are largely robust protective measures and regulations in place following earlier disasters. However, risk assessment has become an important management tool. How does risk play out in relation to work?

Risk and anxiety in the workplace

There is a growing literature within occupational health, especially on psychosocial risk factors in the workplace. Increasingly workplaces run staff surveys in order to ascertain their employees' perception of risk and of overall satisfaction. For example, the Canadian Centre for Occupational Health lists thirteen factors, all of which are classified as psychosocial. What is psychosocial about these factors?

Factors identified include psychological support, organizational culture, clear leadership expectations, civility and respect, recognition and reward, leadership and responsibility, psychological job fit, growth and development, psychological protection, (for example, from bullying and harassment), balance, engagement, workload management, and physical safety. Staff satisfaction has financial implications, since unhappy staff are more likely to be absent and there will be decreased productivity. A higher incidence of accidents, incidents, and injuries has also been identified as a likely outcome.

Psychosocial risk factors are those that connect the perception of individuals to the social context of the workplace, which include reference to mental health and well-being and are framed by psychological concerns, all of which are work based, however. These aspects of risk relate to the psychological makeup of the worker and not of the whole person and his or her life story, which might suggest to the critic that these factors are not really psychosocial. Risk assessment conducted by management may take on board the findings of such surveys, but strategies for risk assessment are likely to be more explicitly concerned with profit margins or in the public sector with outcomes and performance indicators.

Risk in relation to performance indicators, however, might still trigger signal anxieties, for example, in relation to continued employment and the employee's fear of redundancy. Risk is psychosocial even if the risks are less those of physical danger and fear of physical pain and distress. Distress can be experienced individually and collectively. Anxieties in relation to risk, although experienced by individuals who are the target of risk assessment by management, can also be shared as defence mechanisms. Anxiety about risk can lead to **regression** in the expression of hostility and can be disruptive in a number of ways. In changing economic climates marked by banking crises, when economic and financial power geometries are shifting from western economies to others such as the BRIC economies of Brazil, Russia, India, and China, to mention but a few, the risks most likely to motivate anxiety are those related to job security.

These risk factors are also linked to those of health, as is demonstrated by some of the specific factors listed in the Canadian Occupational Health literature. Mental health and mental well-being also constitute risk factors, since ill health of whatever sort can lead to absence and prolonged periods of illness.

Health and risk

Psychosocial risks to health are increasingly being recognized as part of effective management as is securing the well-being of citizens. Health is an important sphere of contemporary life in which risk features prominently and where psychosocial factors can be deemed to be injurious to health and, for example, to positive outcomes following either routine surgery or management of ill health, such as heart disease or trauma as in the case of accidents. Sometimes psychosocial factors are linked to recovery and sometimes to the management of chronic conditions such as back pain, which might be multifactorial. Psychosocial aspects can also be seen to encompass stress, which invokes notions of anxiety in the sufferer that might be multifactorial or might be part of the individual's psyche, and offers recognition of the interrelated elements in the makeup of the self. The discourse of risk can increase anxiety through its attribution of responsibility to the individual, often in highly contentious and problematic ways, for example, in the case of obesity and drug and alcohol dependency. There is a fine line between the autonomy and agency of neoliberal cultures of individualization and guilt and blaming the victim. What a psychosocial approach endeavours to achieve is an understanding of the complex interrelationship between different elements and between psychic processes and the external factors of the social world a person inhabits.

There has been a growing interest in the psychosocial aspects of health ranging from coronary disease and cancer to chronic back pain. Work undertaken in these areas focuses upon the interrelationship between social and environmental factors and the fears and anxieties of the individuals concerned. There is some elision between what is classified as stress and anxiety, and a psychosocial approach is multifactorial and includes physical dimensions as well as mental health. These aspects of the person combine and, for example, stress can be corporeal in its manifestations. What are called psychosocial risk factors can cause physical pain and musculoskeletal disorders (Canadian Occupational Health, 2014). In this sense the psychosocial is able to integrate a whole range of factors and overcome the separation of mind and body as well as psychic and social worlds.

Health is closely connected to health care and the practices of caring, whether caring for the self or caring for others, which was the example with which I started this book. The following case study is one that is well known within psychosocial studies as a seminal text that explores the nature of caring in the particular context of health workers by providing a study of the psychodynamics of a caring institution.

Psychosocial work has a history of exploring the nature of caring. For example, Isabel Menzies Lyth's famous work, 'Social systems as a defense against anxiety', which was first published in 1959, was a study of hospital nurses in a large teaching hospital. This study provides extensive insights into the psychic dynamics of an institution in terms of how feeling states, fragments of experience, and emotions are taken in and given out as well as moved around or circulated by individual members of a social organization so much so that individuals lose parts of themselves in the process within the institution, which becomes part of a projective system. In this case study, the nurses at the hospital were being 'trained on the job', that is, they were expected to work while they were being trained at the same time, and this is what created some identifiable problems. Menzies Lyth shows how the nurses adopted defensive techniques against the anxieties generated by their work. The institution was not able to respond to the needs of individuals in spite of initial aspirations to do so, and the social defence system of the hospital became inflexible and rigid, which each new intake of nurses introjected. This is a particular perspective on group dynamics that sees the group as a small-scale society in which there are different modes of social organization and different relationships, some of which lead to the well-being of participants and some of which generate more anxiety and distress. Menzies Lyth concludes that the social defence system developed in the nursing system in the hospital that she studied was ineffective in containing anxiety in its members. She cites the centrality that Klein accords to anxiety in explaining interpersonal relations and in the defence of personality. Menzies Lyth argues for a psychosocial approach in order to facilitate an understanding of the processes so that social change is possible. Bion ([1962]1991) stresses the importance of understanding these phenomena and relating difficulties within the institution to tolerating anxieties that are released as social defences. Social scientists and social policymakers often fail in their attempts to effect change because they do not take on board the need to analyze anxieties and defence mechanisms. These defensive techniques are encouraged by the repression of anxieties rather than containment, which might have been more helpful and led to the possibility of change, which could have produced a better working environment and improved relationships in the workplace.

In Menzies Lyth's example, attempts to make changes only met with even more anxiety because change was felt to be intolerable. She suggests that it is possible to compare the socio-therapeutic experience with the experience of psychoanalysis where what is most difficult is working with patients whose defence systems are dominated by primitive psychic defence mechanisms.

Menzies Lyth stresses the social defences that are summoned by nurses to protect them from the acute anxieties of organizational life but does not say much about the management structures that influence those anxieties or about the management of risk, which would be possible in this case. Risk, anxiety, and trust have changed in contemporary societies, as the individualization and risk society arguments suggest. Anthony Giddens's particular approach to trust, which draws upon Freud's work, provides one route into engaging with the management of risk in relation to trust as an emotional commitment, a conceptualization that challenges the cognitive, rational strategies adopted by most organizations. In a context in which anxiety shapes the contours of organizational life, there are alternative mechanisms for producing the psychosocial security that is vital to active and positive engagement with situations characterized by risk. Giddens defines trust as 'confidence in the reliability of a person or system, regarding a given set of outcomes or events, when that confidence expresses a faith in the probity or love of another, or in correctness of abstract principles' (Giddens, 1991:34). Giddens's two interpretations of trust are instructive in exploring how defence mechanisms might operate to go beyond containment and institute trust. Giddens distinguishes between two sorts of trust in late modernity. The first is personal trust and the second is trust in abstract systems, which is based largely upon faceless commitments. Personal trust in contrast depends upon face-work commitment so that trust relations are sustained through face-to-face contacts. It is easier to sustain personal trust through the intimacy and friendship that can develop over time in face-to-face contact with professionals or even those in authority positions, whereas the distance of abstract, distance trust relationships that characterize contemporary life generate greater anxiety and limited trust. Thus a reduction of risk and anxiety become more likely in a stable social order, which enables repeated expressions and exchanges based upon personal trust, which acknowledges the emotional human subject who has anxiety at the core of that subjectivity. Risk and trust are closely connected, such that the reduction of risk becomes more possible through mutual accommodation. Risk factors and concomitant anxiety are heightened by more abstract trust and a failure to acknowledge the emotional dimensions of risk and risk management.

This example, although the study was undertaken well before the advent of the risk society in the sociological literature and the practice of risk assessment in most workplaces, is illustrative of some of the discussion in this chapter about the nature of risk and the relationship between risk and anxiety.

Conclusion

Although sociological studies stress the discursive aspects of risk and the idea of the risk society, risk presents a particularly relevant area for psychosocial studies because risk is both social and discursively produced and symptomatic of pain and the expression of inner, often unconscious, fears. This is why it works as a mechanism of social control. The risk society cannot be only the socially constructed product of a series of events because risk is psychosocial in its manifestations and in its expression of deep, often unacknowledged, anxieties. Risk both generates fears and engages with the fears and anxieties that are already part of the mental life and the makeup of the person. Discursive regimes organize and conceptualize risk and even quantify its probabilities, in ever more precise and scientific ways, for example, as a management strategy, but how risk works and is made meaningful in people's lives is related to the preexisting anxiety and fear within the unconscious. At a practical level psychosocial approaches and techniques are increasingly being recognized as providing the means of managing risk through an understanding of how defence mechanisms work and the processes that are involved in defending the self against increasing and even potentially overwhelming anxiety.

Risk is also closely connected to trauma, but they are not the same thing, as the next chapter demonstrates. Although anxiety is based on trauma and the centrality of anxiety to the human condition, and there can be risk assessment of the likelihood of traumatic experience, risk is what is assessed and managed, whereas trauma is the experience itself; trauma is the overwhelming loss of control in the largely unexpected moment.

Questions

1   How would you define risk, and how does risk relate to fear?
2   What is the role of anxiety in understanding the part played by risk in contemporary societies?
3   How does this the issue of risk management impact upon your life – in in the workplace, in the home, in the context of your relationships with others? It may be formalized as in the workplace or more specifically an individual responsibility as in the case of being a parent or a carer of a family member, neighbor, or friend.
4   What can a psychosocial approach contribute to our understanding of the part played by risk in society?

chapter 8

Trauma

This chapter:

1   Explores what is meant by trauma and how trauma is understood in contemporary societies, especially in relation to risk.
2   Looks at the relationships between trauma as an individual experience and trauma as a social situation, using psychoanalytic perspectives.
3   Uses a psychosocial approach to understand the impact of trauma and of traumatic events and the possibilities of therapy.
4   Takes the particular example of the Holocaust to explore the meanings of trauma.
5   Explores some of the ways in which a psychosocial understanding of trauma as an explanatory concept can contribute to contemporary debates.

Introduction

Trauma and the concept of a traumatic experience or set of experiences are frequently invoked in contemporary societies at a range of different levels. The pain and distress of trauma is closely linked to risk, as chapter 7 demonstrated. One element of the risk society is based on the fear of traumatic events, like 9/11 in the US, which generated a whole set of risk aversion strategies and policies aimed at reducing the threat of repeats of such events and which has had impact across the globe in light of the policies and interventions of US and allied governments, where acts of associated terrorism have also been committed. The greater the intensity of actions and interventions designed to limit and contain the trauma of terrorist acts, the greater the fear and expectation of trauma and the greater the experience of trauma, for example, of US soldiers and those of her allies, became. Trauma linked to 9/11 is not restricted to North America.

More recently, following the wars in Iraq and Afghanistan, which included lengthy tours of duty, violent death of colleagues, and severe injuries, there has been a high incidence of complex Post Traumatic Stress Disorder (PTSD), which affects soldiers and their families and requires new modes of treatment. PTSD is increasingly recognized as the outcome of sexual assaults and a range of personal and individual traumatic events as well as the more public visibility of the trauma of war.

Trauma is part of the human condition, and we are increasingly aware of trauma as experienced at a variety of levels. We live in troubled times in which people are interpellated or hailed by the social order into particular subject positions, as philosopher Louis Althusser (Althusser, 1971) argues. In this case these subject positions are habituated by fear and the threat of trauma in many parts of the world. Slajov Žižek suggests that 'we do not know it, but we are doing it' (in Myers, 2003:63). Trauma and the possibility and threat of being traumatized have become part of contemporary life in a variety of ways so that trauma becomes taken for granted.

PSTD has entered the vocabulary, and it has become recognized that, following accidents and bereavements as well as major natural disasters, people are likely to need therapeutic assistance in dealing with momentous, disruptive, and distressing moments and experiences. I am writing this book in 2014, the centenary of the outbreak of World War I, and in reading accounts of people's experience as well as watching plays reconstructing the war and some of its early battles, it seems incomprehensible that the only category available for trauma was 'shell shock' and the most likely treatment for a traumatized soldier was a court martial or to be returned to the front.

This is in contrast to contemporary concerns and the attempts of the US military to redress earlier failure to acknowledge the impact of trauma, for example, upon young soldiers returning from the war in Vietnam in the 1960s and 1970s. PTSD is recognized as a condition that has considerable implications in a variety of areas of personal and social life.

Treatment and recognition of the condition remains contentious, however, for example, in the case of the release on May 31, 2014, of Sgt Bergdahl, a US soldier who had been held by the Taliban in Afghanistan for five years. US doctors delayed Bergdahl's return to his family, even meeting with his family for a short time, as this is deemed too stressful for those who have been kept in captivity for long periods. This case, like many others, is not simply a question of the best treatment for a traumatized individual. Not only are there troubling public policy questions about whether or not the US government should have done a deal with the Taliban to negotiate the American soldier's release in return for the release of Taliban prisoners held in Guantanamo Bay, but also this story is haunted by questions about the traumatized individual's complicity in his capture and the idea that he has 'turned' or been turned. This is the subject of fiction as represented in the television drama 'Homeland' ('Homeland', 2014), which explored the complex and contradictory psychodynamics of a US marine, Sgt Nicholas Brody, who, after eight years of captivity, was welcomed home as a war hero but was also a convert to Islam who was working for Al-Qaeda. These psychosocial contradictions and tensions are explored in the drama but become even more troubling when invoked in relation to the life story of a US soldier.

Trauma at one level might appear to be a personal and psychic experience, which nonetheless has implications for collective and social experience (Rashkin, 1992, 2005, 2009) and includes the representational systems, such as film, in which trauma is so central (Cooper, 2012). Representations of trauma can all be seen as defence mechanisms, which are adopted to both contain and make some sense of events that generate such deep feelings of anxiety and distress. As in the case of the television drama series, 'Homeland', representational narratives explore the possibilities and the anxieties of contradictory inner worlds as well as the materiality of 'what if' (Woodward, 2006), for example, in relation to a US Marine who is 'turned' and joins the 'enemy'. The drama pushes unconscious processes into expression so that anxieties are also relived.

Trauma operates at many different levels. There are the mega events, the pivotal points in history when things happen of such magnitude that they cannot be comprehended. The Holocaust is clearly one such trauma. Traumas like this are also experienced by individuals: Holocaust survivors. Trauma is not only concerned with mega events, of course; personal trauma is recognized within psychoanalysis in the clinical setting (Mann and Cunningham, 2009; Parens, 2008). Contemporary psychosocial studies bring together the psychic trauma of experiences such as the Holocaust (Rashkin, 1992, 2009; Byford, 2008), which are translated into cultural memory and where trauma is manifest as a personal experience and as one that is collective. This chapter brings together the psychosocial insights of the clinical encounter and historical social and cultural manifestations of trauma, which can have global implications, as in the case of 9/11 (Seidler, 2013).

This chapter looks at some particular examples of trauma such as the Holocaust and in particular the use of personal testimonies and representations to explore this trauma and the role of memory and haunting in the case of 9/11.

What is trauma?

Early psychoanalytic work on trauma was strongly linked to hysteria as a manifestation of the pain of having suffered a traumatic event, notably in relations to women. Psychoanalytic understandings of trauma have a long history, which goes back to Charcot's work and Freud's later development of trauma and hysteria, which demonstrated the links between traumatic experience and extreme distress. The relationship between trauma and mental illness was first studied by the neurologist Jean Martin Charcot, the French physician who worked with traumatized women who had experienced violence and abuse and presented symptoms such as uncontrollable weeping, paralysis, and memory loss, at the Salpêtrière hospital in the late nineteenth century. In a somewhat circular argument, since the patients being studied were all women, hysteria became associated with the possession of a uterus, the removal of which had hitherto been recommended as a cure for hysteria. There remain some fragments of memory that Charcot's work was, however, the start of an exploration of the internal processes and external manifestations of trauma, which could have much wider application in many different contexts. Many of the symptoms were very like those experienced by 'shell shocked' soldiers in World War I, for these soldiers' memory and the reiteration and rehearsal of the trauma that they had suffered in the trenches and on the battlefield remerged in their unconscious.

Freud and Breuer were able to suggest that trauma resulted from a disassociation, a splitting of the content of consciousness (Freud and Breuer, 1893). Freud's concerns especially in his earlier work were with the trauma of unacceptable sexual desires within the person, and he privileged intrapsychic theory and phantasy over external traumatic forces, although he did accept the possibility of external forces especially in relation to the trauma of war and of anti-Semitism. Once the internal processes have been addressed and acknowledged including the deep pain of coping with trauma, whatever its sources, it becomes possible to think about not only sources but also solutions.

Freud suggests that the origin of trauma is what overrides the psychic dialectic of pleasure and self-preservation. Trauma marks moments when a state of constancy cannot be maintained and the ego's defences collapse because the psychic apparatus, in a state of low cathexis, that is, a concentration of emotional energy, in Freud libidinal investment, is incapable of binding the dangerous external energies. The outcome is a compulsion to return mentally to the situation in which the trauma occurred, in an endeavour to control the external factors retrospectively by producing anxiety, which will allow a psychic binding of these dangerous stimuli.

Psychoanalysis emphasizes the relationship between trauma and memory and the importance of permitting a voice and representation as key elements in the healing process both for individuals and in cases of the collective experience of trauma. Healing is thus connected to the politics of giving voice to those on the margins and who have experienced the trauma of violent repression and social exclusion.

Following his work on hysteria, Freud argued that in the context of analysis the presenting symptoms were often the result of unresolved trauma. Resolution is only possible if the trauma can be revisited and expressed. In therapy this involves removing the barriers of repression and other defence mechanisms that inhibit expression. Psychoanalysis can thus facilitate putting experience into words so that trauma, for example, can be organized and made objective: it can be seen for what it is and expressed. Catharsis is only possible through giving voice to previously repressed trauma. In other contexts, such as collective trauma, giving voice might be through film, art, drama, or literature. Bion too stressed the value of translating trauma or a particularly powerful or distressing experience into words as a way of containing and assimilating the experience, lest it be too overwhelming to be digested, or to survive (Bion, [1962]1991).

Bion offers a useful way to approach our understanding of trauma, which can be seen as particularly useful for psychosocial studies. His theory of trauma has been very influential in psychosocial studies because he puts trauma at the centre of human experience; indeed we are born into trauma, into an undifferentiated inner state of chaotic disorder. These feeling states of sense impressions burst into the infant's mind. Birth itself is traumatic, however calm and well managed by the mother, because the infant is necessarily bombarded with myriad new sensations when it leaves the security of the womb and arrives in the world as a separate being.

These sensations are unbearable for the infant: the experience of birth is thus trauma, which carries with it a sense of impending death, which would be the only relief. It is the possibility and even the inevitability of death that makes the trauma of birth possible to survive. Without relief, the infant would grow to hate these feelings, which start as 'unthought thoughts' before the infant begins to think more rationally. These feeling states hit the infant's mind in intolerable explosions.

Because the infant is born into trauma in an experience that is so overwhelming and inevitable, in order to survive there have to be ways of managing trauma. Bion argues it is the relationship with the mother that can alleviate the trauma of birth. The baby's mother has to contain these disruptive feelings and the child's distress. Mothers thus provide the emotional care through which the infant's feelings are named and thus limited. Attachment between infant and mother whereby the mother takes into herself the infant's incoherent traumatic emotional states before returning them in a named, understood state, leads to a sense of security for the child. The more the mother is able to do this, the less the trauma of birth will haunt the child throughout the life course.

Attempts to give expression to some trauma may be too daunting a task, for example, in cases like the Holocaust or, as has recently been argued, a collective trauma like 9/11 (Altman and Davies, 2002). However, public expressions and representations such as memorials, films, and plays serve the therapeutic role that is so much part of analysis in the consulting room in cases of personal individual cases of trauma, of speaking that which it is too painful to speak, and of making conscious what has been repressed into the unconscious (Ainslie, 2013).

Whose trauma?

Trauma is also part of contemporary life through its visibility. Trauma is a source of enormous interest and concern, for example, within popular culture and media narratives. Trauma, as represented, for example, in television news coverage and on the Internet where ever more graphic details of the misery of the victims of trauma can be made visible and audible, becomes part of the process through which selves are made as well as a means of dealing with the possibility of such experiences oneself. In the twenty-first century, as Andrew Gross and Michael Hoffman argue, there is a 'victim culture' (Gross and Hoffman, 2004), which can lead to identifications with trauma that privilege the testimony of survivors, largely due to the emotional intensity of such testimony. This has been applied to false testimony, which, rather like Freud's seduction theory where seduction or abuse is an expression of desire and fear rather than an actuality, the memory of trauma too can be subject to distortion. For example, personal suffering can be attributed to a broader human experience, as in the case of Binjamin Wilkomirski's *Fragments*, which Gross and Hoffman describe as the false testimony of a troubled man, which subverts the tendency of trauma theory to identify with victims because the author's trauma is authentic even when his testimony is not (Gross and Hoffman, 2004). The Holocaust, as is suggested in the discussion below, is clearly a tragedy that constitutes trauma on a massive scale, which is why it has attracted such attention. It is also something that seems incomprehensible, and thus all we can do is endeavour to deal with the aftermath. Not all trauma is on this scale of course, and trauma is not only concerned with dealing with tragedy.

Carolyn Steedman (1986) suggests that trauma narratives also offer a way of dealing with the good life and well-being for those who are privileged. Lauren Berlant argues that pain can be mobilized as a means of gaining authority. The socially privileged can deal with their privilege through identification with the trauma of those who are disadvantaged, marginalized, and dispossessed. For example, Berlant suggests that in the US, where the 'pursuit of happiness' is a constitutional right, in this setting, she claims injustice is translated into feeling bad so that conversely feeling good is 'evidence of triumph' (Berlant, 2003:35). Berlant suggests, however, that there has also been a move away from the language of trauma because people hold onto the phantasies of the 'good life' and fail to reject their attachments in spite of increasingly difficult economic and financial situations; the phantasies survive even if the conditions for their survival have changed and deteriorated (Berlant, 2003). Trauma is experienced in different ways and at different levels, although, as Berlant also suggests, in some fields there has been a shift from trauma to affect in making sense of emotion and the pain of intense feelings (Berlant, 2012). Trauma has happened and the trauma of past events is always remembered and revisited. How can these memories be accessed, and how can we explore what the experience of trauma involves?

Trauma and the Holocaust

The Holocaust has been the subject of several studies of trauma because the scale of suffering was so vast and so intense, its horrors so unimaginable yet real. This level of outrage clearly warrants the description of trauma and offers a way of exploring how so enormous a social and political trauma might be lived and experienced. It also invites some very different approaches, although it clearly has psychosocial dimensions. Some studies have focused upon representations, and others have combined personal testimonies with historical accounts. The testimony of survivors is clearly central to any such study, especially those studies that are psychosocial and seek to combine the psychic and the social and to explore some of the lived, emotional experience of trauma.

Trauma on the scale of the Holocaust is a large-scale historical trauma and a matter of ethics as expressive of a crisis of values and of humanity is so traumatic that it is difficult to imagine the story that is being told, or retold. Fred Alford bases his research on personal testimony from recorded accounts held at Yale University. He argues that historical trauma is widely enmeshed with clinical diagnoses of Post Traumatic Stress Disorder because survivors of trauma, such as Holocaust survivors, as the representatives of trauma (Alford, 2011) have undergone so distressing an experience. He argues that from the testimonies he researched people found it difficult to believe themselves what happened to them.

Other recent researchers have also endeavoured to get inside the personal testimonies of survivors in different ways. Jovan Byford works on the interdisciplinary study of social and psychological aspects of shared beliefs and social remembering, especially in relation to conspiracy theories, anti-Semitism, and Holocaust remembrance, which he relates to the connections between psychology and history. This work is psychosocial in its focus upon the testimonies of the survivors of the Holocaust in Yugoslavia, which links the personal and the social in the context of traumatic experience. The institutional, ideological, and cultural context of the production, collection, dissemination, and reception of testimonies collected under communism and after 1989, during the turbulent times of postcommunist transition, and during the dissolution of Yugoslavia is connected to personal experiences. This analysis of Holocaust survivor testimonies produced in specific cultural and political contexts, social and historical contingency of Holocaust testimony is thus interconnected to the complex relationship among, and mutual interdependence of, individual, collected, and collective memory (Byford, 2008, 2013).

Byford uses the particular example of the incarceration of Jewish people at Semlin, which marked the beginning of the second phase of the destruction of Serbia's Jewish population. In the first phase, which lasted between July and November 1941, between five and six thousand Jewish men were murdered by the German army. This was a fate that quickly followed for their families. These traumatic events have attracted the interest of historians for a number of reasons, not least for what it symbolized, notably in the official records of what happened. As Byford argues, the suffering of these Jewish people was remembered and their deaths recorded as a symbolic event in the Nazi campaign of destruction and as a manifestation of Nazi crimes. Remembering is an important element in the experience of trauma and in the defence mechanisms of survivors, that is, memories of their experiences rather than the memory of a crime or of a particular political movement.

More recently different interpretations have emerged, which have generated a rich resource of motifs and images that have reclaimed Sajmište as a memorial space that gives expression to those who suffered rather than as a symbol of a discredited political movement. Its multilayered history has been recovered, and it has become a place for trade fairs and mass entertainment. An appropriate memorial to Serbian Jewish suffering needs to be established so that Belgrade is transformed into a memorial, which would provide a continuous and powerful reminder of the gap in the life of the Serbian capital left behind by the almost complete destruction of its Jewish community. Byford argues that Belgrade and Serbia owe this memorial also to the thousands of other non-Jewish victims who were killed in Semlin between 1941 and 1944 (Byford, 2008).

Byford's work approaches the process of memory and the making of memorials through personal testimonies and an analysis of place and of historical events. Memories are also marked by haunting and the persistence of the recurrence of trauma in the unconscious. Esther Rashkin explores the transgenerational transmission of trauma as another way of exploring its impact and the ways in these psychodynamic hauntings are expressed in texts.

The despair of trauma is in a sense timeless, as Freud argued, and trauma can be marked by a 'lapse of duration' (Laplanche, 1989:242). The testimony of Holocaust survivors attests to the lack of division between past and present, and in the memory of trauma the past is in the present. Rashkin's suggestion that Holocaust survivors' memories are embedded in the psyche haunting seems an appropriate description of what is not entirely repressed but that hovers between the unconscious and the conscious mind like phantoms (Rashkin, 1992). Rashkin suggests that these hauntings, which are transmitted from one generation to the next, are triggered by secrets. Rashkin compares texts, including cinematic representations, as literary texts to explore the relationship between the accounts given by survivors of trauma and their families as expressed in the therapeutic context and the phantoms of guilt and repressed secrets as expressed in film. Texts and representations offer an alternative route into an exploration of memory recovery and the attempts that are made to construct defences against trauma and are particularly expressive of the movement between the conscious and the unconscious mind in the timeless experience of trauma, which is inescapable, the more so because the past is always in the present. The idea of haunting and the timelessness of memory in the experience of trauma is evident in other accounts of traumatic events such as 9/11 in the twenty-first century. These traumatic events, in spite of the volubility that has surrounded them, might also illustrate some silences and what Cathy Caruth describes as something unspeakable, which is beyond words and thus beyond explanation (Caruth, 1995).

Remembering 9/11

Victor Seidler develops work that has been undertaken on the Holocaust and Holocaust survivors, in the context of 9/11, in order to address the question of how traumatic memories can be silently carried so that they become difficult to share across generations. He also cites cultural representations and includes media coverage of the events. There are parallels with the work that has been undertaken on the Holocaust, but Seidler, along with many other commentators, warns against suggesting that these are the same of even very similar traumatic events. Trauma is always experienced within contingent, historical, specific social situations even if the feelings of distress and fear do share many features and qualities. Seidler includes the idea of haunting in his discussion of 9/11 and the memories these traumatic events invoked. He argues that hauntings and psychic legacies are neither fully present nor absent and belong to a liminal domain, which permits a politics of memory. The liminal domain is also one that is marked by the dynamic interaction of the social and psychic as well as of past, present, and future.

Seidler too uses personal testimonies and the accounts people giving of their own experience of the attack on the Twin Towers and their memories ten years later. For example, he describes the story of a woman who survived 9/11 and along with others feels guilt at her own survival. Guilt at having made it when others did not is one of the hauntings that recurs. She seeks to redress some of this guilt by seeking out some record of the person who rescued her. Others find that they can never relinquish the feelings of helplessness that reemerge in relation to subsequent events. Helplessness and dependency are the primary states of human beings such that, as Freud argues, this original helplessness is the source of all moral motivations, which are lived and felt within particular social contexts. The expression of weakness may be culturally proscribed for adults. Within a utilitarian culture it may be difficult to express grief and mourning. As Seidler argues,

> [P]eople can be fearful of their own tears, somehow experiencing this as diminishing their status in the eyes of others. Freud teaches us . . . of the need to give time and space to mourn, of the emotional consequences if these opportunities are missed and of the years it can take to open up the grief that we learn to carry silently as a potential kind of haunting disturbance.
>
> (Seidler, 2013:57)

This haunting is more reminiscent of a state of denial, albeit one in which the memories of the past trauma remain in the present.

Conclusion: Trauma and the psychosocial

In this chapter I have attempted to demonstrate some of the ways in which trauma is psychosocial in that the experience is always personal but also always social. Trauma is the result of distressing events that shatter a person's defences and sense of security such that he or she is overwhelmed. In some ways it seems incomprehensible that the US, the most powerful country in the world, could be said to have experienced trauma, but the example of 9/11 is one that demonstrates the operation of the psychic in the social as well as the social in the psychic. There was enormous uncertainty following the attacks when the US government was unable to identify the source, for example, in a particular hostile nation-state (Woodward, 2002). Deaths were high but not comparable to the Holocaust, but what was significant is the lack of control and consequent fear on the part of a state that has such huge military strength and has the resources to access intelligence that might facilitate appropriate defence against such attack. The properties and distinguishing features of trauma are present on the large scale and in the subsequent defence mechanisms of the state, just as they are in the individual who experiences trauma. Individuals did experience trauma too, of course, but the two areas of experience are inseparable.

The psychoanalytic studies of trauma derive largely from the therapeutic context and the consulting room, but the empirical field has shifted as have the contributions of psychosocial studies, which demonstrates that the two worlds are interconnected and unconscious processes are implicated in the experience of personal and individual trauma as in traumatic events on a large scale.

As the psychoanalyst Earl Hopper says,

> An analyst who is unaware of the effect of social facts and forces . . . will not be able to provide a space for patients to imagine how their identities have been formed at particular historical and political junctures, and how this continues to affect them throughout their lives.
>
> (Hopper, 1996:7)

An analyst who does not take these factors on board cannot be sensitive to the unconscious recreation of these social facts and forces within the therapeutic situation.

Although in the last chapter it was argued that risk and what has been called the risk society is powerfully linked to the experience of trauma and in particular the fear of trauma, they are two different phenomena and each has a distinct role to play in understanding of the psychosocial. Trauma is expressive of such deep and enduring fears and anxieties, often with corporeal and psychic impact, that trauma has been the subject of myriad representations and discursive and symbolic expressions. Trauma provides particular connections to the arts and different forms of expression through which fears are sublimated and on which psychic terrors are projected.

In some ways trauma has become routine, and counselling and therapeutic interventions are everyday practices aimed at containing the distress of trauma. Routine recognition does not minimize or eliminate the distress, though; interventions might even exacerbate anxiety, which is made and remade through the interaction and entanglement of internal psychic anxieties and inner fears that are difficult to contain or reconcile, along with a transforming social world in which trauma plays a significant and even more prominent role.

The idea of haunting plays a significant role in the psychosocial understanding of feelings and of experience, especially in the case of trauma, not least in relation to memory. Traumatic events from childhood may emerge in adulthood triggered quite unexpectedly. Similarly, in the context of multiethnic, diverse societies in which different communities and diverse groups of people have coexisted without conflict for a long period of time, something can happen, the reemergence of memory of past, seemingly long-forgotten trauma, which triggers conflict and new traumatic events. Trauma is political, as the next chapter demonstrates.

Questions

1   Can you think of an example of trauma and the use of the term that demonstrates the relationality of inner worlds and social systems and structures?
2   Think of an example of a film that deals with a traumatic event. How would you use a psychosocial approach to explain and locate the particular example?
3   Which psychoanalytic concepts are most useful in addressing the experience of trauma, whether in the personal or therapeutic context or in understanding larger-scale traumatic events?
4   What is the role of memory and revisiting the past in the experience of trauma?
5   What part do representations, like films, dramas, and literature, play in the containment of trauma?

chapter 9

Politics

This chapter:

1   Looks at what psychosocial studies can contribute to an understanding of politics and the operation of power relations.
2   Explores what psychosocial approaches contribute to understanding contradictions in politics.
3   Addresses feelings and emotion as examples of what occupies the space between the psychic and the social in politics.
4   Uses psychosocial concepts to provide some explanation of big political issues such as social and political inequalities like social exclusion and social class and important contemporary debates like climate change.

Introduction

The application of psychoanalytic theories to international politics and conflict has a long history, not least in Freud's critiques of aggression and the First World War and of anti-Semitism as an intensely expressed form of hostility. Freud's first encounters with anti-Semitism as a boy in Vienna and his later knowledge of horrors of the war, the trauma suffered by soldiers in the First World War, and the hatred expressed by Hitler and the Nazis towards Jewish people among others in Germany in the 1930s must have convinced him of the force of the **death drive** on so large a scale and the importance of analyzing social and political expressions of deeply felt emotions as well as in therapeutic encounters with individuals. Hostility in psychoanalytic theory can be explained by regression (Flax, 1990). Freud was well aware of the traumatic outcomes of war and conflict and the impact of economic and financial oppression resulting from crises within capitalism – and indeed as an inevitable feature of capitalist economies. Freud supported the free clinics set up in Berlin and Vienna in the 1920s to support working-class people oppressed by the inequalities of the capitalist system and provide reasonable mental health care (Danto, 1998, 1999).

Psychoanalytic explanations of large-scale acts of aggression and social exclusion offer enormous possibilities for enhancing understanding of the nature of politics and of the interconnections between the personal and the political (Berlant, 2000). In recent times Slavoj Žižek has written extensively about politics using a combination of Marxist and Lacanian critiques, although I have not devoted space in this book to discussing Žižek's work because he does not identify explicitly with a psychosocial approach. Consequently Žižek does not engage with the same questions as more avowedly psychosocial approaches and is more concerned with applying psychoanalysis to political and cultural phenomena. He applies Lacanian psychoanalytic concepts to the political (Žižek, 1993, 1997) and cultural sphere (Žižek 1992; Žižek and Dolar, 2002) rather than exploring the spaces and relationships between the psychic and the social. Žižek, however, certainly warrants mention, though, not least because of his popularity and visibility as a most prolific creator of a very wide range of texts that bring together Lacanian understandings of the unconscious and subjectivity and a committed communist political critique (Žižek, 1989). One of Žižek's major contributions to psychosocial debates has been the part he has played in putting politics and social inequality onto the agenda of psychoanalytic theorizing as well as using psychoanalytic concepts to analyze power relations.

Žižek has importantly noted that if psychoanalytic practitioners are silent about the dynamics of power and social class, they are colluding with oppression in effect and behaving as if capitalism were natural and inevitable. Psychoanalysts, like their patients, occupy a class position as well as having political position even if it is not necessarily formalized. The neutrality of the analyst is not really feasible, which is not to say that acknowledging a political position necessarily jeopardizes professionalism, only that it is impossible to be politically neutral or to be without social class. The psychosocial response to this has been more about acknowledging class and the operation of power and then to start thinking about the social unconscious, which Eric Hopper suggested included the multiple ways in assumptions are made and unstated. Hopper suggested that analysts could work carefully through their own and their patients' responses in the clinical setting to understand the operation of the social unconscious of which analysts and patients are part (Hopper, 2003). Hopper was drawing attention to the notion of a social unconscious in the context of the risk societies emerging, for example, in the US post–9/11 with the bombing of the World Trade Center and the ensuing conflicts around the world, including particularly the Iraq Wars. The public and the private and the personal and social intersect in particularly dramatic ways, and, as Lynne Layton, Nancy Caro Hollander, and Susan Gutwill argue,

> [C]ivilization incites clinicians to challenge the boundaries that are conventionally accepted as existing between the external world and the internal world, between life and reflection, between extroversion and introversion, between doing and being, between politics and psychology, between the political development of the person and psychological development of the person, between fantasies of the political world and the politics of the fantasy world. Subjectivity and inter-subjectivity have some political roots; they are not as "internal" as they seem.
>
> (Layton et al., 2006:12)

These shifts, which cross traditional boundaries, not only indicate the links between politics and the psychosocial, but they also demonstrate some of the puzzling spaces that psychosocial studies address and that are the concern of this book.

One of the ways in which politics is psychosocial is through an engagement with emotion and feeling. How are politics and emotions connected?

Politics and emotion

'All societies are full of emotion. Liberal democracies are no exception. The story of any day or week of even a relatively stable democracy would include a host of emotions – anger, fear, sympathy, disgust, envy, guilt, grief, many forms of love' (Nussbaum, 2013:1–2). Sometimes these are emotions tied up directly with politics; sometimes they are not so closely enmeshed with politics. The emotions that are invoked and felt in political struggles, for example, against social exclusion and racism or in nationalism and expressions of love for one's country, are clearly political (Borossa, 2012). As Nussbaum argues, sometimes there is a popular assumption that emotions are linked to fascist and hostile regimes, as is so well illustrated in the case in Freud's life, for example, whereas liberal democracies are rational. Nussbaum argues strongly against this view and contends that emotion is necessary to ensure stability. Good political principles as well as bad ones need emotional support for stability; for example, through sympathy and love (Nussbaum, 2013).

Emotions are thus central to the maintenance of 'decent' neoliberal states and, for example, in making the case for love in politics, Nussbaum argues, that far from being inimical to freedom and justice, love is essential to the promotion of autonomy and freedom. Although Nussbaum's approach is largely philosophical and not expressed as psychosocial, she makes important contributions to debates in psychosocial studies, in particular in relation to the part played by feelings and emotions, which are so strongly associated with inner worlds, in the wider arena of governance and of politics. She also draws upon psychoanalytically informed ideas to translate some of Freud's understanding of opposing and contradictory drives, most forcefully expressed as love and hate, into a more nuanced concept of compassion, which can be invoked to counter feelings of disgust, fear, envy, and shame. Nussbaum argues that giving priority to emotion and affect in a study of political and the operations of the nation not only provides deeper explanation of the relationship among people who are the subjects of governance and the processes through which politics work but also provides some prescriptions for action and making changes. She suggests that there are two tasks for a liberal society. 'One is to engender and sustain strong commitment to worthy projects that require effort and sacrifice – such as social redistribution, the full inclusion of previously marginalized groups, the protection of the environment, foreign aid and national defence' (2013:3). The other task that involves the cultivation of public emotion is to avoid the negative emotions such as disgust and envy, which are often expressed against others when the self is defended and protected through the denigration of others. Permitting people to inflict shame upon others, whether at the level of the family or group or in the nation, is extremely damaging and detrimental to any promotion of liberal values of equality and justice, especially when such emotions inform law making, which can be used to justify prejudice and discrimination.

Emotion plays a significant part in the reconfiguration of citizenship and the politics of belonging in the twenty-first century (Roseneil, 2013). Migration is a routine part of life for millions of people in the twenty-first century; as it was in the twentieth century (Berger, 1984), but it is more recently that the contradictions and difficulties and especially the tensions within neoliberal discourses, particularly in relation to citizenship, have become most prominent, not least in the unfinished project of citizenship after orientalism (Isin, 2014; Isin and Nyers, 2014).

Psychosocial approaches suggest different questions that can be asked about the politics of migration and of citizenship both from the perspective of migrant peoples and in relation to the policies and practices that govern migration. Roseneil argues that these issues demand thinking 'psycho-socio-analytically about their affective politics, about the relationship between subjective experience, relational and intersubjective dynamics and socio-historical processes and power relations' (Roseneil, 2013:231) in order to address the particular issues and especially tensions and conflicts that have emerged in the post–9/11 world in which neoliberal democratic understandings – and policies – have been found seriously deficient. Citizenship in this context has to include discussion of the absence of rights as well as the inclusion of T. H. Marshall's traditional features of citizenship as characterized by legal, civil, and social rights (Marshall, 1950) and the processes through which exclusions are made and through which they endure. In multicultural, multiethnic societies that are grappling with the dilemmas of life after orientalist constructions of the 'east as other' (Said, 1978), other factors, not least the emotions and the personal as well as the collective experiences of migration and citizenship, or lack of citizenship, have to be addressed. The two-way processes of affect, which embrace emotions and feelings, play an enormous part in understanding how belonging relates to citizenship and how those feelings of wanting to belong are lived in response to powerful feelings of exclusion and the emotions that motivate exclusion.

Social exclusion, inequalities, and prejudice

Social exclusion includes a range of processes through which some groups of people become marginalized or excluded from full participation in social life and is deeply embedded in social structural inequalities. These inequalities and the social action, for example, in relation to justice and citizenship rights that they inspire, are also connected to emotions, as the last section has shown. How can we use a psychosocial approach to understand some of the dynamics of processes of social exclusion and the myriad ways in which inequalities are perpetuated in contemporary political and social life?

As Adorno and Marcuse demonstrated, xenophobia, racism, ethnocentrism, and prejudice are connected with deep-rooted emotions, with hatred, uncanny desires, anxieties, and overwhelming fears of annihilation. It is only possible to understand these phenomena as the expression of unconscious and unresolved political conflicts within society.

Many, or at least some of us, may have some experiences of having been subject to stereotyping, silencing, discrimination, and exclusion, although it is also the case that, as social beings, a much larger group of us, if not everyone, has to some extent participated in upholding these practices, often unconsciously (Auestad, 2012b). It is the unconscious, the collective unconscious of social beings operating within the arena of politics underpinned by such discriminatory and prejudicial feelings, that the psychosocial addresses. Lene Auestad argues that psychoanalysis can be used to think about the invisible and subtle processes of power over symbolic representation, for example, in the context of stereotyping and dehumanization. She suggests that thinking psychoanalytically about the nature of social exclusion involves self-questioning on the part of the interpreter, whether this is the practitioner, the researcher, or the therapist. Auestad poses the question of what forces govern the state of affairs that determine who is an 'I' and who is an 'it' in the public sphere (Auestad, 2012a). The dehumanizing of outsiders and of others is a common aspect of stereotyping and racialized, ethnicized discrimination, for example, in the case of Roma, travellers, black, and minority ethnic or migrant peoples. For example, discrimination in such cases in relation to migrant people is often expressed in a closure around sameness based on nationalism, which thus excludes those not held within the boundaries of this sameness. The politics of race draws upon a legacy of acknowledgement of the interrelationship between the personal and the political (hooks, 1990), which is reconfigured within contemporary psychosocial approaches (Lewis, 2009).

One possible route into understanding how sameness operates in processes of exclusion and in the expression of extreme hostility and prejudice is viewing discrimination and stereotyping in terms of containment, which draws upon Wilfred Bion's work (Bion, 1962). Containment is the capacity to keep within oneself the parts of the self that create anxiety. The infant is unable to do this and projects anxieties onto the mother. Similarly an individual or a group or even an entire population may have within it such anxieties as are unbearable, and the anxiety this provokes becomes projected onto others, who are the object of the projective identification. They either keep or contain these unbearable parts or project them onto a subentity – a group whose members are even more disadvantaged.

These projections are likely to be denied as are the unbearable feelings of anxiety. Communications and expressions of resistance are also denied expression. The concept of containment has proved to be extremely helpful for deepening both clinical understanding of working with therapeutic impasses and managing unbearable states of mind that emerge for both patients and therapists and the holding strategies adopted more widely in cases of political conflict. Psychoanalytic approaches are able to disentangle silences and what is said in these processes of stereotyping, for example, and reinstall meaning where there was none, at a social as well as at an individual level.

Individuals who belong to a group that has been constructed as 'other' on grounds of race or ethnicity or sexuality are objectified and denied subjectivity so that those individuals are silenced and are not able to speak because the position from which they speak is deemed illegitimate. The politics of race intersects with other axes of power (Phoenix and Pattynama, 2006) to produce challenges to neoliberalism (Roseneil, 2012; Special Section, 2014). Social exclusion and 'othering' are social processes the details of which can be explored so that resistance becomes possible. Thus analysis of processes makes social and political action possible. Processes of 'othering' resonate with considerable force in twenty-first century networks of migration and reconfigurations of globalization and postcolonialism when citizen-ship too is marked by emotional identifications and contradictions.

Differences and sameness

The emotions that are involved in perpetuating social exclusion and inequalities can be extreme and violent, both as emotions and in the practices to which they lead. The hostilities of war are motivated by hatred, which is a troubling notion for rational political scientists. Karl Figlio argues that hatred is rooted more in sameness than in differences. Thus the task of politics is not to manage difference but more to manage the unease of the collective as well as the individual unconscious.

For Freud there was a disjunction between conscious perception of difference and the unconscious phantasy of sameness that provokes hatred, one example of which is the hatred between men and women. Freud based his conception of the **narcissism** of minor differences on this particular difference, and it clearly has application to Figlio's attempt to explain the practice of rape as a weapon of war. It is not an existing difference of such magnitude but unease that can lead to hostility and hatred is generated. As Figlio argues, '[D]ifference has to be estab-lished. There is no pre-existent ego and object. They are mutually created in projection and introjection' (Figlio, 2012:18). He goes on to explore some of the ethnic identities that have to be made through the projection of unease when overt differences are reduced and minor differences matter more.

Figlio cites the work of the writer and broadcaster (and latterly Canadian politi-cian) Michael Ignatieff. This is a twentieth-century example that well illustrates the details of how this form of narcissism works in war-torn former Yugoslavia (in Woodward, 1997; Ignatieff, 1994, 1998). Ignatieff describes visiting a Serbian camp in what he calls 'a village war. Everyone knows everyone else: they all went to school together', but now they are killing each other. Ignatieff asks the Serbian soldiers what makes the Serbs so different from the Croats. The first response he gets is to take a packet of cigarettes out of his pocket:

> See this? These are Serbian cigarettes. Over there they smoke Croatian cigarettes. . . . You foreigners don't understand anything. . . . The question bothers him, so a couple of minutes later, he tosses his weapon down on the bunk between us and says, 'Look here's how it is. Those Croats, they think they're better than us. They think they're fancy Europeans and everything. I'll tell you something. We're all just Balkan rubbish'.
>
> (Ignatieff, 1994:1–2)

At a Serbian bunker Ignatieff is told by Serbian reservists that they 'disliked breathing the same air as the Croatians, disliked being in the same room as them. There was a threatening uncleanness about them' (Ignatieff, 1998:51). As Ignatieff observes, these were people who had never even thought that they were breathing the same air as those who they now so despised.

These are minor differences, for example, in the case of the cigarettes, but minor differences are constructed to project hatred and extreme hostility onto another group of people, about whom those who feel so much hatred had either considered friends and neighbours or not even been classified as different in their daily lives.

Hatred can be made through the operation of the most subtle of differences, which at one historical moment are unmarked and do not matter, but at others it is the narcissism of minor differences that, as Freud argued, can be augmented into large-scale conflict. In his work (Figlio, 2012), Figlio draws on Freud's conception of the narcissism of minor differences to explain some of the acts of violent aggression such as rape and genocide, which continue in the twenty-first century. This collapse of identity into narcissism, both sought and dreaded, is enacted by the rapist in order to destroy the woman in hatred, and to reestablish a difference, but in the ambivalence of the narcissism of minor differences.

There are other ways in which a psychosocial approach can enhance our understanding of difference in the political arena through examples of exclusion, which are more routine than the conflicts that actually lead to war. Other differences between groups of people can generate strong feelings, including those of disgust.

Emotion and social class

In times of widening inequalities globally and within nations, feelings about which have heightened following the economic crises starting in the first decade twenty-first century, social class has returned very emphatically to the agenda of the social sciences. Social class has been called the last taboo for psychoanalysis (Layton et al., 2006). Layton demonstrates how class alliances and class divisions are kept in place through a psychosocial study of the emotions that are embedded in class relations.

Layton follows the sociologist Pierre Bourdieu who argued that class identities carry the distinction of particular qualities and tastes are established through processes that involve rejection of the qualities of other classes (Bourdieu, 1994). Bourdieu's work is not psychoanalytical, but it does feature two aspects that are of considerable relevance to a psychosocial approach. Firstly, Bourdieu draws upon phenomenological ideas and methodologies from Merleau-Ponty (1962), which stress lived experience and people's perceptions of their own lives. Secondly, Bourdieu's concept of habitus includes the dispositions and schemes that people draw upon to make sense of their social situation and, in particular, in this case, the dispositions that inform the distinction of taste by which social classes are differentiated.

Habitus thus refers to the inner world of perception and to the operation of cultural and social norms that operate at the level of the unconscious. Popular understandings of class, like race and ethnicity, are not always conscious, and negative feelings leading to marginalization and social exclusion are often rooted in the unconscious and may form part of the collective unconscious, which had some resonance with Bourdieu's notion of habitus.

Bourdieu argues that there are anxieties resulting from people's attempts to differentiate themselves from those in the lower social echelons as well as the fears of being ridiculed by those in a higher social class. These anxieties lead to class differentiation and are the motor for the reproduction of class divisions, which militate against social mobility and reinforce class boundaries. As has been argued more recently, anxieties about those in lower socioeconomic classes are likely to be much more powerful forces of exclusion and marginalization than deference for those in higher class groupings, for example, in a more recent example of the working-class identity of 'chavs', a group that is despised by the middle classes for lacking good taste (Skeggs 2005; Jones, 2012). ('Chav' is a pejorative term used in the UK to refer disparagingly to the cultural tastes and social dispositions of working-class young people who wish to flaunt their tastes and practices.) Bev Skeggs includes the intersection of other social factors such as class and gender in her account and demonstrates how different social systems combine to reproduce particular versions of marginalization and exclusion, which are expressed as disgust.

The internalization of class relations, which are manifest in taste and in people's phantasies about what those tastes mean and what they represent, is responsible for the reproduction of class divisions and inequalities as well as the material economic forces that generate and perpetuate class structures.

Layton uses an example of the feelings of middle-class professionals when they go shopping in a down-market, cheap store. The following quotation from Layton's small-scale research project describes the experience that led her to undertake her study and provided its title.

> I needed a garden hose and took a friend shopping with me to a store called Ocean State Job Lot. As we left, my upper middle class friend looked disgusted and said, 'That place gives me the heebie jeebies'. I tried to find out what she meant what emotion 'heebie jeebies' describes for her, but as I asked it became clear that the emotion had to do with a disdain, not only for the lower class goods in the store but for the lower class shoppers, shame set in and she refused to keep talking.
>
> (Layton, 2006:51)

Layton goes on to interview other middle-class people to demonstrate the ways in which class is held in place through the experience of such emotions, which include anxiety about contamination, humiliation, and shame. Several of her respondents refer to the visceral, corporeal sensations, notably of the smell of the cheap, discount store with its population of bargain hunters. Class distinctions are embodied through the invocation of sensations of disgust at vulgarity or what is deemed crude.

The converse experience is if the working-class person feels anxiety in the up-market store or the gourmet restaurant where he or she fears being found out as undeserving or not knowing the appropriate codes of behaviour. The heebie jeebies is a way of trying to capture emotions that are themselves disquieting and not easy to pin down. Part of her defence of the small scale of the project and her reliance upon respondents who are known to her is Layton's ability to interpret a response such as the heebie jeebies, which might seem obscure to a researcher who had approached a group entirely as an outsider. Layton also knows her interviewees and can thus situate their responses and come to a better understanding of the relational space between the psychic and the social, which, for example, in the case of the heebie jeebies, provides a dynamic connecting process between feelings and sensation and social systems. If emotion deriving from unconscious forces can be understood to operate collectively in the reproduction of social divisions, other aspects of the social unconscious are in play in different contemporary political debates.

As Layton argues, the emotions that reproduce class distinction and differentiation also have policy implications. Lynn Froggett makes the point that a psychosocial approach to welfare needs to be attentive to the relationship between users, managers, and practitioners in order to provide a rich conceptualization of the subject and the equalizing of the service user and the social worker, which takes on board the emotions and feelings involved in the relationship (Froggett, 2002).

The structure of the unconscious can apply to social systems in different ways, and the field of politics has been a most productive area for psychosocial exploration. The next section engages with a psychoanalytic concept that is then applied to an issue within contemporary society to explore different dimensions of the adoption of political positions. Why do people take up the positions they espouse, in some cases even when the evidence suggests that a different view would be more rational? The next section explores the psychoanalytic concept of perversion and goes on to consider how structures of perversion can be used to explain climate change denial using a psychosocial approach.

Structures of perversion

Freud argued that in the context of sexuality, the infant was born polymorphous and perverse (Freud, [1905]2000). It could go any way, and there are lots of possibilities. Perversion in Freudian psychoanalytic thinking is not tainted by the derogatory connotations and moral judgements of the everyday use of the term. Perversion, and even more especially 'pervert', is used judgementally, for example, in popular observations in the mass media and in everyday exchanges, to suggest practices that are outside the norm and are not only transgressive but possibly dangerous. It is the fear of transgression of norms and the threatened breakdown of a particular social order that makes sexuality and the concept of perversion so political.

The broader psychoanalytical approach to perversion deriving from Freud's work has been inspirational in queer theory in celebrating polymorphous sexualities with ideas about perversion being subjected to critical analysis or used ironically to subvert heterosexist norms. Queer theory too has extended the political application of the psychoanalytic concept of perversion. Within the psychoanalytic framework human sexuality was not fixed but could develop in contradictory ways. In this sense perversion – and contradiction and perversity – are seen to be part of the human condition. Freud's discussion of perversion in the context of sexuality might suggest that it relates to inner drives and offers explanation of the activities of individuals rather than wider social and cultural movements. More recently psychosocial theorists have demonstrated some of the ways in which this concept has application to social and cultural change across a range of areas of experience including those that are the centre of political debates.

Paul Hoggett makes a case for what he calls perverse structures as a way of explaining some of the contradictory social practices and cultures of contemporary neoliberal societies. Hoggett uses Susan Long's work on social defence (2008), which, Hoggett argues, is a particularly good illustration of the mediated space between the psychic and the social and can usefully be deployed to explore some of the psychic shifts within capitalism 'from instinctual repression (Freud, [1929]2010), to repressive desublimation (Marcuse, 1966) and narcissism (Lasch, 1978) and to a culture of perversion' (Hoggett, 2010b:58). Each of these stages is marked by the application of a psychoanalytic concept to a particular set of sociocultural circumstances.

Long picks out five characteristics of the perverse structure: firstly, 'It has to do with individual pleasure at the expense of a more general good' (2008:15).

Secondly, the perverse structure both acknowledges reality whilst simultaneously denying it. Thirdly, the perverse structure does not operate alone but engages others as accomplices. Fourthly, the societies where the perverse structure flourishes are likely to be instrumental, and finally, 'perversion begets perversion' (ibid.:15).

Politics and climate change

What's psychosocial about the climate? It's not so much the climate per se as climate change, and the debate that surrounds it, which has recently become of interest to psychosocial researchers. Is the climate political? Climate change certainly is. The subject is discussed at the highest levels of international politics and subject to highly disputed political arguments, although at the highest levels there is some agreement about targets and what has to be done, especially to protect the most vulnerable nations of the world in relation to carbon emissions and the impact of human-generated climate change usually framed by excessive CO_2 emissions leading to the extremes of flooding and drought and famine (UN Climate Change, 2013). Climate change may be explained in technical ecological terms, but most of the debates are political, in relation to setting targets for reduction of global warming and in greenhouse gas emissions. There is, however, neither agreement of strategies for reaching the targets nor even on the extent of global warming, and one of the issues that is particularly relevant is the widespread denial of climate change and the involvement of human activity in generating the change.

As individuals we are exhorted to recycle waste and to engage in sustainable practices in our household consumption, but is this an individual matter on the one hand and a concern of international organization on the other.

The aspect of the politics of climate change that is of particular interest to psychosocial researchers is the issue of denial. Denial is a concept in common currency in popular culture. Smokers can be 'in denial' about the dangers of their habit; those classified as obese may be 'in denial' about what actually constitutes a healthy diet or adequate physical exercise. In the case of smoking the empirical evidence of the higher incidence of ill health and early death is pretty incontrovertible, but those in denial may persist in their refusal accept the evidence and still express their denial within an evidence-based discourse. Others may say they enjoy it and are prepared to take the risk, but denial goes much deeper. There is a repression of the counterarguments and evidence, even if they are expressed within an evidence-based discourse. Denial is not only a matter for the individual but has wider social and political implications.

In the context of the broad, more explicitly political arena, as was demonstrated in chapter 8, there are Holocaust deniers who argue that even an event of such historical magnitude and horror never actually happened. Denial ever since Freud has been linked to perversion; it is a state of feeling that counters rationality and the evidence. Denial is not only an individual phenomenon, not least when it applies to something as global and all pervasive as climate change. Climate change affects us all.

There is a danger that in subjecting denial to a psychological analysis it becomes individualized, but recently there have been productive developments in psycho-social research that explore what is happening when collectively people are 'in denial' about climate change. Paul Hoggett seeks to avoid the individualizing tendencies of a psychological or psychoanalytic exploration of 'being in denial' by showing how denial is a key element of a perverse culture in developed societies.

Sally Weintrobe identifies three main forms of denial in her work; denialism, when people cannot face the truth, negation which means saying that what is is not and disavowal, where people see the reality of climate change but minimise its significance and emotional impact. She argues that

> negation is the more serious form of denial, as it offers a flat no to reality, but actually disavowal is more serious in its consequences. This is because negation may be the first stage of facing reality and mourning illusion – while it initially says no to the truth. Negation can help when the truth is too much to bear (in Hoggett, 2013).

Weintrobe concentrates on negation and disavowal (Weintrobe, 2012). She suggests that individuals use these strategies of negation and disavowal when things get to be too much to bear, even though they are phantasy solutions and cannot actually effect the restoration of equilibrium that we need. According to Weintrobe, whilst negation offers a flat denial of the reality of climate change, this state can lead to later acceptance, as at least there is a reality that is being negated. Disavowal is nearer distortion and can offer a more enduring way of hanging on to the illusions that there is no climate change problem. Collective disavowal can be fed by media coverage if a particular issue – weather extremes such as flooding or drought or, the example Weintrobe uses, a hurricane – is presented as a single event and not related to a wider pattern of climate change.

Weintrobe cites the case of Superstorm Sandy, the hurricane which hit the US East coast and led to the death of 117 people. She argues that US media coverage gave the devastating event less attention as a manifestation of climate change than might have been expected. In spite of Obama's acknowledgement of the enormity of the problem of climate change following his second-term inauguration in January 2013, feelings of negation and, in particular, disavowal had already been engendered by the nature of the US media coverage and discussion of Superstorm Sandy and the mainstream media marginalization of the political and social issue of the magnitude of climate change.

Through an exploration of a particular contemporary debate it is possible to demonstrate the interconnections between psychic states and social worlds and the dynamic and multifaceted nature of denial as a mental state that is both individual and collective.

Conclusion

What does a psychosocial approach bring to an understanding of politics and of political debates? The examples in this chapter have demonstrated the importance of connecting policymakers and practitioners and the research community in a relational approach to understanding political phenomena and politics at all levels. Psychosocial approaches present challenges, not least because they question assumptions and go beneath the surface to explore epistemic differences between political positions. Such critiques examine what is assumed by researchers about what is involved in making knowledge and the need for critical reflection on 'business as usual' and habitual ways of undertaking research.

In exploring some examples under the umbrella term of politics as has been done in this chapter, distinct areas of concern emerge in psychosocial approaches. Firstly, the lived experiences of emotions and affective depths cut across different disciplines but are central to a psychosocial approach to politics. As Lynne Froggett's discussion of social class demonstrates, emotions and feelings are also constitutive of the lived experiences of class inequalities. Psychosocial approaches are distinctive in taking emotions like anxiety into account when conducting research. Emotion can be of different degrees of intensity, and it is only by engaging with the unconscious, especially the collective unconscious, that it is possible to understand the strong feelings of disgust and hatred that can lead to political conflict. Secondly, in exploring the possibilities of political action there is a focus upon diagnosing problems with what people, whether as individuals or in groups, are actually *doing* in order to meet policy goals whether in promoting social inclusion or addressing the issues of climate change in relation to sustainable practice, and what needs to be changed. Thirdly, there is the sociocultural context in which politics and political action are situated. This includes the values people hold and how these are expressed and how they inform action and how ideas are communicated and disseminated in relation to habits and routines as well as policy statements. The everyday is important to psychosocial approaches. As Karen Henwood argues, in the context of climate change and energy policies, what people do routinely in their everyday lives is what matters, even though energy policy can deliver understanding of the practices in which energy consumption is embedded. The puzzle is how the routine and the everyday are connected to or disconnected from the policies that are made and remade at a global level. Psychosocial approaches offer some routes into addressing this puzzle and the relationship between what people do and how energy policies might be lived and practised (Henwood, 2014). Lastly, there is a shared commitment to psychoanalytic theories and practices, for researchers who are intellectually dedicated to psychosocial approach and for therapists.

Questions

1 What role might the unconscious play in a critique of social exclusion and social class?

2 What is the collective unconscious? How might the concept be applied to the issue of climate change denial?

3 How can a psychosocial approach explain ways in which emotion and feelings are a part of politics and political action as well as personal life?

4 How convincing is the argument that differences are made and reproduced rather than preexisting and given?

chapter 10

Conclusion

This chapter:

1   Sums up the ideas that have been presented in this book in relation to what is distinctive about psychosocial approaches.
2   Reviews the idea of a genuine merging of the psychic and the social and shows how the psychosocial moves beyond the idea of separate spheres and of applying psychoanalytic theories to social phenomena (or social ideas to psychoanalytic encounters).
3   Suggests some of the particular strengths of the psychosocial.
4   Discusses the contradictions and tensions and the limitations of the psychosocial and the ways in which psychosocial studies are addressing them and opening up the possibilities for future work.

Introduction

Some of the ideas explored in this book in relation to both theory and practice are strongly informed by psychoanalytic approaches, whether to textual analysis or to social relations or the relationship between individuals with each other and to the social world they occupy. Therapeutic and clinical encounters have yielded new ideas about how to explore what is happening in the wider social and political world. The discussion has involved an exploration of ideas and methods and their connections and some key concepts and areas that have been important.

The field of psychosocial studies can be seen to embrace not only a wide range of disciplines and methods but also to provide new ideas about the distinctiveness of the approach. Psychosocial approaches demonstrate not only how the social operates within the psychic and how the psychic operates within the social, but also the interconnections between the two. In order to achieve a distinctively psychosocial approach it is necessary to go beyond the entrenched traditional dualisms of individual and social, agency and structure and autonomy and relationality.

One of the most important concepts that has been highlighted in the discussion in this book is that of the unconscious, which generates methods that can unravel its deeper processes and permit an engagement with largely unconscious realms of experience in both individual and social life. An understanding of the unconscious makes it possible to explore mutually constitutive relations between unconscious and social processes. It is the mutuality of these processes that makes them psychosocial.

In order to understand subjects and selves it is necessary to see the psychosocial as a variable and contingent construction that is used to represent people and social situations in the process of making an argument or account. This is a dynamic approach that also explores how we see ourselves and how others see us.

Psychosocial approaches, as this book has demonstrated, also focus upon large-scale phenomena by endeavouring to understand the workings of how the unconscious impacts on individuals' encounters with the social and in turn, that unconscious processes take place in particular sets of social circumstances. As has been argued throughout the book, the psychic and the social are each always present in the other.

The presence of the social in the consulting room in the clinical context as well as in the more explicitly social and sociological critiques of social relations and social forces also permits an exploration of inequalities and challenges the individualism and ethnocentricity with which psychoanalysis has been charged. Feelings and emotions are influenced and inflected by social inequalities as the discussion of social class and politics shows.

One of the most challenging aspects of psychosocial studies is avoiding a focus upon the individual or the social and focusing instead on the processes and how they are contingently used to represent people, mental constructs, social relations, and identities. This involves an engagement with the relationship between culture and subjectivity: that is, the way discursive regimes, social structures, ideologies, and social relations form and constitute us and how they somehow get 'inside' into the inner world and the intersubjective and the relationship individuals have to the social unconscious.

Psychosocial approaches demonstrate how we need new ways of thinking about emotion, memory, and investment as complex constitutive inner/outer meaning-making practices through the intersections of subjectification and agency. A psychosocial understanding shows how psychic life and the social are manifested in particular situations by moving beyond the polarized distinction between discursive and psychoanalytical perspectives.

The discussion in this book has drawn attention to and has attempted to cast an empirically informed theoretical light on the places where the internal and the external do not quite fit together and where individuals and groups struggle with their feelings and sense of self, their own and others' behaviours, including that of the state, and international movements and the discursive positions and social practices that are available to them. By combining the psychic and the social it becomes more possible to enter the liminal spaces between the inner and outer worlds as well as to develop new ways of accessing as well as understanding these spaces.

The main theoretical concepts employed in the psychosocial

This book has highlighted some of the key concepts that have been used in psychosocial work. Relationality is always in play in the exploration of how people's internalized feelings and sense of self relate to the social worlds they inhabit and that inhabit them. The dialectic between inside and outside at all levels is a distinctive feature of the psychosocial, which is why I think putting relationality at the start of the distinguishing features of the approach is so important. The psychosocial is also distinctive in its combination of psychic and social processes, which are interrelated.

Unconscious processes and the ways in which they might be said to operate at the level of the group and in wider cultural forms and social relations are key elements in psychosocial studies, although the unconscious can be read in a wide variety of ways. Although the psychosocial is not the same as the psychoanalytical, it has to be said that some of the concepts that have been most productively borrowed and reworked come from psychoanalytic approaches. This is not the only route that the psychosocial has travelled, however. As chapters 2 and 4 showed, there has also been significant development of sociological approaches and those of feminist theory and from within the field of gender studies. This is what makes the psychosocial interdisciplinary and transdisciplinary.

Another key feature of the psychosocial that is certainly not its unique preserve is the centrality of concepts of self, subjectivity, and identification, which afford a way to understand intergenerational transmission of identity and feelings through embodied practices and meanings, which combine unconscious and conscious elements and emotions and feelings and affect with social and cultural contexts.

Psychosocial studies aim to show how social categories, for example, which underpin inequalities based upon race, ethnicity, and gender, are lived and internalized. The production of unequal subjectivities, especially in relation to social policy discourses and welfare practices, for example, in the context of race, ethnicity, disability, and generation, is also part of the making of socioeconomic and cultural divisions.

Psychosocial approaches break down distinctions between 'inside' and 'outside' and gendered, racialized identifications focusing on the material body, its practices, and representations, as the site of assemblages of psychic and social realizations. The social worlds of organizations and institutions demonstrate, through the psychodynamics of group processes in the situated contexts of agencies operating, for example, in local government, health, and social care sectors and in education, which occupies a place in private and public systems of provision, that are all part of the relationship between inner and outer worlds.

Psychosocial approaches have been influential in focusing upon liminal spaces and in opening up possibilities for theorizing and conceptualizing unconscious intersubjective space, for example, as in Thomas Ogden's analytic third. In this book, we have looked at the particular phenomenon of 'being in the zone' as an example what cannot be thought and is beyond discourse thinking the 'extra discursive' and the 'unknown known'. The 'unknown known', like the experience of being in the zone, may have been unknown at particular points in a person's biography, but the concept suggests moments of recognition as well and the possibility of knowing. Psychosocial approaches present different interpretations, which are nonetheless characterized by an engagement with the unconscious, however expressed and with the emotional and affective properties of relationships, between people and between people and places and people and objects.

The questions posed at the start of the book in the Introduction suggested some of the paths that psychosocial approaches might take. The first particular question might have led to further questions rather than answers – why do people do what they do? In working towards some responses to this question the book has highlighted the need to be attentive to unconscious as well as conscious explanations and emotional as well as cognitive and rational understandings.

The second question was: how can the researcher access and understand psychosocial relationality – how do you get into those relational spaces as a researcher? A useful starting point is the psychoanalytical strategy of listening and of engaging with expressions of unconscious and irrational motivations and endeavouring to be attentive to the silences as well as what is said. Psychosocial approaches frequently deploy a variety of narrative approaches that will allow the interviewee to speak, rather than imposing a preexisting framework of interpretation. The researcher, like the analyst, has to recognize that even in the case of a subject's personal story the expression of psychic life and feelings is always also made within and through a social world that is part of that story. This discussion was framed by the need for the researcher to be careful about the process of interpretation and the necessity of about finding speaking for the subject of research.

Thirdly, there was a question that explicitly related to irrationality and asked: why are people attracted towards some things and people and repelled by others, often in irrational ways that may not be in their best interests? I have suggested that it is not only individuals whose actions are motivated and influenced by repressed feelings that give rise to contradictory outcomes. Repulsion may arise from unmet needs in other contexts, as do expressions of hatred and disgust. Anger can be expressed because of the inner fears and anxieties that have not been and cannot be contained. Anxiety in the management of risk can also lead to prejudice and the expression of seemingly irrational fears.

Fourthly, I asked the question: how useful are psychoanalytic concepts, across a range of encounters and different relations, outside as well as inside the clinical context? Engagement with this question led to discussion of the key psychoanalytic concepts that have most effectively and productively been translated into the wider field of social relations. Anxiety and fear lead to political exclusion and prejudice, and the social unconscious operates according to principles that are similar to those of the individual unconscious. Defence mechanisms are as central to political and social encounters and exchanges as they are within the individual psyche.

Lastly, this question was posed: how do emotions associated with intimate and personal life operate in the wider context of international politics? For example, how might hurt, affection, and hatred operate among and between nations as well as individuals? Emotions and feelings have more recently been put onto the agenda of social theory and social philosophy, partly as part of the affective turn, but also in light of the application of psychosocial approaches. The psychosocial moves beyond the addition of psychoanalytic or even psychological approaches to social theory and demonstrates the intersection and the relationality of the social and the psychic.

The psychosocial is not a meta theory, but it opens up a whole new way of looking at social and personal, relations, politics, representations, histories, and memories, which is only just starting and has enormous potential. This is the start, so I am going to pose some questions in the Conclusion too. Some of these questions relate to reviewing what has been presented in the book, but others involve looking at what other areas might productively be explored and what else psychosocial studies can address.

Questions

1   What are the distinguishing features of the psychosocial studies?
2   What does the psychosocial promise, and what reservations might you have about psychosocial methodologies?
3   How can these features inform new research? What issues are there in contemporary social life that might particularly lend themselves to a psychosocial approach?
4   In relation to the case studies and examples that have been cited in this book, what do you think is particular about a psychosocial approach, and what can the psychosocial bring to an exploration of issues as diverse as intimate relations and the politics of the environment?

Glossary

Affect refers to the two-way relationship whereby something or, more importantly in psychosocial studies, someone, affects and is affected by someone or something else. Sometimes we don't know why we feel differently or why we are picking up on emotions that another person is experiencing. Psychosocial approaches are concerned with finding out how this happens. Affect generates change through a process of transmission whereby change takes place. Psychosocial studies have reclaimed associations of affect with emotion and feeling and seek to explore the intersubjective relationality of affect. Affect remains characterized by dynamic processes that may operate at the level of the unconscious and are not confined to particular emotions but may include a range of feelings and transformations, which psychoanalytic and psychosocial approaches can address through exploring the spaces in between and the nature of the feelings that are transmitted between people.

Analysis can involve the deconstruction of a narrative or an account of experience or, more specifically in psychoanalysis, it is through analysis that the analyst attempts to enable the analysand to achieve some sense of resolution and harmony. The main objective of analysis in the clinical, therapeutic encounter is to enable the analysand to overcome the splits in the psyche that are perpetuated by unresolved primitive conflicts.

Bodies/Body. Although psychoanalytic theories are primarily concerned with interpretation of the activities of the psyche, which is allied to mental processes more than corporeal ones, the body matters enormously in psychoanalytic thinking. Freud sought neurophysical and biological correlations of psychic events (Freud, 1895a), and he went on to explore the connections between psychic and physical states in his studies of hysteria (1985b). Freud makes biologistic assumptions about the naturalness of women's bodies in particular, for example, in relation to sexuality.

Bodies and their internal imaging are central to the developmental stages of the infant; sexual drives emerge as the infant begins to distinguish its body from the mother's. Body parts are distinguished through oral, anal, phallic, and scopophilic stages and through eroticization. Imaging continues to make and remake the self, and, as Freud shows in the case of hypochondria, the subject's attitude to the body might not be congruent with its condition. Feminist critics have been able to use psychoanalysis to show that bodies (rather than 'the body') are psychosocial because there are only material bodies – not a universal phallocentric body. Bodies have sex, colour, dis/abilities. Within a psychoanalytic framework Jane Gallop (1988) sees bodies as sites of resistance that can challenge patriarchal silencing and invisibility, whereas Luce Irigaray (1985) sees female bodies as having enfleshed specific characteristics as well as being sites of inscription that are spoken through rather than produced.

Collective Unconscious is one of Carl Jung's best-known contributions, which has potential for development in psychosocial studies. The collective unconscious was seen to be expressed through archetypes, which are universal preexistent forms that are shared by a people or a society or even by humanity. The collective unconscious forms part of each individual's unconscious.

Containment refers to the process whereby projections or projective identifications from one person are held by another, especially in object relations and Kleinian psychoanalysis. For example, in infancy mothers have to contain infants' destructive impulses. In therapy the analyst contains the patient's projections. Containment is part of the process of establishing trust between people as well as making it possible for a person to own his or her own feelings of envy. The concept has wider applications to the understanding of social processes of holding and the establishment of trust in a huge variety of settings from care homes and classrooms to global conflict where political agencies, governments, and international bodies, entrusted with the responsibility and the capacity for containment either in relation of the subjects of a nation-state or of different agents in an international context, may be unable to contain projective identifications, which may be expressed in terms of violence and anger.

Countertransference, like **transference**, is an everyday experience that is enhanced in the clinical, analytic context. In everyday situations you might feel hostile towards someone even if you have never met that person before. A common response is to think that the feelings of hostility lie in one's own unconscious. Countertransference in the clinical situation is a phantasy relationship that can inhibit rational decision making and prevent the analyst offering the help that the patient needs. Analysts too experience these feelings. In Freud's work, the analyst who is the source of reason and fair play might feel this disruption in the relation as a resistance towards the patient and attribute these feelings to unconscious phantasies. Kleinians stress that the analyst becomes a container for the patient's projected feelings. The analyst, however, can work through the countertransference to explore what is happening in the patient's mind in an iterative process of analysis where the patient keeps checking that the analyst has contained or cared for his or her projections or if they are generating panic. Countertransference is specific and is not the same as emotion and involves intersubjective, unconscious to unconscious communication.

Death Drive is one of the two main groups of drives identified by Freud. The death drive is in opposition to the 'life' drive as developed by Freud in *The Pleasure Principle*. The death drive describes the basic human tendency to reduce tension. In its externalized form this drive can appear to be destructive and aggressive. Melanie Klein developed this Freudian drive to explain what she saw as the innate envy as the pure expression of the death drive in all infants.

Depressive Position is a term developed by Melanie Klein to explain both a stage in development and a state of mind. In the development of the infant, after resolving the paranoid schizoid position, the infant begins to introject split feelings. Consequently loving and destructive feelings and good and bad objects combine in a relationship. Depressive position also refers a state of mind, a way of experiencing the world or developmental stage in Kleinian psychoanalysis. The depressive position follows and largely resolves the paranoid schizoid position so that the infant is able to bring together and introject split feelings. For example, loving and destructive forces can be brought into a relationship with one another, along with the 'good' and 'bad' objects to which they have given rise. Thus love and hate can be connected and people come to realize that objects are ambivalent and not either ideal or evil as two distinct types. Depressive emotions follow as the subject experiences the damage done to objects through the subject's destructive impulses.

Defence includes defence mechanisms through which people defend themselves against inner feelings and emotions that they find troubling or difficult to deal with as well as a strategy used to protect oneself from what are perceived as attacks from others. Whereas the commonsense everyday view might be that we are defensive against the attacks of others, the psychoanalytic emphasis is upon the internal mechanisms of defence. Sometimes we are unable to confront the hostile feelings we have and can only cope with underlying anxieties through a process of therapy, which enable an individual to strengthen the ego sufficiently to confront these anxieties. Kleinian analysts argue that impulses of anxiety have to be confronted from the start. What matters for psychosocial approaches is the idea that defence mechanisms are internal and necessary, so disruptive and great is the potential force of the unconscious.

Desire is most powerfully associated with psychoanalysis, especially Lacanian psychoanalytic theory where the concept of desire is a signifying relation where desire finds fulfilment in the unconscious through hallucinatory and imaginary perceptions. Lacan argues that the phallus, imaginarily and symbolically, is the key signifier of desire in claims, which, however absurd some of them seem now, have generated significant feminist arguments about female desire, for example, in the work of Luce Irigaray who reverses Lacan's patriarchal interpretation and makes the case for female desire. It is worth mentioning the Lacanian interpretation because it offers some explanation of the psychosocial preferences for object relations theories and the need to be attentive to some of the implications of Lacanian psychoanalysis, whatever its strengths in engaging with symbolic and representational systems.

Discourse usually refers to social constructionist approaches in the social sciences, which are often linked to Michel Foucault's work. Foucault argued that that knowledge is produced (not discovered) through ideas, practices, images, words, and ways of being in the world, which shape who we are and what it is possible to think according to specific set of knowledge. Thus psychoanalysis would be a discourse that produces its own knowledge and set of meanings, rather than a way of uncovering what is actually happening and the reasons why people do what they do. Thus it seems antithetical to a psychosocial approach, although some of the methodological approaches of social psychologists do have a great deal to offer psychosocial approaches, for example, in the detailed analysis of texts and of what people say. The deconstructionism of a discursive approach is also useful in approaching the social context of subjective and intersubjective experiences.

Ego is the space in the mental apparatus occupied by consciousness and perception. The ego has the phenomenological status of a self – the 'I' who speaks. The ego has to deal with the troubling and disruptive forces of the id and exercise repression over its excess. In object relations approaches the ego is made through the internalization of lost objects but retains the idea of a stabilizing element within the constitution of the self – a psychosocial space and energy between the tumultuous forces of the id and the constraints of the superego.

Emotions are commonly classified as subjective affective states that have been the subject of psychological more than sociological analyses. Some writers elide emotion with feelings, but there are distinctions that can be made, and the two terms are not entirely interchangeable (see *feelings*). Psychosocial approaches stress the relationality of emotions and the experience of emotion as intersubjective. Emotions and collective emotions are constitutive of social worlds and collective expressions as well as part of subjective experience. Increasingly emotions have been incorporated into exploration of social phenomena, including the collective expression of hatred, fear, and anxiety as well as compassion and sympathy.

Feelings are not limited to emotions; feelings involve being moved and touched in some way. Feelings occur in mind and body and involve the conversion of emotion and affect into something that can be symbolized. Words can cause and express feelings. Feelings are corporeal and physical with embodied as well as emotional aspects. Feelings can be revelatory and can be life changing as well as routine. Feeling is also what makes us human and contemporary society exhorts people to be 'in touch with their feelings', which are not simply set in opposition to rational thinking, for example, as in traditional dualisms, which set emotion against reason. To be unfeeling is more negative than unemotional. To be unfeeling is to lack compassion or humanity, whereas lack of emotion could be lacking the capacity for expression and perhaps overcontrolled. Feelings can be known and represented or symbolized and motivate action.

Gaze. The gaze is an aspect of spectatorship through which privileges and inequalities are made and reinstated through the process of looking and being looked at. Laura Mulvey developed the psychoanalytic concept in the context of film studies to explain the power geometries involved in the process of looking and being looked at in mainstream cinema. Mulvey argued that the male gaze was privileged, and women, for example, always looked at themselves through male eyes. Mulvey has agreed that her initial argument was exaggerated, but later developments of the female gaze and the democratic gaze have demonstrated the usefulness of a concept that brings together what is a psychosocial process in the space between inner worlds of perception and social worlds of inequalities.

Id is the name given by Freud to the area of the mind and of mental life that is home to drives and the repressed unconscious. Thus the id involves the dynamic interplay of unconscious desires and drives including the libido and generates the tensions and pressures of psychic life, which the ego endeavours to resolve.

Identification refers to the process whereby we take in what is outside us. For example, we absorb information from what we see and hear and form different experiences in the world through a constant dialogue between the inner world of the mind and the world outside it. Psychoanalysis suggests that there are particular mechanisms through which this taking in of outside material happens and that external objects, perceptions, and ideas become part of the mind and of the unconscious. Thus self and other, the inside and the outside, are always entangled. Identification is also a constructive process whereby the self can change. For Freud identifications were most powerfully gendered: boys with their fathers in the hope of resolution to the conflicts of childhood. Lacan saw identification as the taking in of representations and thus the process as imaginary, although the self is still the sum of the subject's identifications. Jessica Benjamin sees identification as a form of relationship, for example, through loving identifications, such as the love children have for their parents, whether female or male. Children are able to remake themselves according to their aspirational identification with others, especially their parents. Benjamin's version is more complex and one that has considerable resonance in contemporary psychosocial work.

Imaginary in psychoanalytic theory is not about the richness of the imagination; it is a strategy adopted by the infant to identify with images so that the ego starts to take form through mental identifications. The imaginary begins in the pre-Oedipal stage with the mirror phase as the point at which the infant appears to recognize itself. Throughout the life course the imaginary operates to suggest that wholeness and unity are possible. This unity appears to resolve the fragmentation that precedes it. According to Lacan, the imaginary too is an illusion of unity, which persists throughout adult life and informs the desire to be whole and to achieve what are utopian dreams of wholeness and unity. Luce Irigaray argues for a female imaginary, which contra Lacan is a period of corporeal female expression and of speaking the body in a presymbolic relationship between mother and child, which is outside the patriarchal law of the father.

Internalization is a concept that draws upon the work of US sociologist Talcott Parsons, who uses the Freudian concept of the ego. Internalization is the psychological mechanism whereby personality traits become constituent elements of the ego and the ego's action. Internalization is the process through which people become and take into themselves the norms and values of the society in which they live. Internalization is a unified system of personality and cultural values so that people's personal values and personalities conform to the society. Within Parsons's functionalist sociology the process works and people conform, or there might be some breakdown that would constitute deviancy and require repair.

Interpellation (or hailing) is the term Althusser used to explain the way in which subjects are recruited into subject positions by recognizing themselves – 'yes, that's me'. The process that takes place at the level of the unconscious is akin to hearing someone calling out your name and turning round to respond, thinking 'That's me'. The concept has been criticized because it is seen to assume a self who is already there before being interpellated so that it does not explain the process through which subjects are made, just how they recognize themselves. It has, however, been immensely influential, not least in advertising where consumers are constantly being hailed as the sort of person who would buy a particular product. It offers a really useful and particularly resonant explanation of the moment of recognition or misrecognition, however.

Interpretation is both important in psychoanalysis and very controversial. Interpretation is central to psychosocial approaches and to the legacy of psychoanalysis. Interpretation is traditionally seen as the part of analysis where the therapist explains to the patient the meaning of his or her words and actions – of what the 'talking cure' reveals – and makes sense of the expression of unconscious feelings that have emerged in therapy. This process is central to psychoanalysis, which, following Freud, has claimed that analysis can uncover the truth. 'Psychoanalysis itself might be defined in terms of it as the bringing out of the latent meaning of given material' (Laplanche and Pontalis, 1973:227). Interpretation in this context depends upon an unconscious. Alternative views, for example, developed in object relations, suggest that rather than interpreting the feelings of the analysand, the therapist might 'hold' or contain them. Interpretation might involve suggestions or inferences that the therapist reads into what is said in ways that cannot ultimately be verified or proved. Kleinian approaches rely heavily on primitive defence mechanisms, which stress that early relationships show how actual human feelings and experiences are different from texts. All psychoanalytic approaches assume that meanings lie beneath the surface and can be understood through the process of analysis, whatever degree of veracity and reliability is accorded to the analyst in the process. A productive, sensitive cooperative process of interpretation can benefit individuals and lead to change.

Intersectionality has become an important concept that refers to a theoretical approach that sees different social forces, such as those that shape inequalities of race, ethnicity, disability, and gender as intersecting and cutting across and into each other rather than an additive model that sees such systems superimposing one on another.

Intersubjectivity is used in psychosocial approaches especially to demonstrate relationality. Intersubjectivity means the capacity of the subject to represent another person as a subject in a process of mutual recognition. This is more than a relationship among people because intersubjectivity involves unconscious knowledge and unconscious connections and representations.

Introjection describes the opposite process to projection and refers to the way the subject of phantasy 'takes into itself' objects from the outside world and henceforth preserves them inside the self. Introjection provides a way of understanding how the projections of others can be assimilated into the self; for example, heterosexual male phantasies can be taken in by women. In *Mourning and Melancholia* (1917) Freud noted how a loved object is taken into the subject when the object is lost through death or absence so that if introjection is to take place, the capacity to symbolize experience has to be developed as a way of coping with separation and loss. Melanie Klein went on to link the process of introjection to the emergence of the depressive position. The subject can identify with others by introjecting them so that introjection and identification are also connected.

Jouissance describes heights of pleasure, and it is difficult to translate into English. Psychoanalytically jouissance is set in opposition to 'lack'. Jouissance can be pre-Oedipal or Oedipal with the latter being heavily inflected by male libido, which has led to feminist uses of the concept to refer to female pleasure, which is outside symbolic systems and belongs more in the pre-Oedipal relationship. Julia Kristeva (1982) assigns joiussance to that element of women which exceeds Oedipal laws and patriarchal, phallic symbolic systems. Helene Cixous (1980) presents a critique of the paternal Oedipal jouissance and expresses the alternative jouissance outside the boundaries of heterosexuality. Luce Irigaray has used the idea more frequently as part of the pre-Oedipal relationship, which generates creativity outside that is based in the maternal body as it relates to the child. Jouissance has since been used to express heightened pleasure that goes beyond discourse, as, for example, in the experience of 'being in the zone'.

Life Drive is more or less the opposite of the death drive in that this drive is directed towards self-preservation, pleasure, and unity. The life drive is made up of the ego and sexual drives in psychoanalytic thought.

Narcissism is the love of one's own image. It is based on Ovid's story of the young man who falls in love with his own reflection in *Metamorphoses* and is punished by being condemned to gaze at his own reflection in water, leading to his untimely death. Narcissism is central to the formation of the ego in psychoanalysis, although there are different approaches. Freud used the term to account for different libidinal states and linked narcissism to identification investments in others. Lacan reversed Freud's theory of narcissism, especially in relation to the making of the self through identification with others. Thus Freud's 'primary narcissism' remains a normal developmental phase when the infant has no understanding of anything outside itself and focuses entirely upon itself, whereas secondary narcissism is a more pathological phenomenon for Lacan. Narcissism is based on an investment of sexual energy in the self, but this self is fragile and starved of love and thus needs constant reassurance. The fragility of the self leads to defensive mechanisms in relationships with other people and the avoidance of dependency and intimacy. Narcissism can be applied to the wider society as well as the individual.

Neoliberalism is a term used to describe the form of government associated with free markets and democratic states that are based on the idea their citizens are self-regulating rational individuals. The form of governance has been linked to Thatcherite market economics in the UK and Reagan's approach in the US. Neoliberalism places considerable emphasis upon freedom of the individual and the matter of choice and responsibility. Following the breakup of the former USSR and the demise of communist regimes in much of the world, this form of governance was seen to have become universal. The extent to which neoliberalism is noninterventionist and permits freedom equally to all its citizens has been called into question as a result of twenty-first-century anxieties about terrorism and increased risks. Economic recession has also led to a lack of confidence in the operation of the free market and especially unregulated banking and investment services. For a discussion of neoliberalism and the psychosocial, see the April 2014 Special Section Neo Liberalism in *Psychoanalysis and Culture Special Section* (vol. 19, issue 1, pp. 1–51).

Object refers to the external object of internal drives. According to Freud, the object depends upon the individual's own experience, but there are particularly significant objects, which are present in infancy, notably the mother and the father. As the child develops, it becomes possible to experience whole objects of thought, not just the parts of the person, like the mother's breast. An object in its entirety is still made up of different parts that may be contradictory, although the object is still experienced as whole. For object relations theorists following Klein, the mind comprises representations of internalized objects.

Object Relations is a branch of psychoanalysis, initially developed in Britain, which takes the relation between mother and child in the first year of life as its primary field of study. The theory assumes that from birth the infant engages in formative relations with objects that are perceived as separate from itself. These 'objects' are entities that could be whole persons – the mother or parts of the body, such as the breast – or mental representations. Object relations privileges the maternal object as central to the development of the infant self. The mother–child dyad is characterized by preverbal communication. Melanie Klein, working with children in the late 1920s, transformed Freud's Oedipal drama. Klein describes the infant as inundated by phantasies of aggression against the mother's body, which in turn provoke persecutory phantasies of retaliation, guilt, and desire to make reparation.

Oedipal Complex is an important Freudian conceptualization that was inspired by Sophocles's play Oedipus Rex, first performed in fifth-century BCE Athens. The play tells the story of Oedipus who is condemned by the Oracle to kill his father and marry his mother. In spite of his attempts to avoid this fate, he unknowingly kills his father and marries his mother. In Sophocles's play it is the inevitable fate decreed by the gods, whereas in Freud this is translated into the infant's desire to kill his father and marry his mother. In fifth-century Athens the play was part of a cultural proscription against incest; in psychoanalysis it becomes the incest taboo that has to regulate unconscious desires.

Paranoid Schizoid Position is a characteristic of early infant development, according to Melanie Klein. The position is marked by a constellation of fears, anxieties, defences, and internal and external objects. When the primitive ego is threatened by the death drive, the defence mechanism is activated by the anxiety that the infant experiences. The death drive is projected onto the object, which is the breast at this stage, which is already split into the good and bad breast. Paranoid schizoid mental states persist throughout life and remain characterized by splitting of both self and object into good and bad.

Phallocentric is usually used as a criticism of Lacan's claims that the phallus is the key signifier of meaning in language and all symbolic systems. Lacan argues that this is not fixed or biological, but the counter claim that Lacan's approach is phallocentric suggests that it is. The phallus is not symbolic; it relates to male power and ignores the importance of mothers and of any female imaginary. The phallus is a penis by any other name and is a somewhat crude assertion of patriarchal power, symbolic and material, although Lacan's ideas about the symbolic power of the phallus as a signifier of meaning have been used productively by feminist psychoanalytic theorists like Juliet Mitchell to demonstrate how patriarchy works, rather than seeking to justify it.

Phantasy is the stuff of the unconscious, an important element in the relationship between inner and outer worlds, which occupies the space of the unconscious. Transactions between these private, mental inner worlds and public external worlds are accessible through psychoanalytic theories of the unconscious. Phantasy is thus of considerable interest to psychosocial approaches because phantasies occupy this liminal, relational space in between. Freud first writes of phantasies as daydreams. Daydreams are like nocturnal dreams but they are subject to conscious processes of 'secondary elaboration' as well as drawing upon childhood memories (Freud, 1900:492). Freud believed that cultural forms such as art represent more or less disguised phantasies. Phantasy may also provide a route out of an unacceptable reality. Phantasy has different modes: 'conscious phantasies or day-dreams, unconscious phantasies like those uncovered by analysis as the structures underlying a manifest content, and primal phantasies' (Laplanche and Pontalis, 1973:173). For Freud phantasies were always triggered by the active unconscious and its responses to frustration. The concept has been developed in different ways and plays a large part in Kleinian theory where phantasies are what happens in the mind or the psyche: they are not particular sorts of mental activity; they are happening all the time. Sometimes it is spelled 'fantasy', often in the case of conscious phantasies, which are not illusory because we are aware, for example, that we are daydreaming about what might be even though we know it isn't.

Pleasure Principle refers to Freud's idea that psychic life is governed by drives and the desire to relieve tension. Feelings of pleasure result so that the unconscious works according to the primary process of pursuing pleasure and avoiding pain. The pleasure principle operates in opposition to the reality principle.

Projection is seen as a defence mechanism that involves a process whereby the subject, specifically the subject's ego in Freud (1896), disowns unacceptable impulses by attributing them to someone else so that the intolerable feelings are then seen as coming from the other person. The idea is less developed in Lacan, although he locates projection in the imaginary in order to show how parts of the subject can be transferred from the inside to the outside. More significantly projection has been developed by Kleinian object relations where it plays a crucial role in the mother–child relationship. The infant's phantasized experiences and innate aggression are expressed towards the mother through projection. Wilfred Bion (1967), following Klein, stresses the importance of the intersubjective mother-infant relationship. Bion distinguishes between communicative projection where the mother returns the baby's projection in a palatable form and a pathological projection where the mother cannot tolerate the baby's projection so the baby is forced to persist in its efforts to expel negative feelings.

Psychodynamic is a term which is used to describe the operation of active unconscious forces, which have to be repressed in order to keep them out of consciousness. Psychodynamic theory is a description of an approach that embraces the idea of the unconscious even if the approach is not explicitly psychoanalytic.

Real is the place where the imaginary and the symbolic emerge in Lacanian psy- choanalysis. The real cannot be expressed in words: it is the abyss from which the subject tries to escape into symbolization. Žižek describes the real as that which sticks, like something you have trodden in and that you cannot get off your shoe.

Reality Principle is seen as linked to rationality and order as a characteristic of the ego through the process of organizing and regulating the flow of energy from the id and the unconscious in order to permit the pleasure principle to achieve its aims within the confines of what the external world and the superego can tolerate.

Regression involves the tendency to revert to earlier stages of development, perhaps in seeking the security of childhood practices and dependencies, either in phantasy or more extremely in a regression to serious dependence and narcis- sism. Regression in analysis could be productive through revisiting experiences of earlier life and thus working with the analyst to repair them.

Resistance in psychoanalysis and in psychosocial accounts is more complex and contradictory than the use of the term in everyday language or in politics suggests. Political resistance, especially to oppressive regimes, has very positive connotation, whereas resistance in psychoanalytic thought raises questions about what is being resisted. Resistance may be to internal forces and might be resistance to the process of therapy or analysis. For example, when an analysand refuses to take part in free association, this can indicate to the analyst that there is something important going on and there needs to be further discussion to find out where the resistance is coming from. Although this sense of resistance is somewhat dif- ferent from other uses and understandings, the concept has wider application, for example, in exploring the social unconscious forces in play when there is collective resistance to change or to particular interventions.

Social Unconscious is an emerging conceptualization in psychosocial studies that is used to explore what can be understood as a collective unconscious of shared repressed desires and what can be called 'baggage'. For example, Jessica Benjamin uses the example of women who 'carry a lot of things that are not individual that are what you might call transpersonal in our political unconscious' (in Layton et al., 2006:182). The collective unconscious operates like the unconscious in psycho- analysis but involves a new relationality between personal and social lives.

Splitting refers initially in Freud's work to the split subject who is never quite complete because of the division between the conscious mind and the uncon- scious. Klein argued that the subject is formed out of the opposing drives of the life and the death force and develops strategies to cope with this fragmenta-tion notably through split objects, that is, the internalized, phantasized repre-sentations of external people and bodies. For Klein, splitting starts in infancy when the baby uses projection and splitting to deal with the turmoil of these opposing drives. For Klein, unlike Freud, it is not repression that is the first line of defence but splitting, which is the mechanism we use from the start to try to deal with the conflicting inborn drives. This produces a duality of objects in the infant's mind so that the mother's breast, which is a single object, is split into two – the good breast, which responds to the baby's needs and the bad breast, which doesn't. The baby adopts the paranoid schizoid position. Develop-ment into adulthood involves adopting more sophisticated strategies, but com-plete resolution and total unity are never possible. Klein stresses the split between the opposing life and death drives. Throughout life, and in therapy, the task is to endeavour to achieve greater integration, whilst acknowledging and being attentive to the danger of becoming even more split and fragmented. Splitting is the mechanism that is central to Klein's understanding of how con-flicts are managed. Firstly, the infant projects destructive and good impulses on to an external object; secondly, that object is split into good and bad; and lastly, the introjection of those objects forms a split ego-object within the psyche. Splitting and projection are connected from the start. The ego is at the centre of the splitting process.

Subject. The idea of the subject suggests a singular, unitary, self-reflective being and is often associated with the philosophy of René Descartes and with Enlight-enment humanism and rationality, which privileged the human over the divine. The subject is the agent and instigator of thought and action but also subjected to social forces such as the state. For example, people are subjects of the state. Jacques Lacan argued that the subject is constituted, not constituent, an effect of structures not their cause. Structuralist and poststructuralist approaches have challenged the humanist unitary subject and challenged the idea of an autonomous subject and stressed that subjects are ideological rather than there being an inalienable 'self'. Feminist critics have questioned the gendered assumptions of the subject and, for example, Luce Irigaray has argued that there is a sexually specific subject and that female subjectivity has been oppressed and subsumed by the so-called universality of the phallic subject. Irigaray thus seeks to provide a conceptual, linguistic, and erotic space for the articulation of female subjectivity (1985).

Sublimation is the transformation or diversion of drives into other activities that are more culturally, socially, and morally acceptable. Thus it is a defence mechanism through which sublimation dislodges the object and 'sublimes' it into a fixed position. Julia Kristeva defines sublimation as 'the possibility of naming the pre-nominal, the pre-oedipal' (Kristeva, 1982:11) when the infant symbolizes the pre-Oedipal mother at the margins of language. Slajov Žižek develops sublimation as 'the sublime object of ideology' (Žižek, 1989) in order to explain the role of ideology in capitalist societies.

Superego refers to the third component of Freud's inner world. The superego develops out of the Oedipus complex as the internalization of the prohibition against incest and the (male) child's repressed hatred of the father who has imposed this law. The superego is thus a kind of internal judge and contains some aspirational as well as critical phantasies, although its role is largely to regulate desires and phantasies.

Symbolic in the Lacanian order is in tension with the imaginary and intrudes upon its unity and illusion of wholeness. On entry to the symbolic the infant becomes subject to the structures of language, thus making communication possible. The powers of communication and entry into the symbolic order liberate the infant but also offer constraints because the infant then has to be regulated by an outside law – the law of the father, according to Lacan.

Transference is part of the process of analysis that has received a great deal of attention in recent work, especially that which can be categorized as psychosocial. In Freud's work transference was seen a process of displacement that Freud expressed in his 1905 Dora case study as copies of impulses and phantasies, which emerge during the process of analysis and which are then transferred from the original person to whom they relate in the analysand's life onto the analyst. The transference is experienced as something new, but, without the person knowing, it is actually a repetition of an earlier experience – just transferred onto a new person, the analyst. In everyday life transference is unlikely to be encouraged, but in analysis it can be very productive. For Klein transference became a process in which current emotions were projected into the relationship with the analyst as a means of dealing within anxiety. Because the analyst is not simply a neutral listener who then interprets the analysand's story, transference is linked to containment because for Klein the analyst has to become a mirror to the analysand.

Unconscious. The unconscious is an important – probably the most important – concept in psychoanalytical thinking, especially as the distinguishing feature of Freudian approaches. The unconscious is something very different from conscious awareness or preconscious states: a parallel state to consciousness with its own rules and laws. It has an energy of its own, which is nothing like conscious or subconscious states, although there are points of connection. The unconscious can suddenly interrupt consciousness, for example, in jokes or 'Freudian slips' when people say the wrong word, a word that reveals the wishes or desires that have been repressed from the conscious mind into the unconscious. Dreams also give expression to unconscious forces and repressed desires, albeit in a language of their own. However different the unconscious may be, for Freud the unconscious can be known and can affect our actions, collectively as well as individually.

References

Adorno, T. W. (1938) 'On the Fetish Character in Music and the Repression of Listening' in T. W. Adorno (2001) *Problems of Moral Philosophy*, trans Rodney Livingstone, Stanford, Stanford University Press, pp: 29–60.

Adorno, T. W. (2001a) *Problems of Moral Philosophy*, trans Rodney Livingstone, Stanford, Stanford University Press.

Adorno, T. W. (2001b) *The Culture Industry: Selected Essays on Mass Culture*, New York and London, Routledge.

Adorno, T. W. and Horkheimer (1950) *The Authoritarian Personality*, New York, Harper and Row.

Ahmed, S. (2004a) Affective economies. *Social Text*, 22 (2) pp. 117–139.

Ahmed, S. (2004b) *The Cultural Politics of Emotion*, New York, Routledge.

Ahmed, S. (2010) *The Promise of Happiness*, Durham CA, Duke University Press.

Ainslie, R. (2013) Intervention strategies for addressing collective trauma: Healing communities ravaged by racial strife. *Psychoanalysis, Culture and Society*, 18 pp: 140–152.

Alford, F. (2011, July 5) Is the Holocaust traumatic? *2011 Journal of Psychosocial Studies*, 2 pp: 1–22.

Althusser, L. (1971) *Lenin and Philosophy and Other Essays*, London, New Left Books.

Altman, N. and Davies, J. (2002) Out of the blue: Reflections on a shared trauma. *Psychoanalytic Dialogues*, 12 (3) pp: 359–360.

Auestad, L. (2012a) (ed) *Psychoanalysis and Politics*, London: Karnac.

Auestad, L. (2012b) 'Subjectivity and Absence: Prejudice as a Psychosocial Theme' in Lene Auestad (ed) *Psychoanalysis and Politics. Exclusion and the Politics of Representation*, Karnac Books, pp: 29–42.

Auestad, L. (2014) 'Idealised Sameness and Orchestrated Hatred – Extreme and Mainstream Nationalism in Norway' in Lene Auestad (ed) *Nationalism and the Body Politic: Psychoanalysis and the Rise of Ethnocentrism and Xenophobia*, London, Karnac Books, pp: 41–62.

Bainbridge, C., Radstone, S., Rustin, M. and Yates, C. (2007) (eds) *Culture and the Unconscious*, Basingstoke, Palgrave MacMillan.

Banks, M. (2014, February 14) 'Being in the zone' of cultural work, culture unbound. *Journal of Cultural Research*, 6 pp: 241–262.

Barrett, M. (1991) *The Politics of Truth, from Marx to Foucault*, Cambridge, Polity.

Bauman, Z. (1989) *Modernity and the Holocaust*, Cambridge, Polity.

Bauman, Z. (1991) *Modernity and Ambivalence*, Cambridge, Polity.

Bauman, Z. (1992) *Mortality, Immortality and Other Life Strategies*, Cambridge, Polity.

Bauman, Z. (2001) *Liquid Love*, Cambridge, Polity.

Beck, U. (1992) *Risk Society: Towards a New Modernity*, London, Sage, in conjunction with *Theory, Culture and Society*.

Beck, U. and Beck-Gernsheim, E. (1995) *The Normal Chaos of Love*, Cambridge, Polity.

Beck, U. and Beck-Gernsheim, E. (2002) *Individualization*, London, Sage.

Beck-Gernsheim, E. (2002) *Reinventing the Family: In Search of New Lifestyles*, Cambridge, Polity.

Bellah, R. (1996) *The House Divided*, Oakland, CA, University of California Press.

Benjamin, J. (1988) *The Bonds of Love: Psychoanalysis, Feminism and the Problem of Domination*, London, Virago.

Benjamin, J. (1995) *Like Subjects, Love Objects*, New Haven, CT and London, Yale University Press.

Bennett, J. (2010) *Vibrant Matter: A Political Ecology of Things*, Durham, NC, Duke University Press.

Berger, J. (1972) *Ways of Seeing*, Hammondsworth, Penguin.

Berger, J. (1984) *And in Our Faces, My Heart Brief as Photos*, London, Writers and Readers.

Berlant, L. (2000) 'The Subject of True Feeling: Pain, Privacy and Politics' in S. Ahmed, J. Kilby, C. Lury, M. McNeil, and B. Skeggs (eds) *Transformations: Thinking through Feminism*, London, Routledge, pp: 33–47.

Berlant, L. (2003) Critical inquiry, affirmative culture. *Critical Inquiry*, 30 (2) pp: 445–451.

Berlant, L. (2012) Affect Is the New Trauma, *Minnesota Review*, ns, 71–72.

Betterton, R. (1987) *Looking On: Images of Femininity in the Visual Arts and Media*, London, Pandora.

Billig, M. (1997) The dialogue unconscious: Psychoanalysis, discursive psychology and the nature of repression. *British Journal of Social Psychology*, 36 pp: 139–159.

Bion, W. (1967) *Second Thoughts*, London, Heinemann, pp: 43–109.

Bion, W. ([1962]1991) *Learning from Experience*, London, Karnac Books.

Bion, W. ([1961]2004) *Experiences in Groups and Other Papers*, London, Taylor and Francis.

Bitz (2014) www.open.ac.uk/ccig/dialogues/blogs/what-is-bitz (Last accessed April 26th, 2014).

Bitz film (2014) http://vimeo.com/91256618 (Last accessed April 26th, 2014).

Bollas, C. (1987) *The Shadow of the Object*, London, Free Association Books.

Bollas, C. (1995) *Being a Character: Psychoanalysis and Personal Experience*, London, Routledge.

Borossa, J. (2012) 'The Extension of Psychoanalysis: Colonialism, Post Colonialism and Hospitality' in Lene Auestadt (ed) *Psychoanalysis and Politics*, London, Karnac.

Bourdieu, P. (1994) *Distinction: A Social Critique of the Judgement of Taste*, trans R. Nice, Cambridge, MA, Harvard University Press.

Braidotti, R. (1994) *Nomadic Subjects: Embodiment and Sexual Difference in Contemporary Feminist Theory*, New York, Columbia University Press.

Brennan, T. (1993) *History after Lacan: Opening Out: Feminism for Today*, London and New York, Routledge.

Brennan, T. (2004) *The Transmission of Affect*, Ithaca, NY, Cornell University Press.

Brown, J. C. (2006) *A Psychosocial Approach to Love and Intimacy*, Basingstoke, Palgrave.

Brown, J. (2010) Life Begins At? Psychological Reflections on Mental Health and Maturity' in Judith Burnett (ed) *Contemporary Adulthood: Calendars, Cartographies and Constructions*, Basingstoke, GB, Palgrave Macmillan, pp: 120–130.

Brown, J. C. (2012), 'The Therapeutic Use of Self' in S. Tee, J. Brown and D. Carpenter (eds) *Handbook of Mental Health Nursing*, London, Hodder, pp: 20–54.

Brown, S. and Stenner, P. (2009) *Psychology without Foundations: History, Philosophy and Psychosocial Theory*, London, Sage.

Buckner, S. (2005) Taking the debate on reflexivity further: Psychodynamic team analysis of a BNIM interview. *Journal of Social Work Practice*, 19 (1) pp: 59–72.

Butler, J. (1990) *Gender Trouble: Feminism and the Subversion of Identity*, London, Routledge.

Butler, J. (1993) *Bodies That Matter: On the Discursive Limits of Sex*, London, Routledge.

Butler, J. (1997) *The Psychic Life of Power, Theories in Subjection*, Stanford, Stanford University Press.

Butler, J. (2000). *Antigone's Claim: Kinship between Life and Death*. New York, Columbia University Press.

Butler, J. (2005) *Giving an Account of Oneself*, New York, Fordham University Press.

Butler, J., Laclau, E., & Žižek, S. (2000) *Contingency, Hegemony, Universality: Contemporary Dialogues on the Left*, London, New York, Verso.

Byford, J. (2008). Denial and Repression of Antisemitism: Post-Communist Remembrance of the Serbian Bishop Nikolaj Velimirovic, Budapest and New York, CEU Press.

Byford, J. (2013). The Semlin Judenlager in Belgrade: A Contested Memory. *Discussion Papers*, vol. 3, The Holocaust and the United Nations Outreach Programme, available at www.un.org/en/holocaustremembrance/docs/paper20.shtml (Last accessed June 1st, 2014).

Cambridge Facebook Diversity (2014) www.facebook.com/facebookdiversity (Last accessed March 24th 2014).

Canadian Occupational Health (2014) www.ccohs.ca/oshanswers/psychosocial/mentalhealth_risk.html (Last accessed June 2nd, 2014).

Carry, J. and Kwinter, S (1992) (eds) *Zone 6: Incorporations*, New York, Zone Books.

Caruth, C. (1995) *Trauma: Explorations in Memory*, Baltimore, John Hopkins University Press.

Chamberlayne, P., Bornat, J. and Wengraf, T. (2000) (eds) *The Turn to Biographical Methods in Social Science: Comparative Issues and Examples*, London, Routledge.

Chamberlayne, P., Rustin, M. and Wengraf, T. (2012) (eds) *Biography and Social Exclusion in Europe*, Bristol, Policy Press.

Chancer, L. and Andrews, J. (2014) (eds) *The Unhappy Divorce of Sociology and Psychoanalysis*, New York and London, Palgrave, MacMillan.

Chevalley, A. and Woodward, K. (2014) *Le Temps et Le Sport*, Lausanne, Olympic Museum.

Chodorow, N. (1978) *The Reproduction of Mothering: Psychoanalysis and the Sociology of a Gender*, Berkeley, University of California Press.

Chodorow, N. (1999) 'Toward a Relational Individualism' in S. A. Mitchell and L. Aron (eds) *Relational Psychoanalysis: The Emergence of a Tradition*, Hillsdale, NJ, The Analytic Press, pp: 109–129.

Cixous, H. (1985[1980]) 'The Laugh of Medusa', trans Keith Cohen and Paula Cohen, in E. Marks and I. de Courtviron (eds) *New French Feminisms: An Anthology*, Brighton Harvester Press, pp: 245–264.

Clarke, S. (2006) Theory and practice: Psychoanalytic sociology as psycho-social studies. *Sociology*, 40 (6) pp: 1153–1169.

Clarke, S. and Hoggett, P. (2009) *Researching Beneath the Surface. Psycho-social Research Methods in Practice* (Psychosocial Studies Series), London, Karnac Books.

Clough, P. T. (1994) *Feminist Thought: Desire, Power and Academic Discourse*, London, Basil Blackwell.

Clough, P.T. (2008a) The affective turn: Political economy, biomedia and bodies. *Theory, Culture and Society*, 25 (1) pp: 22–62.

Clough, P.T. (2008b) (De) coding the subject-in-affect. *Subjectivity*, 23 pp: 140–153.

Clough, P. T. (2009, February) The new empiricism: Affect and sociological method, *European Journal of Social Theory*, 12 pp: 43–61.

Clough, P. T. and Halley, J. (2008) *The Affective Turn*, Durham, NC, Duke University Press.

Coleman, R. (2013) *The Becoming of Bodies: Girls, Images, Experience*, Manchester, Manchester University Press.

Coleman, S. (2006) How the other half votes. Big Brother viewers and the 2005 General Election. *International Journal of Cultural Studies*, 9 (4) p: 457.

Cooley, C.H. ([1902]1964) *Human Nature and the Social Order*, New York, Charles Scribner's Sons.

Cooper, A.L. (2012) *Dario Argento*, Champaign, IL, University of Illinois Press.

Coward, R. and Ellis, J. (1977) *Language and Materialism: Developments in Semiology and the Theory of the Subject*, London, Routledge and Kegan Paul.

Craib, I. (1995) Some comments on the sociology of emotions. *Sociology*, 29 (1) pp: 151–158.

Craib, I. (1998) *Experiencing Identity*, London, Sage.

Craib, I. (2001) *Psychoanalysis: A Critical Introduction*, Cambridge, Polity.

Csikszentmihalyi, M. (1975) *Beyond Boredom and Anxiety: Experiencing Flow in Everyday Life*, New York, Basic Books.

Csikszentmihalyi, M. (1997) *Finding Flow: The Psychology of Engagement with Everyday Life*, New York, Basic Books.

Csikszentmihalyi, M. (2003) *Good Business: Leadership, Flow and the Making of Meaning*, London, Hodder and Stoughton.

Danto, E. A. (1998) The Ambulatorium: Freud's free clinic in Vienna. *International Journal of Psychoanalysis*, 79 pp: 287–300.

Danto, E. A. (1999) The Berlin Polyklinik: Psychoanalytic innovation in Weimar Germany. *Journal of American Psychoanalytic Association*, 47 (4) pp: 1269–1292.

Dawkins, R. ([1976]2006) *The Selfish Gene*, 30th anniversary edition, Oxford, Oxford University Press.

Deleuze, G. (1988) *Spinoza: Practical Philosophy*, trans R. Hurley San Francisco, CA, City Lights Books.

Deleuze, G. (1992) 'Ethology, Spinoza and Us' in J. Carry and S Kwinter (eds) *Incorporations*, New York, Zone Books, pp: 625–633.

Deleuze, G. and Guattari, F. (1977) Anti-Oedipus: Capitalism and Schizophrenia, trans R. Hurley, M. Seem and H.R. Lowe, New York, Viking Press.

Dinnerstein, D. (1976) *The Mermaid and the Minotaur: Sexual Arrangements and Human Malaise*, New York, Harper and Rowe.

Edholm, F. (1992) 'Beyond the Mirror: Women's Self Portraits' in F. Bonner, L. Goodman, R. Allen, L. Janes and C. King (eds) *Imagining Women*, Cambridge, Polity, pp: 154–172.

Elias, N. ([1939]1982) *The Civilizing Process: The History of Manners*, Oxford, Blackwell.

Elliott, A. (1992) *Social Theory and Psychoanalysis in Transition: Self and Society from Freud to Kristeva*, Cambridge, MA, Blackwell.

Elliott, A. (2001) *Concepts of the Self*, Cambridge, Polity Press.

Elliott, A. (2004) *Social Theory since Freud*, Roehampton, Psychology Press.

Elliott, A. (2013) *Reinvention*, London, Routledge.

Elliott, A. and Frosh, S. (1995) (eds) *Psychoanalysis in Context: Paths between Theory and Modern Culture*, London, Routledge.

Enduring Love (2014) www.open.ac.uk/researchprojects/enduringlove/ (Last accessed June 1st, 2014).

Evans, D. (1996) *An Introductory Dictionary of Lacanian Psychoanalysis*, London and New York, Routledge.

Evans, M. (2003) *Love: An Unromantic Discussion*, Malden, MA, Blackwell.

Fairburn, W. R. D. (1952) *An Object Relations Theory of the Personality*, New York, New York Books.

Fanon, F. (1967[1952]) *Black Skin, White Masks*, trans Charles Markmann, New York, Grove Press.

Fanon, F. (1963[1961]) *The Wretched of the Earth*, trans Constance Farrington, New York, Grove Press.

Figlio, K. (2012) 'The Dread of Sameness: Social Hatred and Freud's Narcissism of Minor Differences' in L. Auestad (ed) *Psychoanalysis and Politics*, London, Karnac, pp: 7–24.

Finch, J. and Mason, J. (1993) *Negotiating Family Responsibilities*, London, Tavistock and Routledge.

Flax, J. (1990) 'Lacan and Winnicott: Splitting and Regression in Psychoanalytic Theory' in *Thinking in Fragments: Feminism, Psychoanalysis and Postmodernism in the Contemporary West*, Berkeley, CA, University of California Press, pp: 89–134.

Flax, J. (1993) *Thinking Fragments, Psychoanalysis, Politics, and Philosophy in the Contemporary West*, Berkeley, University of California Press.

Foucault, M. (1981) *History of Sexuality. Volume: An Introduction*, trans R. Hurley, Harmondsworth, Penguin.

Foucault, M. (1998) Technologies of the Self' in L. H. Martin, G. Huck and P. H. (eds) *Technologies of the Self: A Seminar*, Amherst, MA, University of Massachusetts Press, pp: 16–49.

Freud, S. (1896) 'Further Remarks on the Neuroscience-Psychoses of Defence' in J. Strachey (ed) *The Standard Edition of the Collected Works of Sigmund Freud*, Vol. 7, London, Hogarth Press, pp: 157–168.

Freud, S. (1921) 'Group Psychology and the Analysis of the Ego' in J. Strachey (ed) *The Standard Edition of the Collected Works of Sigmund Freud*, Vol. 21, London, Hogarth Press, pp: 67–143.

Freud, S. (1926) 'Inhibitions, Symptoms and Anxiety' in J. Strachey (ed) *The Standard Edition of the Collected Works of Sigmund Freud*, Vol. 20, London, Hogarth Press, pp: 77–174.

Freud, S. ([1905]1953) 'Fragment of an Analysis of Hysteria' in J. Strachey (ed) *The Standard Edition of the Collected Works of Sigmund Freud*, Vol. 7, London, Hogarth Press, pp: 1–122.

Freud, S. ([1900]1965) *The Interpretation of Dreams*, trans J. Strachey, New York, Avon Books.

Freud, S. ([1905]2000) *Three Essays on Sexuality*, London, Basic Books.

Freud, S. ([1929]2002) *Civilization and Its Discontents*, Harmondsworth, Penguin.

Freud, S. and Breuer, J. ([1893]2012) *Studies on Hysteria*, Charleston, Forgotten Books in association with the Hogarth Press.

Froggett, L. (2002) *Love, Hate and Welfare: Psychosocial Approaches to Policy and Practice*, Bristol, Policy Press.

Froggett, L., Chamberlayne, P., Buckner, S. and Wengraf, T. (2005) *Bromley by Bow Centre research and evaluation project: Integrated practice – focus on older people*. Project report, Preston.

Froggett, L. and Wengraf, T. (2004) Interpreting interviews in the light of research team dynamics: A study of Nila's biographic narrative. *Critical Psychology*, 10 pp: 94–122.

Fromm, E. ([1940]2011) *The Escape from Freedom*, Edinburgh, Ishi Press.

Frosh, S. (1987) *The Politics of Psychoanalysis*, London, Macmillan.

Frosh, S. (1997) *For and Against Psychoanalysis*, London, Routledge.

Frosh, S. (2002) *Key Concepts in Psychoanalysis*, London, The British Library.

Frosh, S. (2003) Psychosocial studies and psychology: Is a critical approach emerging? *Human Relations*, 56 (12) pp: 1545–1567.

Frosh, S. (2011) *Feelings*, London, Routledge.

Frosh, S. and Baraitser, L. (2008) Psychoanalysis and psychosocial studies. *Psychoanalysis and Society*, 13, pp: 346–365.

Frosh, S. and Emerson, P. (2005) Interpretation and over-interpretation: Disputing the meaning of texts. *Qualitative Research*, 5 (3) pp: 307–324.

Gabb, J. (2008) *Researching Intimacy in Families*, Basingstoke, Palgrave Macmillan.

Gallop, J. (1988) *Thinking through the Body*, New York, Columbia University Press.

Gerson, S. (2004) A relational unconscious: A core element of intersubjectivity, thirdness and the clinical process. *Psychoanalytic Quarterly*, LXXIII pp: 63–97.

Giddens, A. (1991) *Modernity and Self-Identity*, Cambridge, Polity.

Giddens, A. (1992) *The Transformation of Intimacy: Sexuality, Love and Eroticism in Modern Societies*, Cambridge, Polity.

Giddens, A. (1999) *RunawayWorld*, Reith Lectures, London, BBC www.bbc.co.uk/programmes/p00w9s1 (Last accessed November 17th, 2014).

Giulianotti, R. (1999) *Football*, Cambridge, Polity.

Giulianotti, R. (2002) Supporters, followers, fans and flaneurs. *Journal of Sport and Social Issues*, 26 (1) pp: 25–46.

Giulianotti, R. (2005) (ed) *Sport and Critical Sociology*, Cambridge, Polity.

Goffman, E. (1959) *The Presentation of Self in Everyday Life*, Harmondsworth, Penguin.

Goffman, E. (1961) *Asylums*, Garden City, NY, Doubleday.

Goffman, E. (1963) *Stigma: Notes on the Management of Spoiled Identity*, Englewood Cliffs, NJ, Prentice-Hall.

Goffman, E. (1967) *Interaction Ritual: Essays on Face-to-Face Behaviour*, Garden City, NY, Doubleday.

Goffman, E. (1974) *Frame Analysis: An Essay on the Organization of Experience*, New York, Harper and Row.

Greco, M. and Stenner, P. (2013) *Emotions: A Social Science Reader*, London, Routledge.

Gregg, M. and Seigworth, G. (2010) *The Affect Theory Reader*, Durham, NC, Duke University Press.

Gross, A. S. and Hoffman, M. J. (2004) Memory, authority and identity: Holocaust studies in light of the Wilkomirski debate. *Biography*, 27 (1) pp: 25–47.

Grossberg, L. (2010) *Cultural Studies in the Future Tense*, Durham, NC, Duke University Press.

Grossberg, L. (2013) Culture. *Rethinking Marxism, A Journal of Economy, Culture and Society*, 25 (4) pp: 456–462.

Grosz, E. (1994) *Volatile Bodies: Toward a Corporeal Feminism*, Bloomington, IN, Indiana State University.

Guntrip, H. (1961) *Personality, Structure and Human Personality*, New York, International Universities Press.

Hall, S. (1982) 'The Rediscovery of Ideology: Return of the Repressed in Media Studies' in M. Gurevitch, T. Bennet, J. Curran and J. Woollacott (eds) *Culture, Media and Society*, London, Sage, pp: 56–90.

Hall, S. (1990) 'Cultural Identity and Diaspora' in J. Rutherford (ed) *Identity Community and Difference*, London, Lawrence and Wishart, pp: 9–27.

Hall, S. (1992) 'The Question of Cultural Identity' in S. Hall, D. Held and T. McGrew (eds) *Modernity and Its Futures*, Cambridge, Polity and Milton Keynes, Open University.

Hall, S. (1996) 'Who Needs Identity?' in S. Hall and P. du Gay (eds) *Questions of Cultural Identity*, London, Sage, pp: 1–18.

Hall, S. (1997) (ed) *Representation: Cultural Representations and Signifying Practices*, London, Sage.

Hall, S. and du Gay, P (1996) (eds) *Questions of Cultural Identity*, London, Sage.

Hammersley, M. and Atkinson, P. (2007) *Ethnography, Principles and Practice*, 3rd edition, London, Routledge.

Haraway, D. ([1985]2000) 'A Manifesto for Cyborgs' in G. Kirkup, L. Janes, F. Hovendon and K. Woodward (eds) *The Gendered Cyborg: A Reader*, London, Routledge, pp: 50–57.

Harvey, P., Castella, E. C., Evans, G., Knox, H., McLean, C., Silva, E. B., Thoburn, N. and Woodward, K. (2014) (eds) *A Routledge Companion: Objects and Materials*, London and New York, Routledge.

Henwood, K. (2014) http://energybiographies.org/our-work/think-pieces/ (Last accessed April 14th, 2014).

Hochschild, A. (1983) *The Managed Heart: Commercialization of Human Feeling*, Berkeley, University of California Press.

Hoggett, P. (2000) *Emotional Life and the Politics of Welfare*, Basingstoke, Macmillan.

Hoggett, P. (2010a) *Politics, Identity and Emotion*, Boulder, CO, Paradigm.

Hoggett, P. (2010b, June) Perverse social structures. *Journal of Psycho-Social Studies*, 4 (1) pp: 57–64.

Hoggett, P. (2012) *Politics and the Emotions: The Affective Turn in Contemporary Political Studies*, Boulder, CO, Great Barrington Books.

Hoggett, P. (2013) www.open.edu/openlearn/body-mind/psychology/dialogue-climate-change-denial (Last accessed April 7th, 2014).

Hollway, W. (1989) *Subjectivity and Method in Psychology*, London, Sage.

Hollway, W. (2004) (ed) Psycho-social research. Special issue of *International Journal Critical Psychology*, 10.

Hollway, W. (2010) Conflict in the transitions to becoming a mother: A psychosocial approach. *Psychoanalysis, Culture and Society*, 15 (2) pp: 136–155.

Hollway, W. (2011a, January) Psycho-social writing from data. *Journal of Psycho-Social Studies*, 5 (1) pp: 92–101.

Hollway, W. (2011b) In between external and internal worlds: Imagination in transitional space. *Methodological Innovations Online*, 6 (3) pp: 50–60.

Hollway, W. and Jefferson, T. ([2000]2013) *Doing Qualitative Research Differently: Free Association, Narrative and the Interview Method*, London, Sage.

Hollway, W. and Jefferson, T. (2001) Free association, narrative analysis and the defended subject: The case of Ivy. *Narrative Inquiry*, 11 (1) pp: 1–120.

Hollway, W. and Jefferson, T. (2005a) Panic and perjury: A psychosocial exploration of agency. *British Journal of Social Psychology*, 44 pp: 147–163.

references

Hollway, W. and Jefferson, T. (2005b) But why did Vince get sick? A reply to Spears and Wetherell. *British Journal of Social Psychology*, 44 pp: 175–180.

Homeland (2014) www.sho.com/sho/homeland/about (Last accessed June 8th, 2014).

hooks, b. (1990) *Yearning: Race, Gender and Cultural Politics*, Boston, South End Press.

Hopper, E. (1996) The social unconscious in clinical work. *Group*, 20 (1) pp: 7–42. Reprinted in Hopper, E. (2003) *The Social Unconscious. Selected Papers of Earl Hopper*, London, Jessica Kingsley Publishers.

Hopper, E. (2003) *The Social Unconscious: Selected Papers of Earl Hopper*, London, Jessica Kinsley Publishers.

Howson, A. (2005) *Embodying Gender*, London, Sage.

Ignatieff, M. (1994) *The Narcissism of Minor Differences*, Milton Keynes Open University, Pavis Centre.

Ignatieff, M. (1998) *The Warrior's Honor: Ethnic War and the Modern Conscience*, London, Chatto and Windus.

Irigaray, L. (1985) *Speculum of the Other Woman*, trans G. Gill, Ithaca, NY, Cornell University.

Irigaray, L. ([1977]1985) *This Sex Which Is Not One*, trans Catherine Porter with Carolyn Burke, Ithaca, NY, Cornell, University.

Irigaray, L. (1993) *Je Tu Nous: Toward a Politics of Difference*, London, Routledge.

Irigaray, L. (2004) *Luce Irigaray: Key Writings*, London, Continuum.

Isin, E. (2014) (ed) *Citizenship after Orientalism: An Unfinished Project*, London and New York, Routledge.

Isin, E. and Nyers, P. (2014) (eds) *The Routledge Handbook of Global Citizenship Studies*, London and New York, Routledge.

James, W. ([1982]1961) *Psychology: The Briefer Course*, New York, Harper and Brothers.

Jamieson, L. (1998) *Intimacy*, Cambridge, Polity.

Jones, O. (2012) *Chavs the Demonization of the Working Class*, London, Verso Books.

Jung, C.G. (1991) *The Archetypes and the Collective Unconscious (Collected Works of C.G. Jung)*, trans R. F. C. Hull, London, Routledge.

Kaplan, E.A. (1992) *Motherhood and Representation: The Mother in Popular Culture and Melodrama*, London and New York, Routledge.

Kaplan, E.A. (2005) *Trauma Culture: The Politics of Terror and Loss in Media and Literature*, New York, Rutgers.

Kappeler, S. (1986) *The Pornography of Representation*, Cambridge, Polity.

King, C. (1992) 'The Politics of Representation: A Democracy of the Gaze' in F. Bonner, L. Goodman, R. Allen, L. Janes and C. King (eds) *Imagining Women*, Cambridge, Polity, pp: 131–139.

Klein, M. ([1935]1986) 'Mourning and Its Relation to Manic Depressive States' in J. Mitchell (ed) *The Selected Melanie Klein*, Harmondsworth, Penguin, pp: 146–174.

Kristeva, J. (1982) *The Powers of Horror: An Essay in Abjection*, New York, Columbia University Press.

Kristeva, J. ([1974]1998) 'Revolution in Poetic Language' in J. Ruskin and M. Ryan (1998) (eds) *Literary Theory*, Oxford, Basil Blackwell, pp: 451–463.

Lacan, J. (1988) *Écrits: A Selection*, trans Alan Sheridan, New York: W.W. Norton.

Laplanche, J. (1989) *New Foundations of Psychoanalysis*, trans David Macey, Oxford, Wiley Blackwell.

Laplanche, J. and Pontalis, P. (1973) *The Language of Psychoanalysis*, London, Hogarth Press.

Laplanche, J. and Pontalis, P. (1985) *The Language of Psychoanalysis*, 2nd edition, London, Hogarth Press.

references

Lasch, C. (1978) *The Culture of Narcissism: American Life in an Age of Diminishing Expectations*, London, Norton.

Lawler, S. (2014) *Identity: Sociological Perspectives*, 2nd edition, Cambridge, Polity.

Layton, L. (2004) A fork in the royal road: On "defining" the unconscious and its stakes for social theory. *Psychoanalysis, Culture and Society*, 9 (1), pp: 33–51.

Layton, L. (2006) 'That Place Gives Me the "Heebie Jeebies"' in L. Layton, N. C. Hollander and S. Gutwill (eds) *Psychoanalysis Class and Politics*, London and New York, Routledge, pp: 51–64.

Layton, L., Hollander, N. C. and Gutwill, S. (2006) (eds) *Psychoanalysis, Class and Politics: Encounters in a Clinical Setting*, New York, Routledge.

Levy, A. (2005) *Female Chauvinist Pigs: Women and the Rise of Raunch Culture*, London, Free Press.

Lewis, G. (2009) Birthing racial difference: Conversations with my mother and others. *Studies in the Maternal* Inaugural Issue, 1 (1) pp: 1–21.

Lewis, G. (2010) 'Animating Hatreds: Research Encounters Organisational Secrets, Emotional Truths' in R. Ryan Flood and R. Gill (eds) *Secrecy and Silence in the Research Process: Feminist Reflections*, London, Routledge, pp: 211–227.

Lloyd, M. (2007) *Judith Butler*, Cambridge, Polity Press.

Long, S. (2008) *The Perverse Organisation and Its Deadly Sins*, London, Karnac.

Mann, D. and Cunningham, V. (2009) (eds) *The Past in the Present: Therapy Enactments and the Return of Trauma*, London, Routledge.

Marcuse, H. (1966) *Eros and Civilization: A Philosophical Inquiry into Freud*, Boston, Beacon Press.

Marshall, T. H. (1950) *Citizenship and Social Class: And Other Essays*, Cambridge, Cambridge University Press.

Marx, K. (1975) *Early Writings*, intro Lucio Colletti, New York, Vintage Books.

Marx, K. and Engels, F. (1976) *Collected Works, Vol. 5 Marx and Engels 1845–1847*, New York, International Publishers.

Massumi, B. (1996) 'The Autonomy of Affect' in P. Patton (ed) *Deleuze: A Critical Reader*, Oxford, Blackwell.

Massumi, B. (2002) *Parables of the Virtual: Movements Affect, Sensation*, Durham, NC, Duke University Press.

Massumi, B. (2005) Fear (the spectrum said). *Positions*, 13, pp: 31–48.

Maxwell, C. and Aggleton, P. (2013) (eds) *Privilege, Agency and Affect. Understanding the Production and Effects of Action*, Basingstoke, Palgrave.

Mead, G. H. (1934) *Mind, Self and Society*, Chicago, Chicago University Press.

Melanie Klein Trust (1997) *Envy and Gratitude and Other Works 1946–1963* (Contemporary Classics) by the Melanie Klein Trust, London.

Menzies Lyth, I. (1960) 'Social Systems as a Defense Against Anxiety' in E. Trist and H. Murray (eds) *The Social Experiment of Social Science Vol. 1 The Socio-Psychological Perspective*, London, Free Association Books, pp: 95–121.

Merck, M., Caughie, J., Creed, B. and Kuhn, A. (1992) (eds) *The Sexual Subject: A Screen Reader in Sexuality*, London, Routledge.

Merleau-Ponty, M. (1962) *The Phenomenology of Perception*, New York, Routledge.

Midgely, M, (2010) *The Solitary Self: Darwin and the Selfish Gene*, Durham, Acumen Press.

Midgely, M, (2014) *Are You an Illusion?* Durham, Acumen Press.

Miklitsch, R. (2012) *Roll over Adorno: Critical theory, Popular Culture and the Audiovisual Media*, Albany, SUNY.

Mitchell, J. (1971) *Women's Estate*, Harmondsworth, Penguin.

Mitchell, J. (1974) *Psychoanalysis and Feminism,* London, Allen Lane.

Mitchell, J. (2003) *Siblings, Sex and Violence*, Cambridge, Polity Press.

Mitchell, J. and Rose, J. (1982) *Lacan Jacques: Feminine Sexuality: Jacques Lacan and the ecole freudienne*, New York, Norton.

Mitchell, S. A and Black, M. J. (1995) *Freud and Beyond: A History of Modern Psychoanalytic Thought*, London, Basic Books.

Morrison, T. (1989, Winter) Unspeakable things unspoken: The Afro-American presence in American literature. *The Michigan Quarterly Review*, 38 (1) pp: 1–34.

Mulvey, L. (1975, Autumn) Visual pleasure and narrative cinema. *Screen*, 16 (3) pp: 6–18.

Mulvey, L. (1989) *Visual and Other Pleasures*, Bloomington: Indiana University Press.

Myers, T. (2003) *Žižek*, London, Routledge.

Nordquist, P. and Smart, C. (2014) *Relative Strangers Family Life, Genes and Donor Conception*, Basingstoke, Palgrave.

Nussbaum, M. (2013) *Political Emotion and Why This Matters for Justice*, Cambridge, MA, Harvard University Press.

Ogden, T. H. (1994) The analytic third: Working with intersubjective clinical facts. *International Journal of Psychoanalysis*, 75 (1), pp: 3–19.

Parens, H. (2008) *The Unbroken Soul: Tragedy, Trauma and Human Resilience*, London, Karnac.

Parker, I. (2011) *Lacanian Psychoanalysis: Revolutions in Subjectivity*, London, Routledge.

Parker, R. (1996) *Mother Love, Mother Hate: The Power of Maternal Ambivalence*, London, Basic Books.

Parsons, T. and Shils, E. ([1951]2001) *General Theory of Action. Theoretical Foundations for the Social Sciences*, New Brunswick, NJ, Transaction Publishers.

Phoenix, A. and Pattynama, P. (2006) (eds) Intersectionality. Special edition of *European Journal of Women's Studies*, 13 (3).

Pollock, G. (2013) 'Sarah Kofman's Father's Pen and Bracha Ettinger's Mother's Spoon: Trauma, Transmission and the Strings of Virtuality' in P. Harvey et al. (eds) *A Routledge Companion: Objects and Materials*, London, Routledge, pp: 162–172.

Rashkin, E. (1988, Winter) Tools for a new literary criticism: The work of Abraham and Torok. *Dialectics*, 18 (4) pp: 31–52.

Rashkin, E. (1992) *Family Secrets and the Psychoanalysis of Narrative*, Princeton, Princeton Press.

Rashkin, E. (2005) *Response to Death: The Literary Work of Mourning*, Alberta, University of Alberta.

Rashkin, E. (2009) *Unspeakable Secrets and the Analysis of Culture*, New York, University of New York Press.

Redman, P. (2009) Affect revisited: Transference, counter-transference and the unconscious dimensions of affective, felt and emotional experience, *Subjectivity*, 26, pp: 51–68.

Reich, Wilhelm (1970) *The Mass Psychology of Fascism*, New York, Simon and Schuster.

Ribbens-McCarthy, J. and Edwards, J. (2003) *Making Families: Moral Talks of Parenting and Step Parenting*, Durham, Sociology Press.

Riesman, D. (1950) *The Lonely Crowd: A Study of the Changing American Character*, New Haven, CT, Yale University Press.

Rich, A. (1975) *Of Woman Born*, London, Virago.

Rose, J. (1983) Femininity and its discontents. *Feminist Review*, 14, pp: 5–21.

Rose, J. (1986) *Sexuality and the Field of Vision*, London, Verso.

Rose, J. and Mitchell, J. (1982) (eds) *Feminine Sexuality: Jacques Lacan and the École Freudienne*, New York, W. W. Norton.

Rose, N. (1990) *Governing the Self: The Shaping of the Private Self*, London, Routledge.

Rose, N. (1996) *Inventing Our Selves: Psychology, Power and Personhood*, Cambridge, Cambridge University Press.

Rose, N. (1999) *Governing the Soul: The Shaping of the Private Self*, 2nd edition, London, Routledge.

Roseneil, S. (2000) Queer frameworks and queer tendencies: Towards an understanding of postmodern transformations of sexualities. *Sociological Research Online*, 5 (3) pp: 1–19. www.socresonline.org.uk/5/3/roseneil.html

Roseneil, S. (2006) The ambivalence of Angel's 'arrangement': A psychosocial lens on the contemporary condition of personal life. *Sociological Review*, 54 (4) pp. 847–869.

Roseneil, S. (2007, June–September) Queer individualization: The transformation of personal life in the early 21st century. *NORA, Nordic Journal of Women's Studies*, 15 (2–3) pp: 84–99.

Roseneil, S. (2009) Haunting in an age of individualization: Subjectivity, relationality, and the traces of the lives of others. *European Societies*, 11 (3) pp: 411–430.

Roseneil, S. (2010) Intimate citizenship: A pragmatic yet radical, proposal for a politics of personal life. *European Journal of Women's Studies*, 17 (1) pp: 77–82.

Roseneil, S. (2012) 'The Vicissitudes of Post-Colonial Citizenship and Belonging in Late Liberalism' in S. Roseneil (ed) *Beyond Citizenship?* Basingstoke, Palgrave, pp: 231–265.

Roseneil, S. (2013) 'Beyond the relationship between the individual and society': Broadening and deepening relational thinking in group analysis. *Group Analysis*, 46 (2) pp: 1–15.

Rosenthal, G. (1998) *The Holocaust in Three Generations: Families of Survivors and Perpetrators of the Nazi Regime*, London, Cassell.

Rustin, M. (1991) *The Good Society and the Inner World*, London, Verso.

Rutter, M. (1987, July) Psychosocial resilience and protective mechanisms. *American Journal of Orthopsychiatry*, 57 (3) pp: 316–331.

Said, E. (1978) *Orientalism*, London, Vintage Books.

Sartre, J. P. ([1957]1963) *The Problem of Method*, trans Hazel E. Barnes, London, Methuen.

Schoonderwoerd, P. (2011) Shall we sing a song for you? Mediation, migration and identity in football chants and fandom. *Soccer and Society*, 12 (1) pp: 120–141.

Sclater, S., Jones, D., Price, H. and Yates, C. (2009) (eds) *Emotion: New Psychosocial Perspectives*, Basingstoke, Palgrave.

Segal, L. (1997) 'Sexualities' in K. Woodward (ed) *Identity and Difference*, London, Sage, pp: 184–224.

Seidler, V. J (2013) *Remembering 9/11. Terror Trauma and Social Theory*, Basingstoke, Palgrave, MacMillan.

Sennett, R. (1974) *The Uses of Disorder*, New York, Vintage Books.

Skeggs, B. (1997) *Formations of Class and Gender: Becoming Respectable*, London, Sage.

Skeggs, B. (2005) *Class, Self, Culture*, London, Routledge.

Smart, C. (2002) From children's shoes to children's voices? Family Court Review 40 (3) pp: 307–319.

Special Section Neo Liberalism (2014, April) Special Section: Psychosocial Effects of Neoliberalism. *Psychoanalysis Culture and Society*, 19 (1) pp: 1–51.

Stanley, L. (1990) *Feminist Praxis. Research Theory and Epistemology in Feminist Sociology*, London, Routledge.

Steedman, C. (1986) *Language for a Good Woman: A Story of Two Lives*, London, Virago.

Stenner, P. (2014) Being in the Zone: Liminal Reflections. http://vimeo.com/88508051 (Last accessed April 26th, 2014).

Stenner, P. and Moreno, E. (2013) Liminality and affectivity: The deceased organ donation. *Subjectivity*, 6 (3) pp: 229–253.

Stenner, P., Cromby, J., Motzkau, J. and Yen, J. (2011) *Theoretical Psychology: Global Transformations and Challenges*, Captus, Concord, Ontario, Canada.

Stern, D. (2004) *The Present Moment in Psychotherapy and Everyday Life*, New York, W. D. Norton.

Stewart, K. (2007) *Ordinary Affects*, Durham, NC, Duke University Press.

Taylor, C. (1989) *Sources of the Self: The Making of the Modern Identity*, Cambridge, MA, Harvard University Press.

Tee, S., Brown, J., Carpenter, D., Coldham, T., Davies, L. and Faulkner, A. (2012) 'Introduction to the Philosophy and Practice of Mental Health Care' in, S. Tee, J. Brown and D. Carpenter (eds) *A Handbook of Mental Health Nursing*, London, Hodder, pp: 3–19.

Thomas, J. (2013, November) Editorial. *Journal of Psycho-Social Studies*, 7 (1) pp: 1–5.

Turner, V. (1977) *Dangling Man*, Harmondsworth, Penguin.

UN Climate Change (2013) https://unfccc.int/meetings/warsaw_nov_2013/meeting/7649.php (Last accessed April 7th, 2014).

Van Gennep, A. (1960) *The Rites of Passage*, Chicago, University of Chicago Press.

Walkerdine, V. (1986) 'Video Replay: Families, Films and Fantasies' in V. Burgin, J. Donald and C. Kaplan (eds) *Formations of Fantasy*, London, Methuen pp: 167–199.

Walkerdine, V. (1997) *Daddy's Girl*, London, MacMillan.

Walkerdine, V., Lucey, H. and Melody, J. (2001) *Growing Up Girl: Psychosocial Explorations of Gender and Class*, London, Palgrave.

Warner, S. (2011) You only sing when you're winning: Football factions and rock rivalries in Manchester and Liverpool. *Soccer and Society*, 12 pp: 58–73.

Watts, S. and Stenner, P. (2012) *Doing Q Methodological Research: Theory, Method and Interpretation*, London, Sage.

Weintrobe, S. (2012) (ed) *Engaging with Climate Change: Psychoanalytic and Interdisciplinary Perspectives*, London, Routledge.

Wengraf, T. (2001). *Qualitative Research Interviewing: Biographic Narrative and Semi-Structured Method*, London, Sage.

Wengraf, T. (2004). 'BNIM and the psycho-societal challenge: Towards a psychoanalytically informed institutional ethnography, and/or vice-versa, but above all both!' Paper produced for the IRGfPSA Dubrovnik workshop, June.

Wetherell, M. (2003) 'Paranoia, Ambivalence and Discursive Practices: Concepts of Position and Positioning in Psychoanalysis and Discursive Psychology' in R. Harré and F. Moghaddam (eds) *The Self and Others: Positioning Individuals and Groups in Personal, Political and Cultural Contexts*, New York, Praeger/Greenwood Publishers, pp: 99–120.

Wetherell, M. (2012) *Affect and Emotion. A New Social Science Understanding*, London, Sage.

Whitford, M. (1991) (ed) *The Irigaray Reader*, Oxford, Basil Blackwell.

Williams, R. (1976) *Keywords: A Vocabulary of Culture and Society*, Oxford and New York, Oxford University Press.

Winnicott, D.W. (1953). Transitional objects and transitional phenomena. *International Journal of Psychoanalysis*, 34 pp: 89–97.

Winnicott, D. W. (1955–1956) Clinical varieties of transference. *International Journal of Psycho-Analysis*, 37 pp: 386.

Winnicott, D.W. (1960a) 'The Theory of the Parent-Infant Relationship' in D. W. Winnicott (1965) *Maturational Processes and the Facilitating Environment*, New York, International Universities Press, pp: 37–55.

Winnicott, D.W. (1960b) 'Ego Distortion in Terms of True and False Self' in D. W. Winnicott (1965) *Maturational Processes and the Facilitating Environment*, New York, International Universities Press, pp: 140–152.

Winnicott, D.W. (1965) *Maturational Processes and the Facilitating Environment*, New York, International Universities Press.

Winnicott, D.W. (1967). 'Mirror-Role of the Mother and Family in Child Development' in P. Lomas (ed) *The Predicament of the Family: A Psycho-Analytical Symposium*, London, Hogarth, pp: 26–33.

Winnicott, D.W. (1971a) 'Creativity and Its Origins' in D. W. Winnicott (1971b) *Playing and Reality*, London, Tavistock, pp: 65–85.

Winnicott, D.W. (1971b) *Playing and Reality*, London, Tavistock.

Woodward, K. (1997) 'Concepts of Identity and Difference' in K. Woodward (ed) *Identity and Difference*, London, Sage, pp: 7–62.

Woodward, K. (2002) *Understanding Identity*, London, Edward Arnold (then Bloomsbury Academic).

Woodward, K. (2006) *Boxing, Masculinity and Identity: The 'I' of the Tiger*, London, Routledge.

Woodward, K. (2008) Hanging out and hanging about: Insider/outsider research in the sport of boxing. *Ethnography*, 9 (4) pp: 536–560.

Woodward, K. (2009) *Embodied Sporting Practices: Regulating and Regulatory Bodies*, Basingstoke, Palgrave MacMillan.

Woodward, K. (2012a) *Sporting Times*, Basingstoke, Palgrave, MacMillan.

Woodward, K. (2012b) *Sex, Power and the Games*, Basingstoke, Palgrave, MacMillan.

Woodward, K. (2014) 'Boxing Films: Sensation and Affect' in P. Harvey et al. (eds) *A Routledge Companion. Objects and Materials*, London and New York, Routledge, pp: 109–118.

Woodward, K. (forthcoming) *The Politics of In/Visibility: Being There*, Basingstoke, Palgrave.

Woodward, K. and Goldblatt, D. (2011) Introduction. *Soccer and Society*, 12 (1) pp: 1–8.

Woodward, K. and Woodward, S. (2009) *Why Feminism Matters: Feminism Lost and Found*, Palgrave, MacMillan.

Wrong, D. (1961, April) The oversocialized conception of man. *Modern Sociology. American Sociological Review*, 26 (2) pp: 183–193.

Young, R.M. (1994) *Mental Space*, London, Process Press.

Žižek, S. (1989) *The Sublime Object of Ideology*, London, Verso.

Žižek, S. (1992) *Enjoy Your Symptoms! Jacques Lacan in Hollywood and Out*, London, Routledge.

Žižek, S. (1993) *Tarrying with the Negative: Kant, Hegel and the Critique of Ideology*, Durham, NC, Duke University Press.

Žižek, S (1997) *The Plague of Fantasies*, London, Verso.

Žižek, S. and Dolar, M. (2002) *Opera's Second Death*, London, Routledge.

Index